Ride America

Illinois, Indiana, Michigan, Minnesota, Ohio, Wisconsin

Bill Murphy

Arbutus Press, Traverse City, MI

ISBN 978-1-933926-65-0

Manufactured in the United States of America
First Edition/First Printing

Photos are by the author unless otherwise noted
Interior design and layout by Julie Phinney

To every reader:

I hope you will experience the same thrill in discovering America on back roads and in small towns that I have for forty-five years and that, like me, in the end you discover yourself.

Table of Contents

This is Why We Ride 1

Motorcycling in the Prairie State 13
   1. South by Southwest 16
   2. Galena and Savanna Driftless Ride. 19
   3. Ohio River Scenic Route 21
   4. Following the Illinois River 25
   5. Riding the Rock River/Rockford and Dixon Loop 27
   6. Crossing the Line 29
   7. Great River Scenic Byway in Illinois. 32

Motorcycling in the Hoosier State 37
   1. Bluegrass and the Boone Brothers on Route 135 40
   2. The Whitewater Valley Ride. 44
   3. Covered Bridges Over Rocky Waters 47
   4. Haunted Hindostan. 49
   5. Springs, Licks and Great Motorcycling Roads 52
   6. On the Banks of the Wabash. 55
   7. Indiana's Ohio River Segment 61

The Best of the Wolverine State. 65
   1. Michigan's Pinkie 68
   2. Tip of the Mitt. 76
   3. Lake Huron Sunrise Shoreline Tour 84
   4. Rocks, Classic Cars and a Grand River 94
   5. Judge Dexter's Trail. 98
   6. Porcupine Mountains to Brockway Mountain. 101
   7. A Yooper Chemistry Lesson: Iron, Copper, Wood and Water. . . . 106
   8. Pictured Rocks and Historic Bays. 112

North Star Delights 121
   1. Superior National Forest Scenic Loop. 124
   2. Fergus Falls To International Falls 126
   3. Minnesota Driftless Region Tour 128
   4. The Superior Shoreline 130
   5. Grand Rapids and International Falls Ride 134
   6. Mississippi River Bluffs Ride 136

Best of the Buckeye State 139
   1. The Hocking Hills and So Much More 142
   2. Ancient Treasures 147
   3. From the Fort to the Port – Old Route 24 152
   4. The Triple Nickel 154
   5. Ohio's Dragon 156
   6. Nirvana in Eastern Ohio 158
   7. The Ohio River Ride 162

The Badger State's Best 171
   1. Following the Kickapoo 174
   2. Stone Bridges and Blue Mounds 176
   3. The Northwoods Superior Tour 180
   4. Wisconsin's Thumb – The Door Peninsula 183
   5. Riding with Eagles and Hodags 189
   6. The Great River Scenic Byway Ride 195

Great Lakes Circle Tours 203
   1. The Lake Erie Circle Tour 205
   2. The Lake Huron Circle Tour 214
   3. The Lake Michigan Circle Tour 229
   4. The Lake Superior Circle Tour 254

Some Suggested Safe Riding Tips 269

Index 277

This is Why We Ride

Motorcyclists are a self-sufficient independent lot. We have distinctively personal attitudes and motives as to why we love our chosen pastime and our criteria need no validation beyond our own. At the same time, motorcyclists share many of the same reasons for riding, making us a community of individuals with shared values. Different yet similar. Individualistic yet friends with a common passion.

With this underlying thought in mind I am once again boldly, perhaps brashly, embarking on putting thoughts about motorcycle touring in print. This is the sixth in a series of books I've written about motorcycling opportunities in the Great Lakes region. More correctly, my books are about motorcycle exploration. They go beyond simply recommending particular roads and destinations; the books discuss opportunities for two-wheeled adventures and discovery. Because I have long felt that there is much more to motorcycling than simply the riding. Whether it's the bond created with strangers who share the passion, the enjoyment of discovering new places and adventures, or the visceral delight of the machine; it's about more than a simple ride. Though I am the first to admit that I love a great ride on fun roads, this book takes it a step further.

A person's status as a rider establishes his or her ability to think for themselves, which means that writing a book about and for motorcyclists is a daunting task. While bikers are smart enough to accept good advice when they hear it, it's up to the speaker, or writer, to cross the threshold as to whether the advice is credible, useful and based on experience. Passing along information and suggestions among riders is a well-established practice. I have learned about some of my favorite roads by talking with other motorcyclists and have reaped valuable safe riding lessons by listening to their stories. Get two or more riders together and the conversation soon takes on the tone of a professional consultation with ideas about how to make the overall motorcycling experience more rewarding being freely exchanged.

From the beginning, fifteen years ago now, my goal has been to provide information based on actual experience that discerning riders

can use. This undertaking quickly turned from a single direction communication of me writing and others reading to a two-way idea sharing
discussion that I never imagined at the start of this journey. My books
have afforded me the privilege of meeting thousands of bikers throughout
the Midwest. I sat at tables in motorcycle dealerships, hung out at various
motorcycle events talking to groups, attended countless motorcycle swap
meets as a vendor, and spoke at libraries and bookstores with PowerPoint
slides to tell the story of motorcycling to riders and curious nonriders
alike. After these many conversations I've concluded that for all our individual preferences and differences there are many attitudes and desires
that are common regardless of age, gender, length of riding experience
and type or brand of bike we ride. Miles in the saddle have given every
rider similar experiences and we share the same reasons for being in the
saddle in the first place. We can relate to one another and sharing motorcycling stories is one of the most enduring traits that we have in common.

This is not only my sixth book about motorcycle touring, it's my
last. I thought that perhaps my swan song tome should be a book that
proudly boasts about the biking virtues of the North American heartland
(Michigan, Wisconsin, Minnesota, Illinois, Indiana and Ohio and adjacent
areas of Iowa and the Province of Ontario) rather than just one state.
I'm a Midwestern farm boy through and through and I have a special
affinity for this region. It's made up of diverse people and places and I'm
proud to call it home. What better tribute than to write about it for riding
companions with whom I share an abiding passion. So once again bear
with me as I attempt to explore the idea of motorcycling adventures in
America's heartland.

My books are fundamentally about motorcycle touring opportunities
based on three principles – good roads, nice scenery, and interesting
places along the way to make the ride not only fun but also thought-provoking and even educational. To explore things and places that provide a
sense of awe. The totality of these factors is that it's the journey of exploration that's most important, not a destination.

In an attempt to explore the emotional and community aspects of
riding I titled this first section of the book 'This is Why We Ride'. I meant
it as a conversation into the underlying reasons behind our participation
in an activity understood or practiced by so few. The 'why' of our riding
passion is complex and worthy of some words.

Motorcycling is about much more than simply riding to a particular
destination. We don't ride just to get somewhere. If our reason for going
to the places I discuss in the books and following the routes I lay out
was simply in the doing of it we could more easily make the trips in a
climate-controlled car. As motorcyclists we go somewhere not just for a

destination but because of the machine we ride. The motorcycle itself and the road upon which we ride form the basis of why we venture out on a vehicle that is not the most practical means of transportation. We ride because of the motorcycle. If we had to take a four-wheeled car we likely wouldn't even take these unnecessary leisure trips.

To get to the essence of why we ride I suppose a bit of retrospection is necessary. We all have our own reasons for riding and as I noted earlier they are both different and similar. But I do believe there is a historic connection, that part of why we ride has its origins in the past, and that these roots have a powerful emotional basis that transcends generations. When we choose to ride we do it partly to carry on the tradition of a lifestyle and passion whose flame was lit over a century ago and that very flame now burns in our hearts today.

From my perspective there were two golden ages of motorcycles and motorcycling. The first was that amazing period prior to World War One when dozens of manufacturers began making true motorcycles, not just motorized bicycles, and interest in these marvelous machines quickly grew into a passion. A spark erupted into a flame that burned bright for over a decade, circa 1905 - 1917. For several years Americans bought more two-wheeled vehicles than they did the new relatively expensive cars hitting the market. The motorcycle market significantly collapsed after WWI and of course then the Great Depression and World War Two made things worse. Even a post-WW2 brief uptick in interest didn't help much and of course by 1953 there was one major American manufacturer left. Things remained relatively steady into the mid-sixties. But throughout this entire period firekeepers on their BSAs, Harleys and Triumphs kept the flame burning.

The second golden age as I see it was roughly 1966 to 1973. I was caught up in the motorcycling craze of that period, when small affordable machines arrived by the boatload on our shores. Young gearheads realized that these inexpensive bikes were a blast to ride and within their reach financially. This mechanical invasion coincided with the release of many motorcycle-themed movies, with the likes of The Wild Angels, Easy Rider and On Any Sunday drawing large crowds. In the late sixties to mid-seventies there were literally dozens of low budget motorcycle movies showing at drive-in theaters across America. Many of these were attended by groups of newly-recruited youth on their small Hondas and Yamahas. The motorcycle subculture was popularized as never before and awakened dreams of adventure, with a little outlaw flavor thrown in, for a generation more than ready to chase life on its own terms. It was an intoxicating period and many of us saw ourselves as a natural fit in that adventurous and daring lifestyle.

The phenomenon has matured since those halcyon days of "You meet the nicest people on a Honda" or Kawasaki's "Let the Good Times Roll". Imported machines quickly evolved from fun Scramblers with limited road riding capabilities to groundbreaking four-cylinder machines like the CB750 and Kawasaki's Z1. From my world view we are still picking the fruits of this second age of motorcycling. Machines have advanced beyond anything we could have imagined a half-century ago but they are still essentially evolutionary machines from the 1970 breed stock. I believe that electric machines will be the next age of motorcycles.

For many of the kids on those Japanese imports the dream of two-wheeled adventures had to be put on hold due to that contentious Asian War. That reality hit home for me but despite being caught up in the maelstrom I never abandoned the brief pubescent fling with motorcycles I experienced prior to deployment. My fellow Marines and I were fully aware of the dangers in the mountains and valleys of northwestern South Vietnam. But just the same I looked at old Route 9, a narrow serpentine strip of damaged asphalt that wound through the jungled valleys and fantasized about riding a motorcycle on it. Reality and good sense of course overruled my fantasies and I had to wait a few more years before once again being able to pursue my plans for a two-wheeled lifestyle. But I, and uncountable thousands like me, never lost the desire.

My desire became a reality and it has been even better than I envisioned in my youth. I had a lot of company in the 1970s. A substantial number of veterans returned home to motorcycling roots, or took up the activity as a form of catharsis or because the motorcycle cultural phenomenon was so appealing in the sense of leaving mainstream America and entering a world occupied primarily by the few who could relate. There was a lot of societal abandonment taking place at the time. From a military or veteran perspective not a lot has changed. Motorcycling is still very much a part of the lifestyle of those in or having recently served in the military.

After forty-six years on a wide variety of motorcycles I can truly say that my years of riding, and the uncountable associated experiences that I have enjoyed, have given me an underlying source of happiness in my life. No matter the turbulence and the troubles, there was always my motorcycle and the joy it provided.

My many two-wheeling experiences have broadened my life enormously and shown me what can be accomplished by living life to its fullest. On a more cerebral level they have expanded my knowledge and appreciation of this land, its history, and its people. I have motorcycled extensively in every state except Alaska and Hawaii (I've been to those states, just not on a bike) and in this manner have seen America (and much of Canada) up close in a way that would not have happened otherwise. In short, motorcycles and motorcycle riding have enriched my life immeasurably. It's hard to imagine how very different things would have been without this adventurous component. To be sure it would have been less complete and much less stimulating. The adventure and joy I have experienced aboard my faithful horses of steel is beyond measure.

That spark from 1903 is burning brightly today and the motorcycling phenomenon is alive and well to say the least. Over the last few decades millions of men and women, young and old, have joined the ranks of motorcycle riders. People from all walks of life and backgrounds have chosen to ride for as many reasons as there are riders. What is especially encouraging is the number of women who are now owners and riders. As of January 2019, women make up 19% of the motorcycling family. A decade ago it was one-half that number. Young women make up 26% of millennial-age riders, brightening the outlook for the sport's future even more.

Buying a motorcycle isn't based on logic. It's about the machines and the doors to adventure that they open more than any particular rational need that causes a person to consider motorcycle ownership. If rationality and logic were behind it we'd all be riding in small efficient cars. But our heart and soul want something enticingly different, something beyond just rational. And as any rider will try to explain, once a person has experienced the magical feeling of riding a motorcycle down a scenic winding road on a beautiful summer day there is just no looking back; the very same emotions experienced by generations of riders for more than a century.

The infusion of new riders has meant that the lifestyle has been able to broaden and mature. It might be less anti-establishment today but its acceptance across a broader spectrum of society has been nothing but positive. Machines and accessories unlike anything we could have imagined fifty years ago are now the norm because of market demand created by modern discriminating riders. (I recently recounted to a young rider about how 'back in the day' we put newspapers under our shirt in an attempt to block the effects of cold wind on unfaired bikes. I'm not sure if his head shaking was because of how foolish he thought we must have been or because of the pity he felt on our behalf).

We ride for more than just the ride.
We ride to serve, to explore, to discover.

Most people associate street motorcycles with road trips or perhaps cruising the boulevard on Saturday night. But in reality the reasons we ride go far beyond these usual assumed recreational aspects. The motorcycling activities that many riders hold most dear have little to do with commonly held ideas of open roads and desirable destinations. These reasons concern things more important than the mere act of riding, much more akin to public service rather than personal enjoyment. And these forms of service to community, country and our fellow citizens are many.

Non-enthusiasts likely don't link motorcycling with activities such as serving as honor escorts for funerals of military personnel, public safety officers, or government officials. Citizens love seeing motorcycles in civic parades marking special days such as Memorial Day and July 4th, but they might not be aware of events such as the Ride to the Wall or other gatherings, organized or spontaneous, done in honor of those killed or captured in wars. They have no idea how many different events are created and performed by riders purely in the name of charitable fundraising for various beneficial causes. Fundraising events on behalf of kids are the most numerous and have provided millions of dollars for support and research for everything from pediatric cancer to the Special Olympics. We can be proud of the many positive things that we do as a family bound together by these wonderful machines.

Our chrome and steel companions are therapeutic to a degree that even psychiatrists might find hard to explain. There is a reason that many veterans, police officers, firefighters and others in stressful occupations use the motorcycle as a means of enhancing comradeship and emotional health. For countless riders, being a member of like-minded groups and participating in supportive events are an integral part of why we ride. We receive even more than we give in these charity and public service motorcycle events.

One of the mystical aspects of motorcycles is their very presence. They are impressive even when parked and silent, sending a message of latent power and attitude. The essence of these machines creates an impression that can't be duplicated by other vehicles. A procession of motorcycles at a military event, civic parades, fundraising affair or funeral escort sends an unambiguous message of solidarity and respect.

Individuals becoming a supportive community with motorcycles being the common denominator and public service being the objective. Cause, respect and community; all part of why we ride.

But this book is primarily about road riding and discovering the marvelous places off the main highways. Motorcycle tourism is a lifestyle for many of us and being on the road is a significant part of our passion for the sport. Bikers are enthusiastic about getting out for the simple purpose of enjoying a ride and the presence of riders that they enjoy being with. They treasure the companionship of biking brothers and sisters who share the same love of motorcycles and riding and discovering what's over the next hill or around the next curve. These same riders, however, likely find just as much enjoyment in wandering the state or country alone, just them and the motorcycle they trust to carry them to places they would never otherwise see.

There is certainly no doubt about the fact that we can see and appreciate the world around us better on two wheels than on four. Motorcycling puts riders in touch with the world around them as few other motorized activities can. We can never isolate ourselves from our surroundings nor do we want to; rather we willingly immerse ourselves, which is of course part of the attraction. The essence of motorcycling includes not only the mechanical aspects—the leans, the power, the acceleration, the feel and sound of the machine—it involves being part of the environment around us. Motorcyclists want to be part of the real world to actually experience it. We want to be a participant not just an observer or passerby. We accept whatever consequences being on a motorcycle brings because the occasional discomfort is a small price to pay for the enjoyment received.

Motorcycle exploration of course depends on roads. Our wants, however, are different from what most users wish for in a road system. Long distance truck drivers and minivan pilots want highways that are dissimilar from those most motorcyclists desire. They simply want an efficient and smooth roadway to get them to their destination as effortlessly and quickly as possible. For motorcyclists the road itself is the destination. We do not just drive on a road; we become one with the road. A particular road, not a destination, is often the underlying reason a motorcyclist ventures forth in the first place. That concept is what this book is all about. We judge roads not by how efficient they are but by their character. We want roads with sex appeal, roads that twist and turn and excite the soul rather than maximize efficiency. Often, these highways are the 'gray line' roads depicted on state maps. They are two-lane primary county roads that have all the benefits of a well-maintained highway with fewer negative factors.

When it comes to enjoyable biking roads Midwesterners are more fortunate than the general consensus of motorcycle journalists and pundits might suggest. While we do in fact have countless miles of checkerboard roads of the straight and flat variety, a great many roads in the Midwest take full advantage of its varied geography and offer everything that serious riders seek. It became clear to me many years ago based on conversations with riders and travelers who had strong opinions of midwestern states that their knowledge of this region was very limited. Most folks who express negative opinions have never explored it. Instead, it seems that their 'all-knowing' opinions are based solely on observations made while driving across the region on major expressways such as I-70, I-80, or I-75. They rarely got off the main roads or out of the big cities to see the true Midwest, places where beautiful countryside and lightly traveled scenic byways dominate. We are blessed with thousands of miles of rural roads in a scenic landscape that take a backseat to no other region.

The bucolic roads that bikers enjoy aren't like modern roads. They were formed during a time when trails followed the landscape. They adhere to the serpentine meanders of rivers and go over hills and follow ravines and ridges rather than bulldoze through them like modern highways. They provide better motorcycling enjoyment than four lane high speed modern highways and are often in better condition due to less traffic and far fewer trucks. And of course this lack of traffic enhances the back roads experience even more.

For roads to make it into this book as recommended for motorcycle adventures they must meet several criteria: First, they of course have to be paved (this book is for road bikes, not dirt bikes.) Second, the road and area must have riding and scenic appeal. Traffic on the roads can't be oppressive and the general touring area must have something to offer in the way of interesting scenery, history, land cover, geologic features, or other attractions. Third, the road must have character: that is, curves, hills or other qualities that make it an enjoyable riding route. High speed or maximum efficiency is not of importance on these routes.

But there is one more criterion to meet before making it into this book and that is the length of the biking road. There are hundreds of enjoyable roads that we all escape to when we want a quick exhilarating ride near home. Problem is, many of these local favorites are short. They might be amazing but they're often only ten or twenty miles in length. To be considered for this book an enjoyable route, with associated stops, must be long enough to be considered a day ride and in some instances multiple days. Listing the hundreds or even thousands of fun local roads that we all enjoy for a quick ride would fill volumes. And it would be wasted effort as we all know where the nearby roads are when we go out for some peg scraping after mowing the lawn or when taking the long way home from work. These roads aren't the focus of this effort. Scenic and enjoyable routes and associated attractions that a person or group can plan to spend several hours or days enjoying is the motivation behind this book.

There are many reasons why riders prefer rural byways to hectic highways. Enjoyment of the ride is one obvious explanation, as are factors such as scenery and light traffic. But there is one more reason to get out beyond the point where neon turns to woods. America is best seen from its back roads and in its small towns to be fully appreciated and enjoyed. As travel writer Charles Kuralt once famously said, a person can drive an expressway from one end of the country to the other, and never see America.

The rural Midwest has many small cities and villages that still offer the kind of qualities many people yearn for in this rapidly urbanizing monoculture world where unique cultures and neighborliness have been replaced with endless sprawling sameness and personal anonymity. There is very little of interest to be found in sprawling suburbs. Attractive landscapes are found in rural America, and fascinating historical sites are found in old downtowns or in almost forgotten remote places where the forming of America took place two hundred or more years ago. Not along interstate highways or in cookie-cutter suburbia.

We ride to look for America along country roads where friendly smiles and waves are part of the scenery. Kids on bicycles, farmers in pickup trucks, clerks at small stores or gas stations—they all have a ready smile or wave and are happy to make small talk, asking about our motorcycle, our trip, and our plans. They often have good advice as to nearby roads or places that we should check out. This wonderful slice of the American pie still exists but we have to put ourselves in those places where it can be found.

The curiosity of nonriders is a phenomenon that occurs when traveling on a motorcycle. The number of strangers—people who wouldn't pay us a moment's notice if we were another car driver—that go out of their way to inquire about where we're from, where we're heading, how the trip is going and so on is remarkable. It is a very interesting statement on how people view us. I think even those who wouldn't get on a bike on a dare are still fascinated by the sense of adventure that motorcycles, and those daring enough in their minds to ride them, represents. For a variety of reasons these folks can't or don't wish to ride themselves, but they gain a vicarious sense of adventure and understanding of our passion by talking with us about the experience. These folks ponder the same question we often ask ourselves – why do we ride? Hopefully I've partially answered that question in my own way based on my experiences and reasons. I know every reader could add much to the list of reasons why we ride.

There are numerous topics or issues that are common across the Midwest when exploring the backroads. One of them is that some of the most beautiful places to visit have fortunately been preserved in state or national parks or museums. Given the fact that many riders enjoy exploring these places or taking advantage of them for overnight camping accommodations, I have included information for each state's web sites relative to state parks and camping reservations on that state's introductory page. I've also included information for federal parks and lakeshores and for scenic byways programs.

A Few Final Generic Thoughts

All across the Midwest there are historic roads that touring motorcyclists might find of interest. These roads are ridden for a different reason than most. They are the roads or trails that formed our country and were there when horses pulled stagecoaches or wagons loaded with a pioneer family's belongings across them. They were the trails that settled the Midwest and opened up the far west to overland travel. These roads are lined with history; two hundred year old buildings, historical markers describing a pivotal event or battle, and other attractions that have been preserved for our exploring and appreciating. There are many of these roads in the heartland and I encourage riders to check them out. I cover several in detail in previous books. They're not included within this book because they're historic roads, not great riding routes.

So explore the Lincoln Highway (the original 1913, 1918 and 1928 versions, not the replacements that today have been 'improved' to expressway status.) The National Road, the Sauk Trail (US 12 in Michigan and Indiana), The Yellowstone Trail, The Dixie Highway's various versions, Route 66, Grand River Avenue, Old Mackinaw Trail, and so many more. Do a little web surfing and you will find historic roads and trails in your state that perhaps you had never heard of. They have been replaced today by parallel expressways so traffic is light on them and the riding enjoyable and interesting. Part of the motorcycle persona is pushing the envelope, and I believe that means exploring the world around us and discovering our history, not just putting miles under our tires. Wandering with a purpose.

I've been asked in the past why I don't make recommendations as to lodging and restaurants. I rarely do because the desires of touring motorcyclists vary so greatly. Some demand 4-star luxury, some want fast food, more than a few want bar burgers and a beer, and others prefer a bottle of wine, homemade bread and a chunk of cheese in their saddlebag to enjoy at a rustic camp site. And I believe that if a person is capable of riding across the country on a motorcycle they certainly don't need anyone to tell them where to eat or sleep. If there are places that are unique in some manner I'll mention that, otherwise we're all on our own.

And finally, as noted above several times, this book is about much more than taking rides on fun roads. (though that's a key part of it) It's also about exploring and discovering the many manmade and natural attractions along the way. It's about appreciating our history and the beautiful places the Midwest has been blessed with. There are countless points of interest that are found on the tours I describe. Some of the routes were purposely selected because of the sites that exist along the roads as well as the road itself. Don't just ride by them. Stop and explore and learn. There are many more attractions than I specifically mention in the various chapters. I try to touch on a few to enhance curiosity and to provide some interesting details, but I list only a small percentage. Space, and readability, prevent listing every place of interest along a route. I encourage riders to watch for signs, do a little research beforehand, and be aware of attractions along the way – be they old forts or covered bridges, railroad museums or history changing battle sites, historic inns where the likes of Abraham Lincoln slept or waterfalls in a park. There are so many amazing things to see in America's heartland and it would be a shame to simply drive by out of indifference. Option two in the 'do I keep riding or do I stop to check out attractions' issue is to do both – I ride fun routes without stopping just for the enjoyment of the ride, and on other days I ride the same routes with frequent stops for the purpose of discovery and education.

That said, kickstands up – let's ride!

Motorcycling in the Prairie State

Most folks don't equate prairies with enjoyable motorcycling. A common reaction is that prairies need to be crossed as quickly as possible in order to get to desirable riding locales. But the reality is, there are entertaining motorcycling opportunities in every section of The Prairie State.

The geography of Illinois dictates that the best riding is found primarily in four distinct landform areas in the state. First, the northwest corner of the state in what's called the driftless zone. This part of Illinois escaped being altered by the last Ice Age glacier to cover the northern United States. This island of bare land that was surrounded by mile-deep ice resulted in what is today an unaltered scenic landscape of hills, valleys and bluffs of exposed rock. These sorts of landforms were obliterated or at least dramatically altered in surrounding glaciated areas leaving behind the more familiar landscape of much of the northern Midwest. What it means to motorcyclists is that this unaltered area, absent a layer of glacial till and lacking the bulldozing effect of glacial ice, retained a legacy of fabulous motorcycling opportunities with miles of winding roads through undulating land features not found everywhere in the region. Virtually every road in this locale is an enjoyable ride.

The second prime motorcycling opportunity in the state is along the Mississippi and Ohio Rivers. Rocky bluffs border these waterways and winding roads alongside the rivers provide dramatic scenic opportunities along with the enjoyable riding. Designated Scenic Byways follow the course of both rivers in the state. There are also countless fascinating points of interest along these riverside roads.

The third exceptional riding area is similar to the second except that it applies to inland rivers rather than the Mississippi and Ohio. Roads along watercourses such as the Rock and Illinois Rivers are often custom made for enjoyable outings due to their meandering ways. The landscape along waterways is also typically picturesque because trees often line the streams and frame the contours of rivers and their floodplains, offering relief from the otherwise open nature of the countryside. And while bikers favor these meandering riverside roads many drivers of four-wheeled vehicles avoid them due to their inefficient ways. This means more riding enjoyment and less traffic congestion to interfere with our two-wheeled fun.

The final geographic zone for motorcycling adventures is the far southern part of the state. This is where rocky hills and numerous small streams decree that rural roads follow the dictates of geology, curving around hills and along winding creeks. It is also the part of the state where woodlands reign supreme, not farmlands. Large blocks of state and national forests result in scenic landscapes of forested hills where twisting two-lane pavement are the norm.

I believe you will find that routes described in this section meet your standards for the best motorcycling opportunities in Illinois.

- IL DNR State Parks: https://www.dnr.illinois.gov/Parks/Pages/default.aspx
- Parks campground reservations: https://www.reserveamerica.com/welcome.do
- Great River Road Site: https://www.fhwa.dot.gov/byways/byways/2279/maps
- Ohio River Scenic Byway: https://www.fhwa.dot.gov/byways/byways/2286
- IDOT scenic roads: http://www.idot.illinois.gov/travel-information/tourism/scenic-byways/
- Illinois Tourism: https://www.enjoyillinois.com/

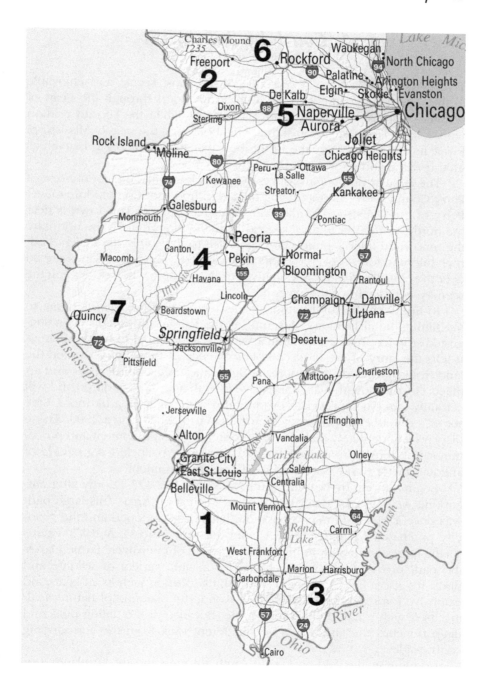

1. South by Southwest

THIS TWO-WHEELED outing is one of the most scenic and enjoyable in the state. One segment of the tour carries riders through the heart of southern Illinois' woodlands and hill country, while the second portion whisks them along the astonishing bluffs bordering the mighty Mississippi River. Its 180-miles truly take in the best that Illinois offers in marvelous motorcycling and scenery.

The circular ride begins and ends in Pinckneyville, the county seat of Perry County. Perry County being named in honor of Commodore Oliver Perry of the War of 1812 Lake Erie Naval Battle fame. This town is near the northern edge of Illinois' rugged Little Egypt region. To the north are the renowned Illinois prairie farmlands but to the south are ancient bedrock hills and forest-covered bluffs interspersed with rocky ravines carved over the eons by streams. Superlatives truly do apply when describing the scenery in this part of the state.

In line with the rural nature of this region Pinckneyville is home to the Illinois Rural Heritage Museum (at 187 Fairground Road). It's a suggested stop for anyone not familiar with the agricultural history of Illinois. It tells the story of the hardscrabble existence of those who worked the land from pioneer days to more modern times. Museum displays and artifacts clearly show the labor-intensive lives that farmers endured and will certainly make us appreciate our modern conveniences a bit more. One set of exhibits explores medical and dental practices circa 1900. Those displays will definitely make us appreciate modern equipment and procedures! The museum's annual Antique Tractor Drive includes a parade of antique tractors, and associated food and entertainment.

Begin the ride by heading south on routes 13 / 127. Shortly after embarking we'll go past the Pyramid State Recreation Area. This large park was once a coal strip mine operation that was abandoned and the property purchased by the state over a several year process. At 19,700-acres it's the largest state park in Illinois. In a region of intensively farmed lands the park provides a welcome home for a wide variety of wildlife and birds. It's also a favorite hunting and fishing location with its 24 lakes and extensive forest and grasslands. It's a wonderful example of nature healing itself with a little help from people. Because of the tailing piles and deep trenches the land has a very different look from the surrounding countryside.

Continuing the laid-back ride south through mostly farmlands our roads are combined to Murphysboro where route 13 splits off and we continue south on route 127. Murphysboro is at the doorstep of southern

Illinois' unique landscape of forests and hills. This ride becomes more appealing south of here.

There are some things to consider regarding the best time of year to make this trip or to visit this vicinity. These seasonal factors can expand the riding season and the list of activities available to riders. Summers can be hot and muggy in southern Illinois. There are events in the cooler months of Fall that are compatible with motorcycling that can make the entire experience more enjoyable, however. Consider timing this ride for September and October to enjoy the Apple Festival, the second weekend after Labor Day, the Murphysboro Riverside Blues Festival in September at the Historic Riverside park, and the Big Muddy Brewfest every October. The Brewfest is a big deal with over one hundred breweries involved. On the first Saturday of each month from April to September Cruise Night is a fun event downtown. Lots of classic iron, both two-wheeled and four.

Murphysboro is in the record books for some unfortunate reasons. Nearly a century ago close to 750 people were killed in an outbreak of F5 tornados in that region of the country. The village of Murphysboro was essentially wiped off the map and 234 people killed, the most in American history for any single city. Other storms and floods plagued the area in later years. It seems to be in Mother Nature's bullseye.

Crossing the Big Muddy River on the south side of town Route 127 is our host again as it carves its way through the Shawnee National Forest and further south through the Trail of Tears State Forest. The scenery and the character of the road will not disappoint as it meanders through the montage of forested hills and fields. The road follows several creeks as it winds through the countryside, including Sugar, Cedar and Cave Creeks. Ten miles south of Murphysboro watch for signs and Pomona Road. The Little Grand Canyon park is less than a mile to the west. It is a dramatically scenic area for a walk through rock formations carved over the millennia by small streams. Adjacent bluffs provide overlooks to view the surrounding forestlands. The canyon hike is discretionary but the overlooks are easy to get to and well worth the time and effort.

Near Alto Pass there are several vineyards that you may wish to check out. Coming into the tiny town of Alto Pass I highly recommend turning onto Main Street and following it to the east side of town to Cliff View Park. The overlook in the park provides wonderful views in all directions. The park is aptly named. To the south the 111-foot high Bald Knob Cross can be seen.

South of Alto Pass route 127 joins route 146 for an eastward jog of about three miles into Jonesboro. Two loops of the National Historic Trail of Tears cross near Jonesboro. For more information about local features check the Trail's web site at: https://www.nps.gov/trte/planyourvisit/places-to-go-in-illinois.htm

At the traffic circle in downtown Jonesboro route 127 heads south again as Main Street and we stay on it for twenty five more wonderful riding miles through the southern Illinois countryside. Just south of the village of Unity route 3 intersects with 127. Turn right onto route 3 and follow it west through the forested hills and then north alongside the Mississippi River. Route 3 is located in the river's adjacent floodplain, or 'bottoms', some of the most fertile land in the country. The bluffs are on the right as we ride north and the river often nearby on our left. As we get further north route 3 is situated at the base of the cliffs adding even more charm to the ride. It's an amazing stretch of road with few peers. Route 3 takes us north all the way to state route 150 at Chester.

Chester is one of the more historic towns in a state filled with history. There are many attractions near Chester to check out, ranging from a statue of the 'Popeye the Sailor Man' character (created by a Chester native son) in the town's Segar Park, to several nearby historic sites preserving the military, Native American and cultural history of the region.

Turn right onto route 150 and ride it the many pleasant miles northeast toward Pinckneyville. It'll 'T' at route 154 which we follow the last few miles east back to Pinckneyville and the end of this very pleasant road trip through a part of Illinois that far too many folks unfortunately never see.

2. Galena and Savanna Driftless Ride

THE ORIGINS of the city of Galena make it one of the oldest and most historic in Illinois. Early French explorers travelled through the area in the late 17th century and found the lead ore deposits that formed the basis of this region's importance even more so than its proximity to the Mississippi River. A boomtown sprung up around lead ore mining and in the pre-Civil War days it rivaled Chicago in importance and population. Galena is home to general and later president Ulysses S. Grant and incredibly, eight other Civil War generals!

The city is on the Galena River, a fact that has caused many problems with severe flooding over the last two hundred years. Floodgates were installed that prevent catastrophic floods today but in prior years the damage was severe. The town is nestled in the scenic hilly country of the driftless area. Horseshoe Mound, just southeast of town near US20 is the highest hill in the area at 1,063 feet; impressive when considering that average elevation in the area is about 630 feet. Galena Grant Park is on the riverfront in town and provides an enjoyable interlude prior to starting out on the ride. President Grant's home is an easy walk from the park on Bouthillier Street.

This outing begins in this historic and charming town and takes advantage of the trademark roads in this region by hooking several renowned motorcycling routes together into a very enjoyable ride. Commence by heading east on Field Street in town, which turns into Stagecoach Trail beyond the city limits. This old winding road closely follows the original stagecoach route that crossed northern Illinois in pioneer days. It's fascinating to follow the same road and see the same scenic sights that several generations of travelers saw in stagecoaches, on horseback, and later in cars. The route is also designated as county route 3.

Stagecoach Trail carries us the twelve miles to Scales Mound and route 4, where we turn south. By the way, Charles Mound is located just outside Scales Mound, at 1,235 feet the highest natural elevation point in Illinois. It's on private property and thus not readily accessible. The 'natural elevation' descriptor is important because the Sears / Willis Tower building is higher.

Route 4, aka The Elizabeth Scales Mound Road, transports us south through fourteen miles of rolling woods and farmlands to US20 and the town of Elizabeth. The road is in constant flux as one curve follows another in a very nice dance in which your motorcycle will be leaning left and then right as it smoothly sails through the sweepers. At US20 turn left toward Elizabeth. Ride three miles and on the east side of town turn right onto Derinda Road / county road 7. This marvelous road will be our host through nearly twenty miles of fabulous countryside all the way to Savanna. As it approaches Savanna the road's name changes to Scenic Ridge Road; and an aptly named road it is.

There are a few things to check out in Savanna, including the Iron Horse Social Club; part museum and part tavern on Main Street. The Savanna Train Car Museum might also be of interest. It's also on Main Street. And of course Poopy's Biker Bar on the south end of town.

To continue the ride get on Main Street / State Route 84 and ride north along the mighty Mississippi River. The scenery is spectacular and there will soon be places to stop to take in the beauty of the area. The first is the Mississippi Palisades National Natural Landmark. Mississippi Palisades State Park is a bit further north. Both offer marvelous scenic overviews.

Route 84 carries us north through the wonderful scenery and dramatic views along the river all the way to the town of Hanover, nestled in a scenic loop of the Apple River. Hanover is billed as the Mallard Capital of the World and this claim to fame is proudly displayed on the water tower with the portrayal of a giant mallard. This title isn't the result of large nearby wetlands and wild Mallard duck populations, however. It's the Mallard capital because the world's largest Mallard duck hatchery is located there. They provide ducks around the world for purposes as diverse as restaurant fare to university research projects. This location was a large Native American village until a dam and mill were built on the river in 1828.

Cross the bridge on 84 / Washington Street and go north a few blocks. You'll see Blackjack Road angling sharply to the left. Turn onto Blackjack and it will eventually, after sixteen miles of smile inducing twists and turns, lead all the way back to Galena.

This is an excellent outing of 75 miles. And while it's short, it's one of the best routes to see the Illinois driftless area up close and personal.

3. Ohio River Scenic Route

THE OHIO RIVER originates in Pennsylvania where it begins life as an already impressive stream created by the confluence of the Allegheny and Monongahela Rivers. It flows for nearly a thousand winding miles as one of America's great rivers, finally ending at the southwest corner of Illinois where it joins forces with the even mightier Mississippi River. All along those impressive miles across the heartland it creates its own landscape and a local culture that depends on and revolves around the river. It is also a living history classroom where countless nation-building events took place at which we can stop to appreciate and learn. For motorcyclists it represents a fabulous opportunity for enjoyable riding on winding roads in the shadow of forested bluffs that guard the river.

The Illinois section of the Ohio River is of course no less impressive or important than upstream sections. Like its neighbors to the east the land adjacent to this river is unique and different than geography and geology to the north. For Ohio, Indiana and Illinois this southern region is the area where hills, rocky landscapes, forests, and curving roads alongside winding streams exist. Prairies, fertile farmlands and straight flat roads might be common in counties to the north but along this river ancient and rugged unglaciated bedrock headlands prevail.

Wanting to avoid the congestion and traffic in the Cairo vicinity we'll begin this ride just east of Cairo in Mound City. The ride ends at Old Shawneetown in the east. This not only follows the best part of the route but also pays homage to the historic presence of Native Americans in the heartland of America.

State route 37 is our host for the first portion of the ride. It's the main street in Mound City and is also signed as the Ohio River Scenic Byway in this portion. This area is known for several Native American burial and ceremonial mounds. Watch for signs to the parks where these ancient earthen structures can be found. Mound City National Cemetery is on route 37 a mile northwest. Dating to Civil War days it's one of the oldest in the country.

Our road initially traverses floodplain farmland, formed over millennia by countless floods and meanderings of the river. This is the landscape as we ride by the villages of America, Olmstead and New Grand Chain, beyond which point SR37 heads north into the interior. Two miles north of New Grand Chain, just past Shawnee Community College, turn right onto route 169 and follow it east to US45. Turn right onto 45 and trail it into Metropolis on the river. There are a couple things of interest in Metropolis. First, you'll want to visit Superman Square at the courthouse to view the superhero and get a selfie with him. Given the town's name it's logical that sooner or later someone would make the connection between the town and the man of steel. In 1972 the Illinois legislature declared that Metropolis was in fact the home of Superman. The city had big plans for the honor including an amusement park and other tourist attractions. Those fell through but in 1986 they did build a seven-foot statue. That original monument unfortunately didn't share the same invincibility as its namesake and was vandalized. In 1993 the town erected a twelve-foot two-ton bronze bullet proof statue, and this version has held up well. Two blocks up the street is a Lois Lane statue, another very fitting spot for a one-of-a-kind selfie.

The second attraction here is a bit more serious and historic. It is Fort Massac, in the state park of the same name on the east side of town. Fort Massac was built by the French in 1757, during the French and Indian War. The French left the fort at the conclusion of the war and it was destroyed by the Chickasaw sometime after 1763. In 1778, during the American Revolutionary War, Colonel George Rogers Clark led his regiment of "Long Knives" into Illinois near the site of the fort at Massac Creek. The fort was rebuilt in 1794 during the Northwest Indian Wars. In the fall of 1803 Lewis and Clark stopped at Fort Massac on their way west to recruit volunteers. The Fort was repaired after being damaged in the 1811 New Madrid Earthquake but was ultimately abandoned in 1814, at the end of the War of 1812, when it no longer served any purpose. The Fort Massac site became the first Illinois state park in 1908. In the 1970s, a partial reconstruction of the 1794 U.S. Army fort was built but in 2002 it was torn down and a smaller but more detailed version fort as it appeared in 1802 was reconstructed which is what we see today.

Follow route 45 around the park and then south to the town of Brookport. This is the location of a Corps of Engineers Lock and Dam facility. It is always interesting to view these impressive structures up close.

On the north edge of this town is Unionville Road / county road 6 heading east. This is our road. Six miles east of Brookport is a fascinating attraction that is worth the 4-mile diversion from the route. Turn right on New Cut Road and follow it the four miles to the Kincaid Mounds. These are among the oldest and most impressive Native American mounds in the area. The site could be more significant than the more famous Cahokia Mounds. Much of the site is owned by the State Historic Preservation Agency, including the important flat-topped pyramidal mounds and the plaza. The eastern portion of the property is privately owned.

Once back on Unionville Road ride east to New Liberty. At that crossroad village turn left onto New Liberty Road. This pavement, which goes through several name changes as it passes through different jurisdictions takes us north along the riverfront to Bay City and Golconda and beyond. The name of the two-laner changes from New Liberty Road to New Harmony Road to Bay City Road. North of Golconda it is state route 146. Route 146 is what we'll be riding for many miles as it curves back east and follows the river to Elizabethtown. Between Bay City and Elizabethtown the landscape becomes more typical of what's expected along the Ohio River. More wooded bedrock bluffs and fewer farm fields.

Pausing in Golconda to reflect on its history is appropriate. First settled in 1798, today, despite its small size, it is the county seat for Pope County. It was once an important river ferry crossing point and this was to play a role in history. In the 1830s thousands of Cherokees crossed the river at this point by ferry as part of the infamous Trail of Tears exodus to Oklahoma. A sad chapter in our history that happened where we stand. The town is a dedicated historic area and has a very nice park on the river to watch the water and view the bluffs in the distance. It's a suggested stop for stretching legs and taking in the attractions and views.

There are a couple reasons to stop at Elizabethtown. If you're there on the first Friday and Saturday in July you can participate in the Hardin County Heritage Festival, with all the usual parades, food, music and activities that make up local festivals like this. The town parties again on the third Saturday in September during the Cave-In-Rock Frontier Festival. Finally, if you enjoy historical buildings check out the Rose Hotel, aka McFarland's Tavern, on the rocky riverfront. The building was originally built in 1812 as McFarland's Tavern, and gradually expanded into a hotel. There is a legend that Mark Twain may have stayed there. It's a designated historic building and a unique place to visit.

East from Elizabethtown 146 eventually "T's" at route 1. At this point turn toward the river to the town of Cave In Rock to visit the state park of the same name. Interesting historical story and geology. The heavily wooded park is named for the 55-foot-wide cave that was carved out of the limestone rock by water thousands of years ago. Going inside the cave and seeing the limestone bluffs along the river in this vicinity is enough to make a person from the Chicago area want to say "I don't think we're in Illinois any more, Toto." The cave served several purposes two hundred years ago, including as a hideout for pirates on the river.

To finish the ride, head north on route one as it shadows the Saline River upstream until it intersects with route 13. Turn right onto thirteen and it'll cut across rich farmlands to Shawneetown (aka New Shawneetown) and a couple miles further to Old Shawneetown on the river. This location was an important one circa 1800 when the federal government had a station here to help administer the Northwest Territory. In 1937 a major flood on the Ohio essentially destroyed the town so officials literally moved it inland to its new safer location.

The Wabash River empties into the Ohio ten miles further upstream marking the Indiana border and creating the fertile, and flat, bottomlands that are the trademark of that corner in both states. With the end of enjoyable motorcycling opportunities the 135-mile ride through history – both natural history and manmade – ends here.

4. Following the Illinois River

THIS ENJOYABLE 180-mile ride alongside the state's namesake river carries riders through scenic pastoral countryside in the heart of the state all the way to the rugged bluffs along the Mississippi River. The ride begins at Bartonville and terminates at Alton. Except for short distances on a few other roads it is almost entirely on state route 100. Before putting kickstands up a suggestion – if you enjoy seeing and learning about heavy duty mechanical equipment visit the Caterpillar Visitor Center up the road just four miles near Peoria before the embarking on the ride. It definitely won't disappoint.

Proceed south on US24 from Bartonville alongside the several woodlands and wildlife refuges that border the Illinois River and its adjacent wetlands and lakes. It's a surprisingly scenic stretch of road between Bartonville and Lewiston because of the wooded floodplain and the several wildlife preserves that the state manages along the shoreline. These natural areas not only make for a scenic ride, they provide critical habitat for a variety of wildlife and help protect adjacent farms and downstream towns from floods. River floodplains are after all exactly that – the low-lying land next to a river that routinely floods to temporarily store excess water.

From Lewiston continue south on route 24 and after almost five miles cross the Spoon River. Immediately after crossing the river turn left onto county road 11. Follow this lightly traveled scenic strip of asphalt southeast to route 136. It's a more entertaining stretch of road than US24 in this vicinity.

Take 136 a very short distance east and turn south onto route 100 and let the fun begin in earnest. Route one hundred traverses a mix of wetlands, woodlands and farmland for mile after pleasurable mile. All along this ride the road is near the wetlands that are a natural part of the Illinois River landscape or are being managed by the state in wildlife management areas. Our road eventually crosses the river at Beardstown and then immediately continues south, paired for a fifteen mile stretch with route US67.

The courthouse in Beardstown is an interesting stop on the ride. Abraham Lincoln once had an important legal case in this court, establishing his reputation as an effective attorney. There is a Lincoln Museum in the courthouse today, as well as artifacts from Native Americans who populated this region in bygone days.

The segment of road south of Beardstown is the least entertaining of the entire ride but it's not bad, just fairly straight road through open countryside. Relaxing and enjoyable, just not exciting. But that changes again after route 100 splits off to the southwest and resumes its pattern of broad sweeping curves in a more wooded landscape.

SR100 "T's" at route 106, joining it for about six miles to the west, crossing the Illinois River. It splits off heading south again at the tiny village of Detroit. Eventually our road works its way back to the Illinois River and follow the stream closely for many miles. Route 100 doesn't disappoint and this is a fun and scenic part of the ride, going through Kampsville and beyond. (Never been there but the Center for American Archeology Museum in Kampsville looks interesting.)

The road crosses to the east side of the river again at Hardin, and after teaming up with route 16 for six miles it once again splits off and heads south on its own with farm fields on the right and rolling woodlands on the left. The geography gets more dramatic near Grafton and the confluence of the Illinois River with the Mississippi. Just north of Grafton the Pere Marquette State Park is a great place to view the dramatic river bluffs. South of Grafton the road hugs the shore of the Mighty Mississippi as we ride the final fifteen miles to Alton.

Route 100 ends in Alton but if you follow the pavement to the east after passing the US67 bridge you'll soon be on Broadway. Fast Eddie's Bon Air will appear shortly; always a popular gathering spot. (Perhaps the largest by liquid volume bar in the world) Or, continue south along the river on route 143 to visit the National Great Rivers Museum located at the locks and dam facility. It's an interesting stop, one of several museums of its type along the Great River Scenic Byway operated by the Corps of Engineers.

This particular ride offers such a nice alternative route at the southern end that I thought I would include that alternate route as an option or better yet, a person could include both options on the ride, it certainly would add fun miles and enjoyable time on two wheels to the experience. Option B involves the portion of the tour south of Kampsville. The above route has the rider on route 100 on the east side of the Illinois River all the way south to Alton. Plan B carries the rider into the narrow peninsula formed by the Illinois River on the east and the Mississippi River on the west creating a U-shaped loop in that peninsula.

At Kampsville go west onto state route 96. Follow it to the Mississippi River and turn left onto Mississippi River Drive. Follow this unique road south to its southern end where it turns east as Schleeper Road and then turns back north as Illinois River Drive along the west shore of the Illinois River. This northbound stretch is particularly scenic. At Hardin turn right on route 16 / 100 to cross the Illinois River and continue following route 100 south to Alton in a zone of bluffs and dramatic river views. If a person rides the peninsular U-Loop it adds about forty miles onto the ride; forty enjoyable scenic miles, that is.

5. Riding the Rock River/Rockford and Dixon Loop

THIS 75-MILE RIDE might be on the short side for this book but it is a tour that should be included regardless. It's a 'circular' route along the Rock River between Rockford and Dixon that has two motorcycling personalities. The first half typifies what motorcyclists want in an entertaining road and scenic area. The characteristics for the return loop area are subtler but it's a fun and relaxing ride just the same.

When feasible given the proper quality of the roads and countryside I think circular day rides have a lot going for them. Having a common start and end point makes an outing easy to plan and accomplish especially if it involves a small group.

Starting in the southeast corner of Rockford, the first half of this ride is one of the most enjoyable in this part of the state. And it couldn't be easier to do; simply follow state route 2 as it meanders southwest along the craggy Rock River. It's easy to forget that one is in the northern Illinois farmlands because of the scenic qualities along the tree-lined river and its occasional view of dramatic rock outcroppings. Route 2 is an enjoyable place for a two-wheeler to bask in the freedom of the open road as it closely accompanies the twists and turns of the scenic river. Dramatic views of rock bluffs and of course frequent glimpses of the river itself add to the picturesque charms of the ride.

Near the town of Oregon, Castle Rock State Park is a recommended stop. The rugged beauty of the parklands makes it more than worth the time and entry fee to enjoy the benefits. The unique bedrock geology adds a special allure to the setting and a distinct twist to a motorcycle ride through the Illinois prairies. The John Deere Historic Site in Grand Detour is also a place that will delight and educate.

Route 2 crosses to the opposite side of the river south of Grand Detour, cutting across a peninsula formed by the meandering river into the town of Dixon. There are a couple interesting stops in Dixon (besides lunch). The first is the Northwest Territory Historic Center, and the second is Ronald Reagan's boyhood home.

To close the loop get back on route two and go about three miles east from Dixon to Lost Nation Road / County Road 1. This turns into Flagg Road for three miles at which point we turn left onto Lowden Road / CR27. This road seamlessly turns into Daysville Road / 5, travelling north to state route 64 across the river from Oregon. Go left on 64 for five blocks then turn north onto River Road at the water's edge, riding it through wooded Lowden State Park and beyond. Lowden Park is another recommended stop, especially to see the giant Black Hawk Statue on the river. River Road lives up to its name and hugs the shoreline all the way to Byron and route 72. Go right on 72 for a mile then turn left onto Kishwaukee Road, which carries us back to Rockford.

Local motorcyclists are aware of this enjoyable riding opportunity but if you're not familiar with it make it a point to head to either end point and make the ride. You will be happy that you did.

6. Crossing the Line

NO, I DIDN'T GET geographically confused or forget what state I'm writing about. Sometimes the long way is the best way, and there are no fences separating Midwestern states so it's okay to do multi-state rides. In an attempt to describe the best rides in the various states I'm focusing on internal rides but there of course are many great routes that cover two or more states. The Great Lakes circle tours are a fine example.

There are two entertaining routes that take in the best of northwestern Illinois and southern Wisconsin's scenic landscapes. The first designated route won't be mistaken for The Dragon but this 115-mile ride is a wonderfully relaxing outing on nice roads. The final stretch through the driftless area near Galena is especially enjoyable. Northwest Illinois and southwest Wisconsin share several unique historic and geographic features. There are many interesting things to see and do along the way so be alert for informational signs and points of interest.

Begin the ride in Freeport. The city of 26,000 is the county seat for Stephenson County and a bustling place. Like so many communities in this state Abraham Lincoln left an indelible mark on this town that remains today in the history books as well as in Taylor Park. The second of the famous Lincoln – Douglas debates was held here in 1858. This particular debate had a strong impact on political party alignments as well as on Lincoln's future. The name "Freeport" was used to describe the policy positions that were cemented in that debate. The event is memorialized in the Lincoln Douglas Debate Square in downtown and a Lincoln statue and monument in Taylor Park.

Leave Freeport via Business 20 heading west. Bus20 joins the main route shortly west of Freeport and at this point twenty reverts to a pleasant two-lane road which we'll ride seven miles to state route 73 just south of the town of Lena. Turn north on 73 and follow this pavement all the way to Browntown in Wisconsin. At the state line the road becomes county road M and crosses the Pecatonica River soon after crossing the boundary. CR-M roughly follows the river as it meanders through the picture-perfect rolling farmlands for several miles. Eventually county road M "T's" at CR-B where it makes a short jog to the left and then continues north again as CR-M. Two miles north of this jog CR-M arrives at the small town of Browntown and ends at state route 11 in town. Ride west on SR11 to explore some of Wisconsin's trademark bucolic beauty. Just west of Browntown we'll cross the Pecatonica River again and then ride the relaxing twenty-four miles across verdant rolling farmlands to the town of Shullsburg.

This historic town, Wisconsin's third-oldest community, was established in 1827 by John Shull. Before being given this name it was locally known as New Dublin because of the many Irish immigrants that settled here. Shullsburg was a lead mining town and the Badger Mine and Museum is an excellent place to explore the history of the town and the livelihood of its early residents. The museum has many artifacts from Shullsburg's nearly two hundred years of history, and touring the 19th-century underground lead mine gives a person an appreciation for the lives of the miners who used picks and shovels to extract this ore from the hard ground (like so many burrowing Badgers, which of course is how the Badger State earned its nickname). Watch for the sign on route 11 for the museum located at 279 West Estey Street at the corner of Galena Street, next to the high school athletic field. The museum and mine are open from Memorial Day to Labor Day. Admission fees are reasonable and well worth the cost.

If you have an interest in mines and mining just be aware that there are two closed mines two miles south of Shullsburg on CR-O. When you reach CR-W the large Calumet and Hecla mine, closed in 1979, is off to the east, and the Mulcahy Mine, where eight men died in a 1943 cave in, is less than two miles to the west. This was Wisconsin's worst mining disaster. You really can't see much from the road but I offer this information just FYI. In addition, a couple miles south of town on county road U is the famous Gravity Hill, where cars allegedly roll uphill. Since I happen to be a strong believer in the inviolable laws of physics it's my opinion that it's all an optical illusion, not mysterious forces or magic at work. Out of curiosity I've read a few articles on the alleged mystery and it seems like a lot of fun and interesting conversation but in the end the fact remains that objects roll downhill, not uphill. Gravity wins every time.

Continuing west from Shullsburg the change in the local landscape quickly becomes obvious as we enter the driftless zone. Nearby are the near ghost town villages of Lead Mine and Benton. A mile west of Benton route 11 "T's" at state route 80, where we turn left and begin our 12-mile ride through the picturesque rolling landscape to Galena. This is typical driftless countryside; a very pleasing mix of woods and fields dissected by a road twisting among the ancient hills.

Galena is nestled in the beautiful hilly countryside of northwestern Illinois. It's a town with a long history and much to brag about, including being the home of general and President Ulysses S. Grant. Grant Park is on the riverfront in town and President Grant's home on Bouthilier Street is an easy walk from the park. The town serves as the hub of the northwestern Illinois economy.

To close the loop from Galena follow US20 back to Freeport. Though a federal highway US20 betwixt the two towns is a pleasing motorcycling road. The stretch between Galena and Stockton is particularly nice though the eastern half between Stockton and Freeport is more typical of central Illinois landscape; verdant and pleasant if not heart racing road-riding excitement. Horseshoe Mound just east of Galena on US20 provides a wonderful panoramic view of the city and surrounding hilly landscape. Three miles east of Galena turn left onto Mt. Hope Road for a short two-mile ride to Thunder Bay Falls; certainly worth the diversion! Eleven miles east of Galena on route 20 there is a scenic overlook that's a nice place to stop for a bird's eye view of the tree covered hills and rolling farmland. The nearly five miles immediately west of the overlook is a particularly enjoyable ride as one traverses the hills and woods of the Tapley Woods Conservation Area.

The second route is a one-way ride that is very easy and enjoyable. Simply stay on state route 78, regardless of which state you happen to be in. The road is one of those pleasant rarities that carries the same title on both sides of the border and carries the two-wheeler stamp of approval for most of its length. Mt. Carroll in Illinois anchors the south end of this ride and Portage, Wisconsin is the northern terminus. In between are 130-miles of enjoyable riding. There is a farmland stretch near Stockton but for the most part the road traverses scenic rolling lands with the pavement meandering around rocky hills and following various watercourses. There is a lot to see within a couple miles of this road, from battle sites of the Black Hawk War to various museums and nearby spectacular parks such as Devils Lake State Park and others, and of course Mt. Horeb's many trolls. Watch for signs and be willing to explore a little as well as ride. There are several interesting historical sites in Portage ranging from an Indian Agency house and Fort Winnebago facility from the 19th century to a World War II museum. And check out the Portage canal, which connected the Fox and Wisconsin Rivers.

I think all will agree that regardless of which side of the border one is on this part of the Midwest is a great place to explore on two wheels.

7. Great River Scenic Byway in Illinois

MANY TOURING motorcyclists who live in a state bordering the Mississippi River have a personal goal of riding that state's portion of the renowned Great River Road National Scenic Byway. The Mississippi River is of course the stuff of legends and the roads that follow the shoreline from the river's headwaters to the Gulf of Mexico are similarly legendary. The Illinois segment is as delightful as any other. Though the designated series of roads that make up the Byway aren't endless open roads carving tight curves against riverside cliffs, there are long stretches outside urban areas that are superb from both scenic and enjoyable motorcycling perspectives. But one has to keep in mind that the roads that make up the Byway are also everyday working roads used for normal commerce and that they pass through industrial towns along the shores of this busy river.

A book about the best roads wouldn't be complete without discussing the Great River Road segments, which in this book involve Wisconsin, Iowa, Minnesota and Illinois. In the other states I detailed the road from the south end to the north, but in Illinois I will flip that, beginning at the north end and following the route south to Cairo. I should note here that normally I do not follow designated shoreline routes exactly but rather take local roads rather than official state or federal routes if the local road is closer to the water's edge and more enjoyable and scenic. For this ride I'm not going to do that, but will rather adhere to the official signed byway from end to end. There are places where local roads are closer to the river but rather than spend pages explaining each temporary diversion, let's stick with the official route this time. Overall it's marvelous though it does involve occasional competition with cagers and big rigs. A final caveat is that there are innumerable things to see and do along this 550-mile stretch of highway. Be alert for signs and be willing to stop and explore a bit, not just ride through like an uninterested passerby.

The designated Byway follows various roads along the river and trying to name each one can get confusing and perhaps even overwhelming. Fortunately the route is quite well signed with the unique Scenic Byway sign and is easier to follow than a list of road names might suggest.

Begin in East Dubuque just three miles south of the Wisconsin state line, riding US20 / state route 84 to south of Galena where 20 heads east and we stick with SR84. This is a typically enjoyable scenic ride for many miles. It's a great place to kick back, listen to the hum of the motor and enjoy the ride. Just north of Savanna the Mississippi Palisades State Park offers excellent bluff viewing and hiking opportunities to see and climb the awe-inspiring bluffs. South of Savanna's busyness the road's charms return. At Fulton, check out the Dutch Immigrant Windmill, and also a Great River Road informational kiosk at the site. A bit further, in Albany, the Indian Mounds Historical Site is an interesting and educational stop. Route 84 is our partner for many enjoyable miles, through Jo Daviess, Carroll, Whiteside and part of Rock Island counties – in fact all the way to East Moline.

In East Moline SR84 departs to the east so we turn right onto state route 92 into Moline. In downtown Moline a fun attraction is the John Deere Pavilion, off route 92 just south of I-74. Lots of big boys' toys. Stay on 92, following it along a westerly bend in the river to just west of Illinois City where we pick up local route 14 south to New Boston. On the north side of New Boston turn left onto route 17, cross the Edwards River and ride a short distance to county road that goes by three confusing names; 76th, Keithsburg Road, and county road 25. Just follow the standard Great River Road signs. This road delivers us to the town of Keithsburg where we turn left onto Main Street for seven blocks, then south on 10th Street, which becomes Keithsburg Road / county road 3 south of town.

At state route 164 turn right into the town of Oquawka, then south again on 164 to Gladstone and US34. Keep an eye out for the covered bridge and information kiosk on 164 three miles south of Oquawka. US 34 transports us four miles to the west and just before hitting the big river turn south on state route 522, riding it south to Lomax and route 96. Get on 96 and as it heads south it will have us hugging the shoreline all the way to the town of Hamilton. South of Hamilton county routes 32, 12, and 7 in succession get us close to the water and to Quincy. On the north side of Quincy take Kochs Lane east two blocks to route 24 and turn right onto 24 for a very short distance. When this main road turns to the west to cross the river just keep going straight ahead south on 3rd Street which becomes route 57 outside of town. Fifty seven carries us south across the 172 Xway to route 96, which finally makes life simpler by taking us all the way to Kampsville. From Kampsville route 100 accompanies the Illinois River and delivers us all the way to Alton. The economic might of the Mississippi River resulted in industrial cities all along its shoreline and at one time Alton was a larger and busier city than Chicago. This area of course is where the Illinois, Missouri and Mississippi rivers join. As a result of this unique geographic happenstance the region played a significant role in the country's history.

Route 143 delivers us to Hartford, just south of Alton and across from the point where the Missouri River joins the Mississippi, which was an important gathering place for westward exploration and expansion. Lewis & Clark were here preparing for their historic expedition. Visit the Lewis and Clark State Historic Site at 3500 New Poag Road in Hartford. The site showcases how the crew prepared for the trip and then embarked on their expedition to explore uncharted territory northwest of St. Louis. It was near this site that the group began their journey on May 14, 1804. The museum has five exhibit rooms filled with artifacts. A film "At Journey's Edge" describes their journey and a 55-foot full scale cutaway keelboat gives the viewer a wonderful look and feel for the boat used on their trip into the unknown. After visiting the museum take a tour of a replica settler cabin to see how settlers in the area lived in the early 1800's. Just a mile away is the Lewis & Clark Confluence Tower, soaring 180-feet above the rivers. There are three observation platforms on the tower.

Route 3 ultimately delivers us all the way to Cairo, with a short diversion onto the I-70 expressway and state route 111 while negotiating the complexities of the East St. Louis highway system. At East St. Louis I highly recommend a stop at the Cahokia Mounds State Historical Site. Take Collinsville Road east about five miles to this remarkable site.

Americans are impressed with the cultural legacy of ancient civilizations such as Egypt or the Mayans and Incas in South and Central America. But there were similarly impressive civilizations and structures right here in middle America. Unfortunately, many were earthen and wood structures rather than stone and they haven't survived as well. Cahokia was the largest and most influential urban settlement of what was called the Mississippian Culture, which developed advanced societies across much of central and southeastern America beginning about 1,500 years ago. At over 2,000-acres in size Cahokia Mounds is considered the largest and most complex archeological site north of the great pre-Columbian cities in Mexico. It was a large and bustling city, larger than the city of London eight hundred years ago. The complex is the only UNESCO World Heritage Site in the Midwest.

The mounds are a short ride east of 111. It's easy to come back and turn left onto 111 to continue the byway south.

South of East St. Louis the byway is inland several miles in places. There are points of interest along the way to check out, some of which require a short side trip. One of these is the Fort de Chartres State Historic Site on route 155 west of the tiny town of Ruma. This former French fort was originally built in 1720. It is from here that the monarchs of France ruled a large portion of the New World. There are many other sites of interest that are equally captivating and impressive. If only there was time to visit all of them. They don't get much better than along this river of history.

Sixty miles south of the East St. Louis area is the historic town of Chester, situated high on a river side bluff and the home of Popeye and so much more. Actually it's the home of the creator of the Popeye character, Elzie Segar. There is a statue of Popeye in the Segar Park in town.

An event called Popeye's Picnic is a festival held the weekend following Labor Day each year.

Interestingly, in 1842 Charles Dickens visited Chester during his North America tour, and in the late 1850s Mark Twain stopped here several times on his riverboat duties, staying at a local hilltop hotel. Fort Kaskaskia State Historic Park is also nearby at the mouth of the Kaskaskia River. Interestingly, because of a change in the river channel years ago an island was formed near here that is the only part of Illinois that is located west of the Mississippi River.

The Byway continues to be a scenic and fun ride almost all the way to Cairo. Only the last few miles are in the flat delta area near the Mississippi and Ohio River confluence. Going to Cairo to see the actual point where they join is a memorable part of this trip. There is a small 'confluence park' that isn't in great shape any more but the state of the park doesn't hinder the impressive view of the powerfully flowing muddy waters as they join forces.

For the sake of not providing several confusing (and boring!) pages of exact route designations and turns I've been somewhat superficial in my directions. The scenic byway route is well marked overall with signs, though the placement of signs at every turn can't be guaranteed. The primary place for confusion is in large cities, but these urban areas can be negotiated in whatever manner the rider feels most comfortable with. Certainly the route can be followed even in urban areas. Some may wish to simply go around cities and pick up the river road beyond the city limits rather than try to follow the byway through downtowns. That's often been my remedy if there isn't an attraction in the city that I wanted to visit. After all, it's the open roads beyond urban centers that are the focus of this book and these rides, not congested town centers. The official route outside large cities is well marked and easy to follow. So two tips – avoid downtowns if wished by skirting around them, and secondly, watch for signs for the dozens of points of interest along the byway that will enhance the experience of this tour immensely.

Historic filling station on Route 66 in Illinois

Motorcycling in the Hoosier State

When driving through this part of the country folks are often fooled by the geography and scenery along I-80 and the other interstates that crisscross the Crossroads of America. Expressway travelers rarely see the true story of the region they're driving through. But like other states in the Midwest Indiana offers excellent motorcycling opportunities. Indiana's back roads and small towns are wonderful places to explore though underappreciated and relatively unknown to nonresidents. There are myriad natural and manmade attractions. And of course the purpose of this book is to do more than just suggest some great riding roads. I also want to tell the background stories of places so that the land and the people who shaped it come alive, enabling an appreciation of the events and people that forged what we see around us today.

The state can be divided into three distinct geographic zones. In the southern one-third, which is the most popular motorcycling destination, riders find meandering roads through beautiful countryside, forests dissected by twisting pavement laid alongside walls of ancient bedrock, waterfalls and caves, white water streams, rustic covered bridges, and of course all the delights that motorcycling along the Ohio River offers. Throw in unique small towns and sites of fascinating historical importance and this region can keep a biker smiling for an entire season.

Central Indiana has miles of pastoral country roads through its bountiful farmlands and woods, and roads that meander as they follow rivers such as the Wabash, the Whitewater, the Tippecanoe, the Mississinewa and the St. Mary's – storied streams of history, legend and song. The northern portion of the state is lake country where scores of inland lakes are nestled in the rolling glacial hills, and the blue waters of Lake Michigan stretch north beyond the horizon seemingly forever. Majestic sand dunes that have made their home in the middle of a continent on the shore of this great lake add to the charm and wonders of this beautiful state.

Fundamentally this book is about the best motorcycling roads in the Midwest. I believe that even on the best riding roads the motorcycling experience can be enhanced if one seeks out interesting places during the ride and delves into the stories behind those attractions. Fascinating discoveries about our country are waiting for us out there. All we have to do is slow down and look. Indiana truly is a wonderful place to explore by motorcycle on its back roads and through overlooked small towns. It's time to explore the Indiana that most people don't see because they're in a hurry and as creatures of habit they oftentimes don't venture off familiar routes. Maybe their reticence is a blessing in disguise because that means less traffic on the roads that we enjoy as motorcyclists.

- Ohio River Scenic Byway Site: https://www.fhwa.dot.gov/byways/byways/2286
- Indiana State Parks: https://www.in.gov/dnr/parklake/
- Indiana Tourism Board: https://visitindiana.com/
- Scenic Byway Program: https://www.in.gov/indot/2827.htm
- Indiana Dunes National Lakeshore: https://www.nps.gov/indu/index.htm
- Indiana Motorcycle Events: https://www.cyclefish.com/motorcycle_events/INDIANA

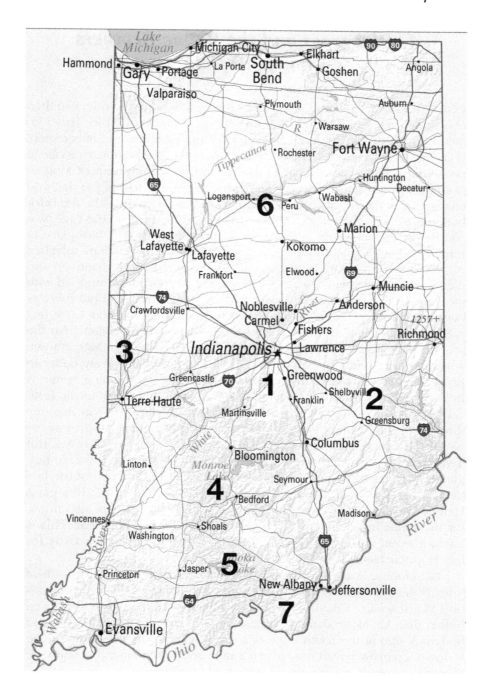

1. Bluegrass and the Boone Brothers on Route 135

POINT TO POINT rides are sometimes the best because the rider can then choose whatever option they want for the next phase of a trip. This 125-mile ride, located in southern Indiana's celebrated forest and hills region, is one of the nicest rides in the state. The outing begins in Martinsville, a prototypical Midwestern town of 12,000 and the county seat of Morgan County. It's their status as county seat that allows me to suggest that you take a look at the county courthouse in town before leaving. The red brick building was completed in 1859 and is one of just a few pre-Civil War courthouses to still stand in the state. Martinsville is also the birthplace of John Wooden, famous college coach and basketball hall of fame member.

Start the adventure by riding east on route 252 to Morgantown and then turning south onto route 135. Route 252 is a decent riding road with pleasant scenery and enticing sweeping curves and hills. About midway between Martinsville and Morgantown is Mt. Nebo, which at 1,000 feet is the highest point around, at least three-hundred feet higher than the average elevation for the area. The real excitement begins at Morgantown when we turn south on route 135. The ride gets progressively better in Brown County and its many attractions. Our first entertaining venue is Bean Blossom—home of the famous Bill Monroe bluegrass music festival. This renowned event has been taking place since 1967 at this tiny town and it's now apparently the largest bluegrass music festival in the world. This place really gets hopping when the stars are in town. But if you're into bluegrass music you already know all this, if you're not, give it a try, all those good people can't be wrong. The site of the festival, which was owned by Mr. Monroe, is also the site of the Bluegrass Hall of Fame and Country Star Museum. Bean Blossom is also home for the Bean Blossom BikerFest held in September each year. This is a major event with top-notch entertainment. Get your tickets early for this popular bash.

Bill Monroe is unquestionably loved in this area. Route 135 north of town is the Bill Monroe Highway, and the Bill Monroe Memorial Bridge is on 135 just south of Bean Blossom. But an attraction that goes back even further than Mr. Monroe and bluegrass music is the Bean Blossom covered bridge. A sign at the south edge of town points it out. The rustic bridge is down a narrow paved road about a mile and I recommend making the short trip to see it. It's in a pretty setting and traffic won't be an issue.

Route 135 just keeps getting better and better the further south one rides. About two miles south of Bean Blossom watch for signs for a scenic overlook on top of Dug Hill. At 920 feet in elevation it gives a nice panoramic view of the surrounding Yellowwood State Forest.

After a short but fun trip south from Bean Blossom we come upon Nashville. This is the kind of bustling small town you'll either want to ride straight on through and avoid the crowds and traffic, or you'll like its touristy charms and want to spend time browsing the stores that line the main street and watch the crowds. It's a popular destination with crowds that belie its size and location. Summer weekends can be trying if you want to stop to shop or eat here, so time your arrival if you can. In fact, this entire area is best explored on a weekday. In addition to the sightseers and tourists the weekend finds many horse trailers being pulled down route 135 to enjoy the horse-riding opportunities in beautiful Brown County State Park. You'll enjoy the area no matter the day or season, but just be aware that for pure motorcycling fun the Monday—Friday period works best if you can arrange it. One fun attraction in Nashville is the Brown County Pioneer Museum and Log Cabin Jail. You might want to check it out before heading south again on 135.

South of Nashville the road becomes heavenly. If you've been seeking motorcycling Nirvana—rejoice; you found it. The tight curves will challenge the most adventurous riders and the overall ambience is fabulous. After many miles of motorcycling paradise you'll come to a ninety degree turn in the road and there ahead of you is the tiny and very cool town of Story. Formed in 1851 by Doctor George P. Story, the town never turned into the bustling metropolis he thought it would. Instead it remained a small charming community deep in the woods. The entire village was placed on the National Registry of Historic Places early in 2019 – and by the way, as of this writing, the entire town is for sale for a mere 3.8 million dollars.

Of special interest is the Story Inn and the historic building it occupies. If you've never been there take the time to park in the lot in front of the inn and take a look around. Better yet, go in and grab a bite. You'll be glad you did. Standing on the old-fashioned front porch of the inn modern motorcycles look out of place parked near the antique gas pumps. In their place one expects to see Indian Chiefs, Hendersons and Harley knuckleheads, with their leather-helmeted and goggled riders standing on the porch praising the virtues of their machines. Perhaps the ghosts of those riders still haunt the inn, basking in the sights and sounds of today's motorcycling experience and happy to see that the adventurous attitude is still alive and well.

South of Story the riding pleasure continues unabated as I35 snakes through the Hoosier National Forest until Freetown. The entire stretch of I35 from Morgantown to Freetown is fabulous. The fun continues for several miles south of Freetown and the road doesn't straighten out and escape the forest until a couple miles north of US50. In order to continue following I35 jog east on 50 for less than three miles at which point our road continues south. It goes through pleasant but mostly open farmlands for several miles before entering the woods and hills again north of Salem. This stretch is once again marvelous with made to order motorcycling ambience.

The route goes straight south through Salem as Main Street. I recommend parking your bike along Salem's attractive courthouse square to see this city and its 19th-century architecture up close. The courthouse is one of the most beautiful in the state, and much of the downtown square is a national historic area. There's a lot going on in this pleasant Midwestern town. Races at the Salem Speedway, classic car shows downtown, a pioneer village, railroad museum, and more.

Salem was perhaps the hardest hit town in Indiana during the Civil War. Businesses and homes in the town were looted and the railroad depot and many rail cars burned by troops under Confederate General John Hunt Morgan's infamous raid into Indiana and Ohio in the summer of 1863. The marauders stole whatever they could carry with them before departing on July 10, 1863.

Between Salem and the old capital of Corydon I35 is just plain fun. You will enjoy the relaxing ride through pleasing countryside and light traffic.

Corydon was the first capital of Indiana from 1816 to 1825, when the capital was moved north to Indianapolis reflecting the movement of settlers from south to north. The historic limestone capitol building is an interesting place to visit and is right along our route through town. Just up the street from the old capitol building, at 419 Capitol Avenue is historic Branham Tavern, a log building first licensed as a tavern in 1809. Corydon's other claim to fame was the Civil War battle fought just a mile south of town on July 9, 1863. In this battle a group of local militia and civilians was defeated by a much stronger force of Confederate cavalrymen led by General Morgan. Colonel Lewis Jordan, leader of the Indiana militia and volunteers, finally surrendered after Morgan began shelling the vastly outnumbered fighters, and the town, with cannon fire. Take Old I35 in town south a mile to the battlefield park.

Upon heading south out of Corydon route I35 loses the fabulous riding category it enjoyed to the north of US50 but for mile after mile it's an enjoyable ride that definitely won't disappoint. The same can be said for the fun miles south of Corydon to the Ohio River. Four miles north of the river watch for signs pointing out Squire Boone Caverns. The actual caverns are on Squire Boone Road three miles east of route 135. Squire Boone, and his more famous brother Daniel, discovered these caverns and underground stream in 1790. At the site today there is an interpretive center and restored mill. So exchange your helmet for a raccoon skin hat and spend a little time with the Boone brothers.

Sometimes a person has to constantly monitor their map or GPS unit to follow a route. The beauty of this ride is that we just stay on one delightful road for virtually the entire distance. More fun and less worry about making a wrong turn on this quintessential motorcycling adventure through some of the best of the Midwest.

2. The Whitewater Valley Ride

RIVERS AND MOTORCYCLES make a marvelous team. Not that bikes and water are compatible but rather because rivers often have adjacent roads that offer excellent motorcycling potential as they mimic the meandering watercourse. This is certainly true in southeastern Indiana along the Whitewater River.

We'll put our kickstands up in Cambridge City on the famous and historic National Road to begin this 120-mile point-to-point ride. The history of Cambridge City is linked with the Whitewater Canal (which we'll see later in this ride) and the city's location on the National Road. This location made it a strategic town for commerce and movement of people west. Before leaving Cambridge City I suggest a stop at the Vinton House on Main Street. The building is at the former intersection of the original 19th century National Road (Old US40) and the Whitewater Canal. The canal's turnaround basin was just a few feet from its rear door, bringing passengers and goods from the east. The building's location was so central that at various times it served as a stage coach stop, a telegraph office, a mail office and even a recruiting post during the Civil War. The 36-room Vinton House Hotel provided lodging for guests traveling on the Whitewater Canal.

From Cambridge City route 1 carries us straight south to Connersville. At that point the river and road combo become more scenic and enjoyable as we continue south on state route 121 from Connersville. This entertaining road is often tight on the tree-lined shore of the West Fork of the Whitewater River and it's a continual series of sweeping curves with nary a straight stretch south to route US52. Turn left onto 52 and shadow it to the unique village of Metamora and the Whitewater Canal district.

Metamora is a tourist town and partly living museum that survives on its history and location. The setting is both scenic and historic. I find it an agreeable place to visit because there are often different events going on, or simple things like sidewalk musicians that add a pleasing ambience and charm. Take a ride on a canal boat or a short train ride to really experience the history of the town. It's a fun place to park the bike, buy an ice cream cone and walk and gawk, even if you don't do anything more than that. But I recommend a stop at the Whitewater Canal State Historic Site. Enjoy a ride on the Ben Franklin III canal boat, pulled by Belgian horses. Visit the old grist mill and check out the Duck Creek aqueduct, which actually carries the canal over the creek on a bridge. Very unusual. To get to the park turn right on Pennington Street and go one mile. This canal played a major role in the early development of Indiana before the days of railroads and navigable roads.

The ride continues east on US52 and the fun increases as the road closely accompanies the twists of the adjacent river. The road between Metamora and Brookville is short but very nice. Bedrock ledges along the river provide a dramatic scenic touch and stand as mute evidence to the power of moving water over time. The East Fork joins the West Fork at Brookville and the river departs, continuing southeast to meet its fate in southwest Ohio where it joins the Great Miami River and ultimately the Ohio River. Just before reaching Brookville on US52 Skyward Adventures Zipline Tours might be of interest for some. It's a large operation and offers zipline tours close to a mile in length. For the more grounded, check out the Brookville Historic District in downtown. Many architecturally interesting and stately old buildings make up the national historic district.

Follow 52 southeast from Brookville for five miles and then turn right onto route 1. This lightly traveled scenic pavement carries us south to the town of Greendale. The segment of this ride on route 1 is typical southern Indiana hills, forests, and rocky bluffs interspersed with small farms and towns. With the exception of one short stretch through farmlands south of Brookville the landscape is a scenic montage that pleases the eye and the road is a fun strip of asphalt that will at least partially satisfy the road racer within.

Coming into Greendale route 1 ends at US50, near the Hollywood Casino on the river. Turn right onto this highway and ride it along the Ohio River west through Greendale, Aurora and the fifteen miles to Dillsboro. Turn left onto North Street / Old US 50 just east of Dillsboro. North Street goes into the downtown section of this small town where it also becomes route 62. Near the west edge of Dillsboro route 62 veers southwest as Sunset Street / 62 (at the elementary school.) Remain on route 62 for the last leg of the ride. This laid back road takes us southwest all the way to Madison, on the Ohio River. Our road teams up with route 129 for several miles and then split off on its own again south of Cross Plains. It once again joins with route 250 for a few miles, but this teamwork doesn't detract at all from the ambience. Route 62 is a joy to ride with its constant curves and the scenic countryside. Upon approaching North Madison turn left at the traffic circle and head south on US421 into Madison and the Ohio River shoreline. Route 421 courses alongside Crooked Creek for three miles and it's a surprisingly nice ride for being so close to a good-sized town.

Madison is a good town to spend a little time exploring. It was initially a major gateway into the Indiana Territory because of its location on the Ohio River. It was platted in 1810 and named in honor of President Madison. The town benefitted from early beliefs that it might become the capital of the new State of Indiana, an action that was just a few years from being approved by the US Congress. As a result early residents created a city with broad boulevards and stately buildings. Downtown Madison retains that original attractive appearance and has many buildings listed on the National Registry of Historic Places, including Lanier Mansion State Historic Site. If you like bluegrass music Madison hosts a free festival at the fairgrounds the first Saturday of each month, and during the summer there are several car shows that attract some marvelous classics. Rockin Thunder River Tours offers a unique way to explore the waterway with their jet boats. On the more tranquil side of adventure check out Clifty Falls and Hoffman Falls in Clifty Falls State Park adjacent to town. And of course a person can spend time just sitting on the shore of the mighty Ohio River at the small but strategically located Lamplighter Park, watching river traffic struggling against the powerful current and viewing the hilly scenery on the opposite shore.

3. Covered Bridges Over Rocky Waters

THIS SHORT BUT SCENIC ride in the west central part of Indiana is an example of the many different features that encompass the state's motorcycling opportunities. It's proof that there is much more to Indiana than corn fields and flat straight roads. The tour takes advantage of the unique geology and the bedrock landscape that is a product of ancient forces. But the geologic underpinnings have many tentacles. This is a beautiful region of forests, rivers, caverns and waterfalls, stone escarpments, and rustic covered bridges. These all exist because of the geologic makeup of the area. It's certainly one of the prettiest parts of the state due to the totality of the attractions and natural beauty it possesses. There are many opportunities to explore and enjoy the rugged beauty of the land in Shades and Turkey Run State Parks but there are also attractions that exist directly because of the landscape. Things such as historic buildings and covered bridges. And did I mention wonderful motorcycling roads?

Let's begin this relatively short circular ride in Crawfordsville, located on Sugar Creek. It's the county seat of Montgomery County and home of Wabash College and of Ben-Hur. The Rotary Jail Museum is a highly recommended stop prior to starting the ride. It's one of only three jails left in the country built on a rotating platform, and apparently the only one that still functions. The sixteen-cell jail is two stories high and the rotating mechanism weighs thirty tons. It's quite amazing, and easy to find at 225 N. Washington Street. And old county courthouses are always impressive structures to admire even if just from the adjacent courthouse square.

On the southwest corner of Crawfordsville state route 32 goes west from US231. Ride 32 about thirteen miles west to route 341. This initial stretch is pleasant enough but is a poor harbinger of the fabulous riding that awaits. Go south on 341 five miles to route 234 and turn back east. Two thirty four is our host for about ten miles, which includes some very scenic and enjoyable pavement as it carves through Shades State Park and along Sugar Creek. In this vicinity Sugar Creek certainly qualifies as one of Indiana's most scenic streams.

There are a few serious hairpin curves on route 234 so be watchful for scenery gawkers who might cross the double yellow. The park is a great place to stop and enjoy the sights and read the signs for local attractions. The geology is impressive and dates back about 12,000 years when melting glaciers to the north unleashed a torrent of water which carved impressive gorges in the native sandstone.

Continue east on 234 past the park to its junction with route 47, and turn right. Forty seven heads southwest for five miles then goes due west where the fun begins again in earnest in Turkey Run State Park. At US41 turn right and continue the ride in the park. Once again this is a perfect place to expand your horizons by seeking out the many other attractions nearby, especially local covered bridges, historic mills and other old buildings, and impressive stretches of river tumbling through sandstone bedrock cliffs. There are walking trails and nearby vendors offer canoe, kayak and tubing runs on the river. Three covered bridges are nearby, Narrows, Wilkins Mill, and Cox Ford and Deer's Mill bridge is near Shades State Park. In total, there are 31 covered bridges in Parke County, each one unique.

After exiting park property head north on US41 to US136. All told, we'll be on 41 for fifteen miles. Follow route 136 as it gently meanders eastward through Hillsboro and Waynetown back to Crawfordsville. This final route is a relaxing riding as it follows the tree lined curves of Coal Creek between US41 and Waynetown. In total this tour is a short 85-miles but with the many potential things to see and do in the two beautiful state parks it can and should easily be a daylong adventure.

4. Haunted Hindostan

THIS 90-MILE RUSTIC ride takes advantage of the remarkable southern Indiana geology, traversing the familiar landscape where motorcyclists love to roam. And as is the case with other tours, there is a significant amount of history and fascinating manmade attractions to explore.

Begin the ride on the west side of Columbus at Mill Race Park, where the Flatrock River and Driftwood River join. The park is a great place to gather and walk, with its covered bridge and scenic trails. Before leaving Columbus you might want to visit the impressive Bartholomew County Veterans Monument on the courthouse square. It's just a few blocks from the park on eastbound state route 46.

When ready to leave town cross the Flatrock River westbound on 46 and then immediately turn south onto state route 11. We will be on route 11 for just under five miles and then turn right on 450 Street. Ride this a mile west, beyond the I-65 expressway where it seamlessly becomes state route 58; the road we want to carry us to Freetown.

The road to Freetown gets progressively better and is a great way to start off a day's ride. The scenery is typically southern Indiana (which means it's a pleasant mix of wooded hills, small rivers, and neat farms tucked against the hillsides)

Route 58 joins with SR135 for a mile south from Freetown and then continues westward through the Hoosier National Forest and the villages of Kurtz and Norman Station. The fun continues almost all the way to Bedford. Two miles east of Bedford the road takes a turn to straight west and the next few miles become open and then urbanized as we skirt around Bedford to the north, remaining on 58 until we reach busy route 37, a divided highway on the west side of town. At this point route 58 abandons us heading off to the north so we want to go south on 37 a short distance in town until we see 16th Street. Turn right onto 16th Street, follow it west just a block and then turn left onto route 450. This really nice biking road angles southwest for many miles through another portion of the Hoosier National Forest and ultimately to the town of Shoals.

There are many enjoyable miles to ride before reaching Shoals, however. There are few straight stretches of the road and a multitude of sweeping curves creating an enjoyable ride with enough character to challenge peg scrapers if so desired. In the village of Williams you might want to park the bike at a small park on the East Fork of the White River and enjoy the ambience. Just a mile west of town is the Williams Covered Bridge which is certainly worth a stop. (Turn left onto Huron and Williams Road, the bridge is a short distance to the south)

Route 450 roughly shadows the White River fork southwesterly as it meanders in a fairly hilly combination of wooded land and farms. It's a real nice mix of scenery and entertaining riding. Four fifty ends just north of Shoals. At this point we turn south / left onto US50 / 150 into the town of Shoals. Shoals is a small town that straddles the river, and despite its small size it's the county seat of Martin County. To learn more about the region stop at the Martin County museum located downtown in the old courthouse. The unique geology of this area has resulted in some of the most impressive cliffs and rock outcroppings in the state. In fact, along the river just north of town in the Jug Rock Nature Preserve is Jug Rock – at sixty feet high and twenty feet in diameter the largest free standing formation of its kind east of the Mississippi River. Along the river in Martin County there are other unique and beautiful rock formations. If you're into this sort of thing definitely plan to spend some time here exploring the geological attractions found nearby. The local geology has resulted in many springs within a few miles of town. These springs were instrumental in drawing early settlers to the area.

A noteworthy historic item for Shoals occurred in 1861. Early in the Civil War troops from Indiana were rushing to Washington D.C. to protect it from attack. In those days Martin County had many southern sympathizers (most of the early settlers in southern Indiana came from southern states). As the troop train was going over a bridge spanning Beaver Creek the rails gave way causing a terrible accident that killed forty Indiana troopers and injured over one hundred more. Though never proven it was long suspected that local southern sympathizers, members of the Knights of the Golden Circle, were responsible for the crash

Motor down US150 south from Shoals and in two miles route 550 carries you five miles west through the national forest to Hindostan Falls. There is a well-marked paved road heading south for the final short distance to the diminutive but scenic waterfall on the East Fork of the White River. The falls are formed by a sandstone ledge that crosses the river at this point. A public fishing site at the location provides a place to park the bikes and enjoy the scenery.

Things weren't always this calm at this location. Hindostan Falls was a booming community called Hindostan two hundred years ago. With a population of 1200 in 1820 it was one of the largest towns in this part of Indiana. Hindostan boasted two mills, a hotel, a post office and even a couple small factories. Ferries made their way between the river's two banks and houseboats moored on its waters. All that's left of the community are some square cuts in the flat rocks where one of the mills used to be anchored and stories of ghosts haunting Hindostan Falls. There is a very good reason for the ghost stories. Just when things seemed to be going so well for the booming community in this idyllic setting many of its townspeople were wiped out by an unknown disease, perhaps yellow fever or cholera or possibly even the plague. Homes where entire families had died were burned to the ground and mass graves, some holding a hundred or so, were dug and then hastily filled up. History isn't always positive nor does it always end well but the stories of where we came from are always fascinating just the same.

The falls and park are a fitting place to end this particular ride on some of Indiana's best roads.

5. Springs, Licks and Great Motorcycling Roads

THIS RIDE WILL HAVE motorcyclists saying "Wow!" many times during the course of the day as they marvel at the magical road carrying them and admire the natural beauty found along the way. They might find themselves spending nearly as much time stopped to admire various attractions along the way as cruising the delightful biking roads that are found on this day ride.

I suspect by now you gotten the impression that a significant part of the motorcycling experience for me goes beyond the ride; it also involves admiring the wonders of nature and the manmade features that dot the landscape. Something I've noticed over the years is that the most interesting built features are either in the old urban cores of our cities and towns, or in the countryside. You don't find things of lasting beauty and historical significance in the 'burbs. Suburban areas were built, and continue to be built, with a throw away attitude. Make a quick profit, use the building for a few years, and then abandon it when it's no longer profitable. But that wasn't the ethic folks had when they built the stately courthouses, churches, railroad depots or other significant buildings in our old towns. Nor was it the prevailing attitude when our ancestors built the barns, covered bridges, or other rural monuments that stand proudly to this day in testimony to their craftsmanship and their faith in the future of this country.

So, on this ride we're going to enjoy the best of both worlds – the natural beauty and enjoyment found while riding down fun roads in a beautiful landscape – and the lasting impression of some of man's notable handiwork found in rural southern Indiana.

We begin and end our ride in West Baden Springs and French Lick; sites that owe their existence to the unique geology of the area. Mineral springs had attracted wildlife and Native Americans to this locale for untold centuries. Places like this were called licks by early explorers and settlers because wildlife came to these salt springs to lick salt from the springs. Early French explorers were always on the lookout for licks for practical reasons. They too needed the salt available at these sites, and they also knew that such springs were almost always to be included in the travel routes established centuries earlier by Indians. This meant that salt licks and springs made logical places to build outposts from which they could interact with the Indians; trading various goods for furs that they then shipped back to Europe. Early explorers didn't just wander through the wilderness. They followed long-established land and water trails created by the aboriginal peoples and migrating animals. Salt springs were often found along these trails. The potential of developing the Baden Springs and French Lick area was realized quickly by settlers and in the 1840s the first hotel and resort was built. Its fortunes reflected the economic and political events of the country; struggling during the Civil War and later economic downturns or periods of war, and prospering mightily in the late 19th and early 20th century when health spas were all the rage. Another much more exclusive resort was built in 1902 at the West Baden Springs. French Lick and West Baden Springs had firmly established themselves as resorts where the upper-crust could gamble and enjoy the various amenities that health spas and exclusive hotels provided.

Both towns and their resorts suffered a decline in the late 1900s, but in recent years have enjoyed an impressive renaissance. The West Baden Springs resort – the so-called eighth wonder of the world – is completely rebuilt. If you don't want to spend the night there you can take tours of the building and grounds for a $10 fee. There are new casinos and hotels in French Lick to support the new-found popularity of casino gambling by the masses. These resorts no longer depend on the wealthy for their existence; it's the average working folks that now support them. A just-completed new casino in French Lick looks every bit a Mississippi River sternwheeler complete with water splashing off its faux water wheel.

Another attraction in French Lick that bikers might be interested in is the Indiana Railway Museum and the French Lick Scenic Railway. There are many interesting pieces of railroading history, including steam locomotives, cabooses, passenger cars and so forth on display outside of the museum (many of which are utilized as part of the scenic railway excursions) and of course more railroading paraphernalia displayed inside the old depot museum. You might want to enjoy the nearly two-hour train ride through some of the most scenic countryside that Indiana has to offer, including through the 2,200-foot Burton Tunnel. Their web site is www.indianarailwaymuseum.org/ and phone is 1-800-74-TRAIN.

After seeing the various manmade wonders in the French Lick vicinity let's get our motors running and start the fabulous ride by motoring south on route 145. This road quickly becomes especially nice as one rides south and leaves the hustle and bustle of the resort area behind. All that urban busyness is quickly replaced by a rolling forested landscape punctuated by beautiful Patoka Lake. Our road crosses narrow arms of this manmade lake in several places, offering opportunities to park the bike and enjoy some relaxing time sitting on the shore gazing at the blue water and wooded hills that surround the lake. Route 145 makes a westerly jog along state route 64 and then continues south at the tiny town of Birdseye. With the exception of a short stretch where route 145 intersects with the I-64 expressway it is a fabulous riding road. It has everything a mo-torcyclist out looking for a good time wants – hills, curves that will wear down the sidewalls of your tires if that's your wish, beautiful scenery, and light traffic. This stretch of road shouldn't be taken lightly though. Its curves are often tight and there are no shoulders alongside the asphalt; only trees, and the occasional serious drop off that will ruin a rider's day real fast if exuberance exceeds control of the bike.

Ridden with skill route 145 is a wonderful ride. It's the kind of road a person would ride every day if he or she lived close enough. We'll take it south to state route 37 and then 237 all the way to the small town of Cannelton on the Ohio River. Turn at the main intersection in Cannelton toward the river to view the amazing flood wall that lines the shore. It might not be pretty but it sure is impressive! Also, take a gander at the old Indiana Cotton Mill building. It's been fully restored and the building re-tains its marvelous original architecture and impressive bulk reminiscent of the day when buildings were built of local native stone, and meant to last for centuries. The floodwall and the old cotton mill building are ex-amples of impressive manmade structures that we can admire and marvel at the engineering and construction skills that it took to build them. And of course the Ohio River itself is a natural wonder with few peers. Its current is the embodiment of unstoppable power, and one cannot help but be amazed at the size and beauty of this river and of the beautiful landscape it flows through.

For the second half of this fun ride we'll head back north on 37, but instead of following route 145 we'll stay on route 37 as it twists and turns its way northward through the scenic low hills of the Hoosier National Forest. At St. Croix and the US64 highway we'll continue north on old 37 which rejoins route 145 after a short westerly ride on Indiana route 64 at Eckerty. One forty five carries us once again through the wooded lands surrounding Patoka Lake for the last few entertaining miles back to French Lick.

I think everyone who rides it will agree that this enjoyable 105-mile loop deserves to be included in a list of Indiana's best motorcycling op-portunities.

6. On the Banks of the Wabash

IN INDIANA THERE is no river more famous than the Wabash, celebrated in song and poetry. It is so revered that the legislature designated it as the state's official river (one of only three rivers in the country having been recognized as an official state symbol). It's also one of the most scenic in the state because much of it remains in its natural condition. As is the case with many rivers, adjacent roads along the Wabash River create excellent motorcycling opportunities that we will take advantage of. This particular river ride is also intellectually interesting because there is so much history to explore along the 220 scenic miles.

Like so many place names in this country the name of this river can be traced back to Native Americans, in this case the Miami nation. They gave the stream the name Wah-Bah-Shik-Ki, which meant roughly "pure white". The river got this name from the condition of the stream in the Huntington area, which in pre-settlement days had a clean and clear bottom of limestone, giving it a white appearance. The French fur traders pronounced the Indian name as Quabache, and the Anglo settlers then pronounced the French name as Wabash.

The Wabash served as one of the most important water routes in the interior of the continent from the 1600s well into the 1800s. For centuries the watershed divide just south of Fort Wayne was a portage location whereby travelers could move between the Great Lakes region to the Mississippi and Gulf of Mexico. The value of this waterway changed from one of military importance to a vital economic link in the 1830s when the Wabash-Erie Canal was dug parallel to the river, connecting Lake Erie and the Mississippi with a water route that required no portage. Ironically, after taking over a decade to build, and essentially bankrupting the young state of Indiana, the canal operated at full capacity for only a decade when it succumbed to a more modern form of transportation – the railroad. It has its place in history firmly entrenched, however, as the longest canal system ever built in the country. Only one canal in China can claim to be longer than this historic canal dug alongside the Wabash.

We'll follow the river in this ride along the most scenic portion, from Huntington to the bluffs south of Terre Haute near the village of Merom. Commencing this ride in downtown Huntington, the Lime City, take Park Street / Business 24 westbound. I suggest this starting point because there are three points of interest on the west side of town that are worthy of a stop before actually beginning the ride. The first is the beautiful sunken gardens in Memorial Park. The gardens are in an old quarry and have been elegantly constructed with fountains, a variety of flower beds, and places to sit to admire it all. It's a unique site to see a park setting surrounded by high stone walls. Parking for the garden is on the opposite side of the street just past an attractive stone bridge, under which one walks to gain entry to the garden. Continue west on Park Street and it joins seamlessly with route 24 on the west side of town. Immediately west of the route 24 / route 9 intersection is the Forks of The Wabash Park and museum in the event you wish to explore the interesting history of Native Americans and early Europeans in this strategic region. A very nice walking trail at the site just happens to be on the old canal's towpath. A very short distance west of the park is Sheets Wildlife Museum. This building houses a collection of about 200 mounted animals from around the world, as well as providing displays and information about the broad ecological story of wildlife and scientific game management. The museum is the work of one Sumner Sheets, a local resident and worldwide traveler and hunter.

With these three possible stops behind us, begin the expedition along the Wabash by continuing west on route 24, known as The Hoosier Heartland Highway. This portion of route 24 is a nice road with pleasing scenery, sweeping curves and a hilly landscape that might not be at all what many expect to find in this part of the state. Route 24 takes us around the outer edges of the city of Wabash. On the southwest corner of town, just as the new divided highway US24 heads straight west again, you'll see a sign for Old 24 / Business 24. Turn left off the main highway onto Old 24 and ride this attractive old road west into Peru.

If you look closely you can see some old canal remains along this stretch of road east of Peru, and a sign just east of the town of Peru notes the prior location of the canal. Through the city of Peru our road becomes known as Main Street and also as business 24. The International Circus Hall of Fame and the Circus City Festival Museum are located nearby. The Circus City Museum is on Broadway a few blocks north of Main Street and the International Hall of Fame is on Peru Circus Lane off route 124, south of the river and just a bit east of town. The HoF site is both a functioning circus in the summer and a collection of rare and amazing circus paraphernalia. In the last century there has been more circus activity in Peru than anywhere else on earth, so these folks know what they're doing.

To continue on the trip ride Main Street west through town where it then acquires the name of Logansport Road. The route is easy to stay with as it's the same road alignment, just given different names as it passes through various jurisdictions. Logansport Road hugs the railroad tracks as it heads west out of Peru, crosses U.S. 24, and then proceed in a westerly direction through the picturesque countryside, picking up the name Lewisburg Road just before entering the town of Logansport. Riding through Logansport our roadway becomes known as Market Street, then

Broadway Street due to a one-way street jog, and then Market Street again west of downtown. It's also signed as business 24 through town. West of the intersection with U.S. 35 on the west edge of town it becomes U.S. 24 again and we continue west on it. This may all sound a little confusing but once on the road you'll find that it's easy and logical to follow straight through from Peru to west of Logansport.

About two miles west of Logansport turn left onto Georgetown Road for an amazing cross-country trip along the river southwest to the town of Delphi. The turn from route 24 onto Georgetown Road is well marked. There are two signs at the turn we want to make – one pointing to the village of Georgetown and the second to the Towpath Training Center.

Very shortly after turning south on Georgetown Road we begin hugging the river, which by this point has become quite wide. The river shadows us and often be in view between here and the city of Delphi. The region is only lightly developed and the river looks natural as it flows in a landscape of woods and farmland. After slightly less than four miles we arrive in the burg of Georgetown itself, and a 'T' in the road. To the left is a bridge over the river. We, however, want to take a right turn and in about a half-mile we come to another 'T' where this time we turn left. After a couple miles we come to yet one more 'T' where we again turn left onto Towpath Trail. From this point on there are distinctive 'Towpath Trail' signs depicting the canal and mule towpath that ran beside the canal. We remain on Towpath Trail for many miles through a beautiful area. The road is narrow and lacking a center line or shoulders. Traffic is light and there are many curves making the scenic ride wonderfully entertaining. Stick with the "Towpath Trail" signs as the road quite closely parallels the river. There is one point about mid-way where we have to make a left turn to remain on Towpath Trail, but it's marked. Eventually the road crosses the river and picks up the name Carrollton Road. South of the river the road has been improved and is much more typical of a well-maintained primary county road. Carrollton Road delivers us to the historic town of Delphi from the north, becoming Wilson Street through town, eventually taking us to a stop sign at state route 25. Turn right onto route 25 taking it just a couple blocks west to the main intersection at the courthouse. Turn right at this corner to get to Canal Park, and a beautiful stone arch bridge over a remaining portion of the Wabash and Erie Canal in the park. This is one of the better preserved vestiges of this once incredible canal system that stretched from Toledo on Lake Erie to the Ohio River at Evansville.

Abandon the main highway and take the old road for the ride between Delphi and Battle Ground. In downtown Delphi get on West Main Street and head west a few blocks. On the west side of town that road turns into Old State Road 25 and heads to the southwest along the river. This old route follows closely along the wooded shores of the Wabash and is a much more pleasant ride than the new nearby four-lane highway version of Route 25. A heads up, at a point three miles southwest of Delphi we have to make a right turn to remain on Old 25 as the road splits at that point and we remain on the right fork. The scenic route takes us through the village of Americus and gradually the landscape changes as we approach Lafayette, but we're not going all the way into the big city just yet. Four miles past Americus turn right onto route 225 and take it across the river to Prophetstown State Park and the Tippecanoe Battlefield Park with its memorial and museum. This park protects and tells the story of one of the more important events in Indiana's history. I don't think I'm the only one who recalls high school history class every time I hear the word Tippecanoe, as in the "Tippecanoe and Tyler Too" slogan used in the 1840 General William Harrison and Martin Van Buren presidential election. I make a "No Tests" promise for this trip, so just relax and enjoy the ride and appreciate the important historical context of the river and places along it.

When done touring the Battle Ground park site continue the downstream trek. Riding conditions change quickly west of I-65 when we enter the Lafayette / West Lafayette urban area. Route Old 25 joins Route 25 and becomes Schuyler Avenue when entering Lafayette. The easiest route (unless you're a Lafayette / Purdue local and know the area well) is take Schuyler Avenue the very short distance to the I-65 expressway and get on I-65, taking it three miles north across the river to the River Road / route 43 exit. Head south on this road. The River Road designation is what we want, disregarding the route 43 options. Motor down River Road south for seven miles as it closely follows a north / south run of the river. When you cross US52 River Road swings westward for several enjoyable miles as it parallels the Wabash again but on a westerly swing. After only about three miles you'll come to the entrance of Fort Quiatenon Historic Park, situated on the banks of the river. This is a historic site dating back to 1717 when the French established a fort and trading community here. The fort changed hands several times during the shifting fortunes and control of the region in the next century by the French, Native Americans, British and Americans. It's a pretty setting and a great place to take a break and some pictures.

Continuing west, the name of River Road changes to Base Line Road and then Division Road and several other local road names as this primary county road follows near the river all the way from Lafayette nearly to the town of Williamsport. Name changes are irrelevant to us as we just continue to stay on the same tarmac without pause. This stretch of local road even appears on the map as one of gray line roads favored by motorcyclists. It's an enjoyable motorcycling byway across the countryside. You'll pass a golf course, continuing west a couple more miles toward the tiny village of Green Hill. There's a southerly jog just east of Green Hill on to County Road 1150, where you turn left then quickly right at the jog onto road 675. Another quick jog and just before the village of Green Hill turn left onto county road 1125 and one more jog west to county road 1100. Ride this road south and it makes a west turn as Independence Road. Independence Road is our guide for several miles as it shadows the twisting river and its adjacent wooded floodplain. This is a really cool stretch of road and it's easier to follow than the complex description might suggest. The route takes us to a four-way stop in the small town of Independence, and we continue straight west through this crossroads town.

Independence Road eventually ends at state route 55, which we take left / south a very short distance to U.S. 41. Turn right onto 41 and in turn take it only a short distance to state route 28, where we turn left and go into the pleasant town of Williamsport; home of Indiana's highest, though intermittent, waterfall. The falls are located in a pretty rock valley right in town, just two blocks from route 28. Turn at the courthouse and make the short ride, guided by signs to the small park. Even if it's mid-summer in a dry year and there is no cascading water over the cliff it's still a pretty setting and an impressive geologic site. If you care to take a short but strenuous walk there is a trail down to the bottom of the valley from the small parking lot.

Upon leaving Williamsport continue west on route 28 about four miles to state route 263, and turn left. Route 263 takes us through the town of West Lebanon and then south for several miles through some especially pretty countryside. Route 263 earns the 'fun motorcycling road' award, with lots of hills and curves in a picturesque rolling and wooded region. There are several small streams in this area that flow south to the Wabash River, and over the millennia they have carved a varying landscape of hills and lowlands, both of which remain tree covered today while the occasional level land is cultivated, resulting in an attractive montage of nature's art.

The fun of 263 eventually ends when the road terminates at route 63 on which we continue our southerly journey, following the Wabash as it begins its major turn southward. We'll be on route 63 many miles, in fact all the way south to well beyond Terre Haute, to a small town called Merom perched on the bluffs high above the Wabash River, not too far north of Vincennes. Route 63 exhibits several personalities as we ride south. From the point we pick it up south to Cayuga it is straight and quite flat, through mostly open countryside. Between Cayuga and

Terre Haute the road begins to meander a bit and the land becomes more wooded and rolling. South of Terre Haute route 63 turns into a nice lightly traveled two-lane biking road that will have you grinning again.

Route 63, like this ride, terminates at Merom and Bluffs Park. You won't want to miss this opportunity to park in the lot at the edge of high bluffs overlooking the river and a view of the Illinois countryside spreading to the far western horizon. It's a wonderful location for a break, a walk, and of course those mandatory selfies.

The Wabash River continues for many more miles south until it joins the Ohio River west of Evansville. But the landscape becomes progressively more open and flat from this point southward so we'll end the Wabash River Run on a natural high at the Merom bluffs.

Reconstructed blockhouse at Fort Quiatenon, originally built on the Wabash River by the French in 1717.

7. Indiana's Ohio River Segment

JUST LIKE THE GREAT LAKES are obvious must see features in the north-ern part of the Midwest, providing fantastic motorcycling opportunities, such is the case with the Ohio River on the region's southern boundary. The Ohio is one of the nation's most important, historic and scenic rivers. It is a stroke of luck that roads following the meanders of the river on both sides are renowned motorcycling roads with all the features wanted on such routes. To make the case even stronger the river road offers dozens of places to stop to explore the natural and manmade attractions along the Ohio River from one end to the other.

The ride along Indiana's portion of the Ohio River begins on the southeast corner of Evansville at Angel Mounds State Park. Follow the signs just east of Evansville, at the intersection of I-164 and state route 662 to this awe-inspiring place where the work of generations of Native Americans has been preserved. The ceremonial mounds are amazing to behold especially when one remembers that they built those mounds, and over a mile of stockade that was sixteen or more feet in height, to-tally by hand. From about 1100 to 1450 A.D. the community that existed here was the largest in all of what is now called Indiana. It was a bustling self-sustaining city that grew its own crops and traded with other commu-nities in distant places. A museum at the park does a good job explaining the life of those early occupants with interpretive displays and artifacts. A person doesn't have to travel to Peru or Guatemala to see the impres-sive handiwork of pre-Columbian Americans—the Ohio River Valley has many sites where we can stand in awe of the extraordinary accomplish-ments of these advanced civilizations.

Continue east on route 662 just a few miles to the next recommend-ed stop—the town of Newburgh. This attractive village is situated on the river and has done a nice job developing the riverfront in a manner that focuses on people being able to walk along the river to enjoy the beauty of the landscape. Newburgh has many shops and restaurants and browsing the various attractions and historic buildings makes for an en-tertaining travel break. It's a walkable community so park the bike and stroll around a bit.

Just beyond Newburgh route 662 ends and we seamlessly pick up state route 66 to continue our eastward journey. The Newburgh Lock and Dam park just east of town is a nice place to get a good look at the river and the navigation system. Though an enjoyable ride in this initial portion, Route 66 can be fairly busy between Evansville and US Route 231 with its main bridge over the river into Kentucky. East of Route 231conditions improve noticeably. There is much less traffic and the road gains motorcycling character with its scenery and fun hills and curves.

East of Cannelton Sixty Six really comes alive. As one rides east across the peninsula formed by the meandering river the road entertains with tight curves and hills in a landscape of forest and rock. Sixty Six leads deep into the Hoosier National Forest and for mile after mile it carves through some of the best motorcycling the Midwest has to offer. Along the way there are many interesting sights and places of noteworthy historical importance. Just south of Derby you'll notice a historical marker for the Hines Raid of 1862. This was a raid by Captain Hines, part of the Morgan's Raiders Confederate cavalry, that made incursion into northern states to locate sympathizers, obtain horses and supplies, and harass Union troops behind their lines. Most of the raiders were later killed or captured in an ambush near Leavenworth on June 19, 1862. Fascinating events occurred right here in the Midwest and Indiana—we need look no further for stories of high drama and excitement than right in our own backyard.

Route 66 intersects with state route 62 near the tiny crossroads village of Sulphur. They continue east as a combined route but after several miles 66 splits off to the north and we continue the wonderful riding on route 62 eastbound. Very shortly after leaving the national forest boundary is the village of Leavenworth, perched high above the river on a bluff. Plan to park the bikes in the roadside parking area in town and walk across the road to the overlook for stunning panoramic views up and down the river and of Kentucky to the south as the river flows far below in a graceful tree lined curve through the hills. If it's lunch or dinner time you're in luck because the Overlook Restaurant is also located on this bluff. The restaurant has been wowing its customers with the view and their food for several decades.

Continuing east route 62 delivers us to Corydon, the first capital of Indiana from 1816 to 1825 when the capital was moved north to Indianapolis reflecting the movement of settlers from south to north. The historic limestone capitol building is an interesting place to visit and is right along our route through town. Just up the street from the old capitol building, at 419 Capitol Avenue is historic Branham Tavern, a log building first licensed as a tavern in 1809. Corydon's other claim to fame was the Civil War battle fought just a mile south of town on July 9, 1863. In this battle a group of local militia and civilians was defeated by a much stronger force of Confederate cavalrymen led by General Morgan. Colonel Lewis Jordan, leader of the Indiana militia and volunteers, finally surrendered after Morgan began shelling the vastly outnumbered fighters, and the town, with cannon fire. Take Old 135 in town south a mile to the battlefield park.

The countryside gradually changes as we continue east on 62 towards the cities of Clarksville and Jeffersonville, across from bustling Louisville, KY. Forests are replaced by farmland, with an interesting mix of crops, including tobacco and the occasional vineyard along with the more customary staples such as corn and beans. Right in the middle of all this tranquility you pass through the village of Lanesville, and if it's lunch or dinner time give the Hogs Tavern a try. It's a biker-friendly eatery and tavern where riders are always welcome and the food is always hearty and served with a smile, and motorcycles are always part of the conversation.

Proceeding east, shortly after passing the intersection with route 11 you come to Edwardsville where we leave route 62 and turn east onto Corydon Pike, a part of the official Ohio River scenic route. The first few miles of Corydon Pike are lots of fun with tight curves cutting through rock hills, but the land gradually levels as we enter Clarksville. Things change quickly as our river route leads through an urban area. Clarksville and Jeffersonville are not without their charms, however. Notice the fabulous old houses and historic buildings lining the streets of Clarksville. They reflect a different time and circumstances. Clarksville history is long and fascinating. The town was chartered in 1783 by the Virginia legislature, with land given to George Rogers Clark and his men. The early town was also a staging point for the famous Corps of Discovery by Meriwether Lewis and William Clark, younger brother of George Rogers Clark.

The towns of New Albany, Clarksville and Jeffersonville stand shoulder to shoulder along the river. A person can go through town if they wish to see local attractions, or they can take the beltway Xway around and pick up route 62 east of the urban area. To go through town, the route is marked by the official Ohio River scenic route signs, so watch for them. Turn off 62 onto Corydon Pike which delivers us to route 111. This becomes Spring Street. Then a trip down Randolph Street deposits us on Riverside Street, which as its name suggests is tight on the water. Riverside becomes Utica Street as we ride east. Take Utica Street east to Allison Street where a north / left turn takes us away from the river temporarily. Follow Allison through the typical urban traffic and surroundings to 10th Street—with a large Meijer store at the corner to guide you. Turn right on 10th, which becomes route 62 again a few miles east of town.

Or a person can take 62 on the west side of all this where it joins US64. Go east on 64 and then take I-265 further east. This beltway ends north of Jeffersonville, conveniently at state route 62, which we use to continue our ride.

Upon leaving Jeffersonville our trip takes a definite northeasterly turn as we work our way upstream. For the roughly 7 miles between Jeffersonville and Charlestown route 62 is a divided four-lane highway but traffic isn't bad and the ride is easy. East of Charleston the road reverts to two lanes again and the riding conditions and scenery improve considerably. We join with route 56 near Hanover and then ride through the nice town of Madison, another river town that has taken full advantage of that fact. It's a great place to stop and walk around, taking in the various shops and attractions, and enjoying the ambience of the river front. Clifty Falls State Park can be accessed off route 62 making it convenient to stop here for some waterfall viewing and hiking in its picturesque ravines. The park's campgrounds accommodate all types of camping, or you can really indulge your basic instincts with a stay at the park's lavish Clifty Inn.

In Madison route 62 departs to the north and we continue east on 56. The remainder of the tour between Madison and Aurora is especially enjoyable because the road runs tight on the shores of the river in large part. In the Swiss village of Vevay route 56 parts company and we continue straight ahead on route 156, only to pick up route 56 again further along. Our final part of the ride takes us through several small villages such as Patriot and Rising Sun (home of an 1845 courthouse—the oldest in Indiana) and the historic tiny village of French, as we make the run into Aurora after 220-miles of Ohio River adventure.

It makes sense to end this ride at the riverside park at the south end of Aurora where we can park the bikes and take one last long look at the river. I hope you also gain the same level of appreciation for the history and beauty of this region that I have as a result of this tour. It's nice to mix enjoyable motorcycling with discovery and exploration, and this ride makes it easy and fun to do just that.

The Best of the Wolverine State

Michigan is a destination state for motorcyclists from all parts of the country. At the Mackinac Bridge, Sleeping Bear Dunes, Keweenaw, The Soo and similar popular gathering points I notice license plates from all states and provinces. They come because Michigan has what motorcycle tourists seek; beautiful scenery, unique attractions, pleasant riding conditions and weather, and importantly, fabulous roads.

Being surrounded by the Great Lakes gives Michigan a unique geographic footprint. And within the boundaries of this state are the physical features that riders find so attractive; the 11,000 lakes and 36,000 miles of rivers, forested wilderness, some of the most stunning state and national parks and lakeshores in the nation, giant sand dunes and stunning sea cliffs, two hundred waterfalls, beautiful farm lands, more lighthouses than any other state, orchards and vineyards, and of course the more than 3,000 miles of Great Lakes shoreline. Connecting these marvelous places are countless miles of winding two-lane pavement.

Michigan is blessed with more public forest and park land than any state east of the Mississippi River. There are world class trout streams, and copper mines that have been in use for thousands of years. Two of the oldest permanent cities in the nation are located here, and ocean-like shorelines where one can gaze at horizons of endless sweet water. Michigan's name is derived from michi-gama, loosely meaning "great water" in Native American language. Michigan also has some of the oldest and most fascinating historical sites in the nation. This land was the envy of European kings long before the first loggers, miners and settlers arrived. These historical sites attract thousands of bikers every summer at places such as Sault Ste. Marie, the Mackinac Straits and Mackinac Island, the Keweenaw Peninsula, Cross Village, Mackinaw City, St. Joseph, Fort Gratiot and sites all along the Great Lakes shorelines from Monroe to Marquette.

Come for the scenery, come for the solitude of wilderness waterfalls, come to explore the history of places older than colonial America, come to see things that won't be seen anywhere else, come to enjoy the countless miles of winding asphalt that dreams are made of, come to stand in awe at any number of places.

Michigan truly does have it all, especially fantastic motorcycle adventures.

Si Quaeris Peninsulam Amoenam, Circumspice—If You Seek a Pleasant Peninsula, Look About You—the fitting motto for Michigan.

- State Parks and Trails web site: http://www.michigandnr.com/parksandtrails/
- State Parks camping reservations: https://www.midnrreservations.com/home
- Michigan Tourism Office: https://www.michigan.org/
- Sleeping Bear Dunes Lakeshore: http://www.sleepingbeardunes.com/
- Pictured Rocks National Lakeshore: https://www.nps.gov/piro/index.htm
- MI Department of Transportation: https://www.michigan.gov/mdot/
- Michigan Scenic Byways: https://www.michigan.gov/mdot/0,4616,7-151-9621_11041_11209---,00.html
- Michigan Motorcycle Events: https://www.cyclefish.com/motorcycle_events/MICHIGAN

1. Michigan's Pinkie

ONE OF THE EPIC rides in Michigan includes the Leelanau Peninsula in the northwestern Lower Peninsula. When a Michigander tells a stranger about this unique region he or she will point at their pinkie finger. The open hand technique of graphically depicting what part of Michigan they're referring to is a common communication tool for natives.

To say that this area is unique and that a ride through it is impressive is a clear understatement. This tour highlights the abundant natural wonders of the region, including massive sand dunes and towering bluffs, horizons that include blue water and islands as far as the eye can see, forests, vineyards and orchards, hills and curves, legendary roads and more. The route I've laid out takes advantage of the best roads, resulting in a mix of premier state or national roadways and two-lane ribbons of amazing asphalt maintained by regional counties. A significant portion of this 180-mile adventure takes riders through state and national forests and the Sleeping Bear Dunes National Lakeshore.

I suggest making it a two-day trip because there is so much to see and do along the way. Wineries, museums, lighthouses, walking trails, and of course the magnificent Sleeping Bear Dunes all deserve your full attention, and being an active participant rather than simply passing through the region requires more daylight than what is contained even in a long summer's day. This makes an overnight stop at the midpoint, at or near the fascinating old fishing village of Leland, an ideal and most enjoyable arrangement. If you do plan to spend the night at a motel, bed & breakfast, or campground in this area reservations are recommended.

We'll start the tour in Manistee, a Great Lakes port city nestled between Manistee Lake on the east and Lake Michigan to the west. Spending some time exploring the historic downtown section of Manistee is a good way to start this tour of discovery. Several notable restored buildings from a more gilded age will delight your architectural senses and taking in museums and shops will satisfy anyone's curiosity. The Manistee Historical Museum in downtown Manistee is a particularly interesting stop where one can learn about the history of this part of the state.

Upon departing downtown on US-31 head to the north end of Manistee Lake to tour two very different but interesting ships. Manistee after all is a port city so nautical attractions are a natural fit. The two ships are at the same dock so touring them both is easy. First, we'll explore the *SS City of Milwaukee*. This impressive steamship sailed across Lake Michigan, winter and summer, ferrying railroad cars as part of the Grand Trunk and Ann Arbor Railroad. The ship was built as an ice breaking vessel in order to make those treacherous cold weather runs across this stormy and dangerous lake. The ship is a National Historic Landmark and is the last of the traditional rail car ferries. The *Milwaukee* saw service from the 1920s to 1981. It is open for tours from Memorial Day through September. Touring the engine room is especially attention-grabbing.

The second ship is the *USCGC Acacia*. This 180-foot Coast Guard buoy tender was built during World War 2 and spent her entire career on Lakes Michigan and Huron, maintaining buoys, lighthouses, and other navigational aids.

In addition to permanent attractions you might want to plan your trip around some of the annual summer events hosted in Manistee. The city hosts a number of fun events – some of which might be expected given the location and others that may surprise folks. On the 'expected' list is the National Forest Festival held in late June, and the Hops and Props festival in September, which highlights craft beers and of course the region's boating heritage. Grapes on the River in July might surprise some folks, but this festival of local wines and music is definitely a crowd pleaser. And the Thunder at the River motorcycle rally, sponsored by Rolling Thunder of Michigan and the Little River Casino Resort in June, just might make your list of favorite things. This motorcycle event has a strong military and veterans focus.

Unless you want to visit the Little River Casino at the junction of US-31 and M22 a few miles northeast of Manistee, I suggest leaving the main route for several miles as we begin our ride north from Manistee. At the north edge of town Route 31 makes a sharp turn to the east. At this curve Lake Shore Road heads due north. I recommend taking Lake Shore Road, aka Old M-110, along the Lake Michigan coast through Orchard Beach State Park to Portage Lake where it curves east to meet M22. This route is not only much nicer it keeps you away from the traffic congestion near the casino at the US31 and M22 intersection.

Lake Shore Road is a curvy scenic road with the benefits of less traffic and commercial development that also offers nice lake views. Following the pavement as it curves around the south shoreline of Portage Lake takes you ultimately to our main host highway - route M22. A left turn onto 22 starts this journey in earnest as it circles Portage Lake and heads back toward the Lake Michigan coast. Onekama, which bills itself as the gateway to M22 is the first town encountered. This water-based village hosts Onekama Days in early August and if you enjoy celebrations that include car racing, music in the park, beer and steaks, and much more plan your trip accordingly.

The road then meanders its way north over hills and past forests and orchards rarely more than a couple of miles from Lake Michigan. Views of the lake shimmering in the distance are common. M22 is one of the most iconic and popular riding roads in Michigan. It is a destination road that riders and drivers make it a point to experience at least once in their lives. No matter where you are in Michigan you see cars with an M22 tourist decal stuck on their rear window or bumper.

M22 and the other roads on this tour are quintessential "Up North" roads. They exemplify the kinds of roads, scenery, geography, and land cover that people have traveled to northern Michigan for generations to enjoy.

Watch for a hilltop MDOT roadside park in the Arcadia vicinity. Located on the Lake Michigan side of the road the scenic lookout offers magnificent views of the lake and forested hills. It is a popular and consequently occasionally a congested attraction so even if you don't plan to stop there slow down and pay special attention when you see the sign announcing the site because traffic is affected by cars pulling into or out of the parking lot on this curvy and hilly road.

The road's delightful pavement soon delivers happy motorcyclists to the sibling towns of Elberta and Frankfort on opposite shores of Betsie Lake. Elberta was once a major link in the trans-lake rail system, though today it capitalizes on sand dunes, fishing, and the Lake Michigan beach as its primary claims to fame. Frankfort is a somewhat larger town with a popular waterfront park and downtown eateries that attract the faithful year after year. The shoreline bluffs near Frankfort are a favorite gathering place for hang-gliders, and throughout the summer these colorful gliders can sometimes be seen soaring high above the beach. The long walk out to the Frankfort pier lighthouse is a great way to see the lake and this old but one-time very important navigational light. On a windy day mighty waves breaking over the concrete pier keep sensibly cautious folks on the shore.

Continuing north on M22 delivers riders to the Point Betsie Lighthouse about four miles north of Frankfort. This historic light, in service from 1858 to 1996, can be found at the end of Point Betsie Road. A paved road leads to the lighthouse and museum, now operated by Benzie County. It is possible to climb the stairs to the top of the light tower for a marvelous forest, sand and water vista but a ticket must be purchased in the museum. It's well worth the small price. The permit also includes a tour of the adjacent lighthouse keeper's home.

Close attention is required at the parking area at the end of the road as there is much sand on the road and if you get off the pavement you'll immediately find yourself in loose and deep sand. Not a good situation for heavy touring bikes. This stop can be, and should be made, but just do it with care if on a heavily-ladened motorcycle.

Just a few miles beyond Point Betsie M22 enters the marvelous Sleeping Bear Dunes National Lakeshore and continues its graceful and winding way north to the town of Empire. The story of Empire's founding is a tale of one person's bad luck being another's good fortune. In the winter of 1863 the locale had just a few scattered settlers living in the woods. A Great Lakes schooner pulled into the nearby small natural harbor for refuge but ended up getting frozen in the ice and damaged too badly to sail again. The name of the schooner was Empire, and the quick thinking and practical locals used the abandoned ship as a school. The next year, with a nascent lumber industry taking hold enough people lived in the vicinity that a post office was established.

At the junction of M72 and M22 in Empire is the Sleeping Bear Dunes National Lakeshore headquarters – on M72 a block east of M22. You will be glad that you stopped in to learn about the history and geology of the area and to pick up information. A map of the area is highly recommended and the park service offers excellent tour guides. The motorcyclist in particular should get a park map since some of the attractions are on unpaved roads. Keep in mind that the primary soil type in this area is sand and loose gravel, so a dirt road that looks ridable can soon turn to deep and treacherous sand. Best to know which attractions are accessible via two-wheeler before committing oneself. Having said that, the majority of the most popular sightseeing spots are accessible by way of paved roads.

When northbound, a left turn at the M72 / M22 intersection in Empire takes one through this small town and another left turn at the west end of the 'downtown' delivers you to Wilco Road, a marvelous road that works its way up a high hill to a parking area for the Empire Bluffs. Wilco Road can also be accessed about two miles south of town. There is a walking trail about three-quarters of a mile in length (1.5-miles round trip) that leads to breathtaking views of majestic dunes and Glen Lake to the north, Point Betsie to the south, and unsurpassed vistas of Lake Michigan. The viewing area on the top of the dune is over 500-feet above the Lake Michigan beach. It's a recommended stop, an easy walk on a well maintained trail, and a great place to stretch your legs through typical dune forests and meadows. The access road and parking lot are motorcycle friendly. In fact, the short ride up the curvy road from town to the parking area is a delight and you will wish for more.

Native Americans created the story of the sleeping bear long ago. As the story goes, a forest fire on the west side of the big lake caused a mother bear and two cubs to swim across Lake Michigan to safety. The mother made it but the two cubs drowned becoming North and South Manitou Islands, which can be seen in the distance. The mother waited on the beach and is now in the form of the sleeping bear dune.

About two miles north of Empire the road forks, with M22 heading northeasterly to Glen Lake and Glen Arbor and points beyond, and M109 going straight north. I recommend taking M109 to access Pierce Stocking Scenic Drive—a seven-mile long narrow, one-way, paved motorized trail through the dunes. It doesn't have a straight stretch anywhere, and while you can't go fast, the tight curves and hills plus tremendous scenery make for a most pleasant ride. You can also park at several locations for short walks to view the dunes and lake. When you can begin to absorb the true scope of the sand dunes in this area and realize that they exist up and down the east side of Lake Michigan, you begin to appreciate the fact that Michigan contains more freshwater sand dunes than anywhere else in the world. An entry fee or pass is required to use Pierce Stocking Scenic Drive.

Heading north on M109 past the west basin of Glen Lake takes you to two recommended attractions – the Glen Haven Historic District and a short drive west to a maritime museum commemorating the U.S. Life-Saving Service Station at Sleeping Bear Point. The D.H. Day State Park is also in this immediate vicinity, offering a place to camp if so desired and reservations made.

Eventually M109 completes its loop and goes east to the resort village of Glen Arbor where it terminates at M22, which becomes our riding partner once again as we continue our shoreline journey up the west side of beautiful Leelanau Peninsula. A couple miles east of Glen Arbor M22 enters a gorgeous area of wooded hills and the road winds its way through enchanted countryside.

Eventually M22 leads to the charming Village of Leland, which is squeezed between Lake Leelanau on the east and Lake Michigan to the west. A short river flows through town connecting Lake Leelanau to Lake Michigan. What's called Fishtown is located along the river in town and buildings that once served the commercial fishing industry now provide various goods and services for tourists. Fishing craft still anchor in the river at Fishtown. Not surprisingly, Leland is also a good place for fresh fish meals.

Early fall is an especially nice time to tour this area as the colors are wonderful in early October and spawning salmon can be seen jumping the old dam trying to make their way upstream. Traffic is also lighter, especially during midweek after Labor Day. The Leelanau Historical Museum in Leland is a good place to learn about the history of this distinctive area.

Cruise north on scenic M22 along the west shore of Lake Leelanau and a few miles beyond Leland at the northern tip of Lake Leelanau you will see county road 641 / Lake Leelanau Drive going south along the lake's east shore. That's the road we want. A sign informs of the upcoming intersection about 100-yards before Lake Leelanau Drive / CR641. Ride south five enjoyable miles on this entertaining road until it "T's" at Eagle Highway. This is a stretch of road where it's probably better to relax and enjoy the ride rather than aggressively attacking the many curves. The road is fairly narrow with no shoulder, and driveways are quite common. There would be little space for reacting if a car should suddenly pull out of a driveway as you're exiting a curve at high speed.

Upon reaching the end of the road at Eagle Highway turn right and in a minute you'll stop again at route M204. Turn right onto 204 and cross the short channel across hourglass-shaped Lake Leelanau to the village of the same name. On the west shore immediately turn left onto county road 643, aka Lake Shore Drive, along the south basin of long and lovely Lake Leelanau.

Stay on CR643 / Lake Shore Drive as it winds southwest ten miles until it "T's". Turn left and very quickly turn left again at the next stop sign, going into the small town of Cedar. Signs at each stop make the location of Cedar obvious. At the main intersection in the Village of Cedar (4-way stop signs and caution light) turn right toward the tiny burg of Maple City on Bellinger Road / CR616. At the stop sign and caution light at Maple City's main intersection (there is only one) turn left onto County Road 667 / Lewis Road and take it the roughly five miles south to M72. Turn right onto 72 and follow it west two miles at which point M72 makes a 90-degree jog to the north, but we turn left onto County Road 669 just prior to the curve. CR 669 is our guide south almost ten miles to highway US31.

A word about CR669. This is one of those wonderful roads in northern Michigan that traverse several counties. This category of pavement is comprised of county-maintained primary roads and thus kept in good condition, but have noticeably lighter traffic than state or federal highways. They also keep the same numeric designation regardless of which county you happen to be in even though the local name changes. Signs that provide both identification and directional information are common along these roads so they are easy to follow. In the case of County Road 669, it carries the happy rider 38 pleasing miles from M72 south to state highway M55, carving a scenic and enjoyable driving route through Leelanau, Benzie, and Manistee Counties.

At US31 a very short right / west jog is required. You will immediately see the sign for the Platte River Fish Hatchery as the turn is made. If the science of Ichthyology has always fascinated you, or perhaps you just have an interest in fishing and fish hatchery operations, swing in here for a tour of the facility. This is the location of the landmark 1966 planting of salmon in the Great Lakes, which as the saying goes – changed everything.

We must go west on 31 just about a quarter mile from the hatchery and turn left or south again on CR669 (now called Thompsonville Road), at the sign pointing south toward Thompsonville. This stretch of roadway provides a relaxing and pleasant ride, replete with all the scenery and characteristics of fun asphalt that a road must have to be spotlighted in this book. It is our host for about twelve miles of rolling mostly forested lands – through the village of Thompsonville to Springdale Road. Just before reaching Springdale Road you'll have to stop at M115 and then continue south a short distance. Thompsonville Road turns to gravel south of Springdale Road as we enter Manistee County. But CR-669 continues as a paved route, making a westerly jog at this point.

Turn right onto CR669 / Springdale Road and after three miles it makes a sharp curve to the south again as Healy Lake Road – that's our road and it's yet another very nice stretch of motorcycling byway as it bisects the Pere Marquette State Forest. This area is noticeably less hilly than we enjoyed to the north but the scenery is fine and wildlife abundant. A watchful rider may see deer, turkeys, eagles, and perhaps even a bear. Healy Lake Road enters the Village of Kaleva and becomes Osmo Street in town. Stay on this north / south alignment to the center of town and 9 Mile Road, where you need to turn right and jog to the west a half-mile. Nine Mile Road is the main east-west road through town. After making the westerly half-mile jog turn left onto High Bridge Road and continue south. Again, signs for CR 669 mark the way.

Before leaving Kaleva, however, I suggest a stop at the famous Bottle House, a home built in 1941 out of 60,000 glass bottles obtained from a local bottling factory. The building now houses the Kaleva Historical Museum, and is located at 14551 Wuoksi Street. Wuoksi Street is on the north side of town; you'll pass it when coming south on Healy Lake Road / Osmo Street. Kaleva is an interesting small town with a strong Finnish ethnic background. The name is derived from The Kalevala, the national epic poem of Finland.

Continuing south on High Bridge Road takes you to the backwoods village of Brethren and then over the famous Manistee River just north of M55. The village of Brethren was formed in 1900 as a colony of the German Baptist Brethren Church. Brethren's most famous resident is no doubt actor James Earl Jones, who spent his school years there. A teacher in Brethren helped Jones overcome a serious stuttering disability, which essentially caused him to not talk for years, allowing him to pursue a career in acting.

The Spirit of the Woods Folk Festival is held in Dickson Township Park in Brethren on the third Saturday in June, and has been since 1978. True to its roots, the event continues to please with music, crafts, dance, and much more. With a name like Spirit of the Woods some folks might assume that it was a 1970's touchy-feely hippie gathering that survived and evolved. Well, they'd be wrong, and off by several hundred years. The concept of spirit of the woods is a Native American idea. Imagine the state of Michigan covered by an ancient forest comprised largely by centuries old pine trees reaching far into the sky. And then imagine the sound of the wind blowing through that unbroken forest of towering majestic pines. That's the mystical sound that the Ojibwe heard for generations. One of the two theories for the word "Manistee" is that it is an anglicized form of the native term for "the spirit of the woods".

High Bridge Road derived its name from an 80-foot high wooden railroad bridge that once crossed the river near this point. It has since been replaced with a steel bridge. The Manistee was a famous lumbering waterway from the mid-1800s to 1920. Massive rafts of logs were floated down the river and dozens of sawmills once lined its banks. The Manistee River is fed by many springs and is less prone to freezing over in the winter than other rivers. As a result logging could often be done year-round. The Manistee today is a highly-prized recreational river used by fly fishermen, canoeists and others for outdoor recreation. A large public access site is situated on the north side of the bridge. It can serve as a spot to take a break and take a peek at the river and the people who enjoy catching the trout and salmon that inhabit its clean cold waters. Being located in the Huron-Manistee National Forest and classified as a Wild and Scenic River by the federal government it enjoys protection from excessive development and degradation. Once M55 is reached, head west about fifteen miles on this fun riding road through the forest back to the city of Manistee.

It is easy to overuse superlatives on this tour because one really does see some of the most unique and beautiful scenery in the Midwest on some of the most enjoyable roads to be found anywhere. The views of Lake Michigan, majestic sand dunes, and beautiful forested and hilly countryside blend together for a truly memorable ride.

2. Tip of the Mitt

THE NORTHERNMOST portion of Michigan's Lower Peninsula is a traveler's delight with all the charms that an adventurous explorer seeks. Forest-covered hills, lakes and rivers that are widely renowned for their beauty, and charming small towns - each with its own unique history and stories to tell. To this mix add miles of serpentine ribbons of asphalt and hundreds of miles of Great Lakes coastline and it all adds up to a motorcyclist's dream come true. This tour encompasses the best of Michigan's fingertips region, taking explorers through locations and on roads that are destination places and roads for riders from throughout the Midwest.

I considered calling this tour A Ride Along the World's Largest Lake because of the many miles of Lake Michigan and Lake Huron coastline it follows. Technically speaking, these two lakes are actually one huge lake because they're connected at the Straits of Mackinac. A "lake" is defined as a body of water completely surrounded by land. That definition applies to these two Great Lakes only if one considers them to be one extremely large lake, bigger even than Lake Baikal in Siberia, generally defined as the world's largest freshwater lake.

This ride starts and ends at Mackinaw City—a journey's end for thousands of motorcyclists from around the country every year. It's no wonder that so many vacationers and travelers, whether on two wheels or safely ensconced in a four-wheeled vehicle, include the Mackinac Straits region in their travel plans. With the scenic delights provided by the waters of two Great Lakes and the amazing sight that the Mackinac Bridge presents, coming for the scenery alone is reason enough. Add in attractions like historic forts, lighthouses, marinas filled with impressive sailboats, historic sites and museums, unique shopping opportunities, and miles of enjoyable roads, and it makes coming to this region truly a no brainer. But the destination isn't the driving force for the discriminating adventurer. It is the journey that counts, and discovering this region via the most scenic route is more important than simply following the most efficient highway. The route I've laid out here carries travelers along the most scenic sections of Lake Huron and Lake Michigan coastlines, as well as through miles of some of northern Michigan's most striking countryside on roads filled to the brim with smile-inducing appeal for motorcyclists and car drivers alike.

Mackinaw City could take a chapter of its own, but I think once a person is there the things one can do are obvious. Just park the bike, walk around, and take it all in. Mackinaw City is small enough so that a person can cover everything without having to drive from place to place.

Historic Fort Michilimackinac and the Old Mackinaw Point Lighthouse are interesting places to see, and of course if you're there for more than a day include a trip to Mackinac Island on one of the ferries that provide hourly service. Restaurants are plentiful as are fudge and tourist shops. I've always thought that one of the many benefits of traveling by motorcycle is that a person doesn't have room to carry unnecessary things, and that's a good excuse to spend less money at the ever-present tourist stores at places such as Mackinaw City.

To start the trip, head west on Central Avenue, the main east-west street in town. Central Avenue "T's" at Wilderness Park Road. Already there is a choice to make. If you wish to visit McGulpin Point Lighthouse turn right at this T intersection and the lighthouse is a half mile to the north. When done visiting the light head south from that T intersection to begin the tour. Wilderness Park Road becomes route C81 at the first curve as you begin the drive along the lakeshore west toward Wilderness State Park. Shadow the curves along the shoreline, staying on C81, which turns south at the general store and gas station. C81 becomes Cecil Bay Road, which we ride south to Gill Road. Turn right and trail this curving lightly traveled pavement. It becomes Lakeview Road without any fanfare with a curve to the right. Ultimately Lakeview Road becomes Lakeshore Road and heads south along the Lake Michigan shore through a section of sand dunes.

There is one somewhat tricky point, and that occurs when you come around a curve just beyond the sand dunes. Sturgeon Bay Road goes straight ahead to the east, but we want to veer right and continue riding south along the coast. There is a sign just past the curve that points south to Emmet County Scenic Route 1; that's the one we want. Take this right turn onto Scenic Route 1 and you'll be on the Lake Michigan coast on Lakeshore Road again. (I was last on Lakeview and Lakeshore Roads in 2018 and noticed that they are developing some rough stretches. It's definitely still worthy of the ride but there are scattered potholes so ride accordingly.)

Follow Scenic Route 1 south and in a few minutes Cross Village will welcome you to its historic realm. This small village, called La Croix prior to 1875, is one of the oldest settlements in Michigan. Native Americans, especially the Ottawa, have lived here for many generations. The first Europeans showed up in the mid-1600s. Local historical lore claims that legendary explorer and missionary Father Jacques Marquette placed a large white cross on the top of the bluff overlooking Lake Michigan at this spot and a mission was established here at that same time.

If you like Eastern European foods, and lots of it, plan on Legs Inn in Cross Village for lunch or dinner. They serve great food in an out of the ordinary stone and timber building, with unique ambience and a wonderful view of the lake thrown in for free. Dozens of old stove legs form a balustrade around the upper portion of the exterior of the building, thus its name. This is a highly recommended stop even if you're not hungry. Go inside to have a look around and before leaving have your picture taken in front of this one of a kind building. A person can also take the path to the rear of the building for a magnificent view of Lake Michigan from high above the water. This restaurant is a destination for folks from around the Great Lakes region so plan on a wait on summer weekends. But that's not all bad, as while waiting for a table there is a lot of exploring to do.

Beginning at Cross Village Lakeshore Road continues southward as state route M119, one of the most scenic roads in Lower Michigan. M119 is also called the Tunnel of Trees. Designated as a State Scenic Heritage Route, 119 is the one state highway for which an exception has been made for shoulders and tree trimming— there is none of either. What it does have are occasional glimpses of the lake from high on the shoreline bluff, and many, many curves. Use caution, as the road has its share of gawkers and it really is narrow with no shoulders and trees line the edge of the blacktop. It's also a popular bicycling route, which adds another reason to drive cautiously. Average speeds on M119 will only be thirty miles per hour or less.

Signs along the road tell the Native American and early explorer history of the area but unfortunately there usually isn't room to pull off to read them. This region has a long and fascinating Native American history. As you ride south on the serpentine asphalt you go through two tiny corner villages, Good Hart and Middle Village. The village of Good Hart in particular has an interesting history. The village derives its name from a 19th century Native chief whose name translated to Good Heart in English. But the history goes back centuries before the white men arrived on these shores. On the lakeshore bluff at what is today Good Hart once stood a large tree that angled out over the lakeside bluff. That tree was a landmark that various tribes used as a location to rendezvous, including a strategic meeting after the sacking of Fort Michilimackinac in 1763 as part of Pontiac's Rebellion. When French Voyageurs arrived the site received the name *L'Abre Croche*, or Crooked Tree. A book by the same name tells the story in detail. Both the French and English versions of this term are still commonly seen today in the M119 and Harbor Springs area.

Just south of this spot is a sharp corner called the Devil's Elbow. One might assume that motorcyclists gave such a fitting name to this precarious curve but the true story is even more thought-provoking. Indians attached the name following a plague many years before. According to legend, a flowing spring in this ravine was believed by Indian tribes to be the home of an evil spirit who haunted the locality during the hours of darkness. Devil's Elbow is a tight hairpin curve and demands the respect of motorists today so give the devil his due.

Continue the splendid journey down M119, stopping at the one or two places where there is space to pull over at the top of the bluff overlooking the lake. The scenery is spectacular. Stay with 119 to the well-heeled resort town of Harbor Springs where you may wish to park and walk. There are plenty of stores and restaurants in this attractive municipality that is happy to take your money in exchange for quality souvenirs and food. Harbor Springs comes by its name naturally – it fronts on one of the best harbors on Lake Michigan and early settlers found many fresh water springs in the area. Two hundred years ago this locale had the largest Native American population of any place in Michigan.

M119 follows the north and then the east shores of Little Traverse Bay and it eventually joins with highway US31 and at this stoplight we'll turn right into the lively small town of Petoskey. This city is a perfect manifestation of the natural and manmade history of this region. It sits on a hill overlooking Little Traverse Bay. Sunset Park, on the north edge of town, is a picture-perfect place to park and admire the natural beauty of the bay. And to make it convenient the park has two levels - an upper level perched atop the rock cliff and accessible from US31, and a lower level at the lakeshore with a beach and walking trail for your entertainment.

Petoskey is Ernest Hemingway's post World War One hangout and there are several places in town that one can visit where he hung his hat. One place that is worthy of further exploration is Jesperson's Restaurant, located at 312 Howard Street in the downtown section. This hangout was Hemingway's favorite eating and socializing spot. The restaurant is still well known for its home cooking and delicious pies.

Another suggested stop, whether you're a Hemingway fan or not, is the Depot Museum. The old railroad depot has been restored and now serves as the local museum, with a section devoted to the famous writer. The impressive building is reached by turning right onto Lake Street from US31.

Leaving Petoskey stay on highway 31 along the coast to the next unique coastal town - Charlevoix, which is squeezed between Lake Charlevoix and Lake Michigan, the two being connected by a canal. A drawbridge carries the highway over the canal and on occasion it's raised to allow large boats, mostly sailing vessels with tall masts, to pass through. There is a small park next to the canal that makes a fine place to park to further explore the town. Large sailboats moor at the marina on the inland lake and are fun to observe. A walking path alongside the canal allows easy access from town out to the big lake.

This stretch of US31 was part of the West Michigan Pike a century ago. That dirt trail carried the first overland tourists, including the Hemingway family, from places such as Chicago to northwestern Lower Michigan. That was the start of this part of the state transitioning its economy from a forestry, farming, and commercial fishing economy to tourism.

Continue south on 31 out of Charlevoix almost 12 miles to the intersection with County Road C-48 at the crossroads village of Atwood. Turn left on C48 and this fun road transports us through the town of Ellsworth and ultimately deliver us to East Jordan. C48 has the qualities of a fun motorcycling route. It's called The Breezeway and courses through an engaging landscape of hills, forests, farmland and orchards.

At East Jordan pick up state route M32, one of northern Michigan's most popular roads of discovery, linking East Jordan in the west with Alpena on the Lake Huron coast. Enjoy the curving highway as it makes its way through a variety of landscapes, ranging from forests to potato farms, to the tourist center of Gaylord; aka the Alpine City. Gaylord offers any service that one might need, from food and lodging to mechanical repairs.

Continuing east from Gaylord motor down the scenic and very enjoyable motorcycling road through Johannesburg and Vienna Corners, a couple tiny villages that were once bustling lumbering centers. If you look closely the buildings that were busy centers of commerce a century ago are still visible. The winding pavement eventually arrives at Atlanta; Michigan's Elk Capital. Atlanta had its beginnings in 1881 when Alfred West, from southern Michigan, bought land here and built a sawmill. Mr. West was a Civil War veteran and the landscape around his new northern Michigan home reminded him of what he saw near Atlanta, Georgia, as a soldier in the war. He decided to apply the name to the new town he hoped to build on the 45th degree of latitude in the northern Michigan wilderness. This is Elk country so keep your eyes peeled for these large ungulates, as well as their smaller and more troublesome cousin the whitetail deer. There are plenty of both in the Atlanta and Gaylord areas so drive accordingly.

From Atlanta continue east, rolling through pleasant and agreeable miles on M32 to the town of Hillman. The landscape will look familiar with rolling forested lands broken by occasional farming activity. The ride is most enjoyable if not technically challenging.

As we approach Hillman, the normally east / west alignment of M32 turns straight north for a few miles. At Hillman it makes a ninety degree turn to the east again. But at that curve we want to continue straight north into the town of Hillman, on what turns into Montmorency County Road 451 (aka regional county road F21). This long primary county road is our host north all the way to US23 and Rogers City on the Lake Huron coast. Between Hillman and Rogers City our road makes several eastward curves and jogs, but it's easy to follow, just stick with the signs and the double yellow line on curves. It's a nice road with light traffic through pretty countryside and with a laid-back ambience.

One of the easterly jogs occurs in the small village of Hawks, in Presque Isle County. Just east of Hawks is the tiny town of Metz. Though it's not part of this trip, it's worth noting the presence of Metz, and recalling a terrible day in October 1908 when a forest fire destroyed the town and killed almost all the people in a train, mostly women and children, who were attempting to escape. The train was a rescue effort loaded with fire refugees trying to flee east to escape the flames. Tragically it derailed because the rails had been warped by the fire two miles east of Metz. A state historical marker near the site commemorates the tragedy. That was one of the last truly devastating forest fires that swept across Michigan after the lumbering boom. If there is a bright side to this tragedy it is that it helped awaken a conservation movement that was instrumental in restoring Michigan's natural environment, ultimately giving today's citizens the treasured gifts of state and national forests and parks.

At US23 turn left toward Rogers City. We're going to quickly turn west onto highway M68 but before making that turn I suggest continuing into the town and exploring the marina district and waterside park.

M68 goes due west out of Rogers City for several miles when it makes a ninety degree turn to the south. At that curve is a sign for the Ocqueoc Falls. Take the falls namesake road straight ahead for two miles to visit the falls. The Ocqueoc Falls, on the Ocqueoc River, are the only true waterfall in Michigan's Lower Peninsula. These falls, over limestone ledges across the river, probably wouldn't get a second notice in much of the northern Midwest, but though a Yooper might scoff they are picturesque nonetheless. A short path from the parking lot leads right to the falls. The whole area is scenic, traffic is light, and crowds are non-existent. After visiting the falls turn south onto Ocqueoc Road and ride it back to M68.

M68 travels west to the town of Onaway, which derived its name from a fictional character from Longfellow's epic poem Song of Hiawatha. It is officially enthroned as the Sturgeon Capital of Michigan because these primitive fish leave Lake Huron to spawn in the nearby Black River. A century ago Onaway was known as the steering wheel capital of the world. Steering wheels, and many other automobile parts were made of wood at the time. Onaway area forests had an unlimited supply of Sugar Maple and Walnut – dense hard wood that made excellent components, including wooden steering wheels. Until a fire destroyed the factory in 1926 virtually all steering wheels for auto manufacturers, with the exception of Ford, were made in Onaway. (Henry Ford utilized his own forests and factory in the Upper Peninsula for his wood automobile accessories.)

Take a look at the unique building on the west side of town locally called the Onaway courthouse. In 1909 this building was built for the purpose of serving as a courthouse, hoping to convince the state legislature that the seat of county government should be in Onaway, not Rogers City, but the effort failed. Today this much-photographed building houses the local historical society.

Continue west from Onaway a couple miles to Black River Road and turn right. This enjoyable county road goes straight north four miles and then curve west, eventually working its way along the west side of Black Lake and along the Black River through the village of Alverno towards the Lake Huron port city of Cheboygan. Black River Road is a very pleasing, if not adrenaline pumping, ride through woodlands and old farmlands that are inexorably transitioning back to native forests and swamps.

On the south side of Cheboygan Black River Road turns straight north, becoming known as Butler Road in town. Butler Road delivers us to highway US23 on the east side of town next to the Cheboygan River. This is noteworthy because this river is one end of what's called the Inland Waterway. This waterway is a series of lakes and streams connecting Lake Michigan and Lake Huron, allowing small watercraft to cut across the tip of the state. The route includes the Cheboygan River, Mullett Lake, Indian River, Burt Lake, Crooked River, Crooked Lake, Iduna Creek, and Round Lake at the west end. There is a museum in Alanson that tells the story of the waterway.

Like many coastal towns in the northern tip of the Lower Peninsula the history of Cheboygan is long and interesting. Native Americans, especially the Ottawa and Chippewa, lived here for centuries, trading with other tribes throughout the region. The French showed up in the 1700s and the mouth of the Cheboygan River served as a fur trading station. As the fur trade died down the lumber economy was just getting started. By the mid and late 1800s Cheboygan was a major lumber port. White Pine logs were floated down the Cheboygan River where sawmills turned them into lumber that was loaded onto ships and sent to booming cities across America.

Turn left onto US23 in Cheboygan and follow it northwest back to Mackinaw City along the beautiful Lake Huron shoreline for the final leg of the trip. There are a couple roadside parks along this route that give access to the Lake Huron shore. Bois Blanc Island looms offshore. This is a marvelous stretch of road that'll keep a smile on your face. Watch for signs for Mill Creek Historic Park, a state park that is a highly recommended stop if you enjoy old mechanical equipment, or if you like to fly through the air on zip lines. Mill Creek is a reconstructed water powered lumber mill. They do a fine job of demonstrating old equipment and explaining how virgin pine was turned into usable lumber 150 years ago.

This fun mitt tip route is 265-miles long, but be sure to include a few hours for stops and fun activities along the way. The entire area is in the heart of vacation and resort country so there are plenty of resources for food, lodging, camping and other services and activities.

I didn't do the math, but we probably only touched about one percent of the total shoreline along the world's largest freshwater lake!

3. Lake Huron Sunrise Shoreline Tour

MICHIGAN'S LAKE HURON shoreline from Port Huron to Mackinaw City is 380-miles of wow. For mile after beautiful mile there are awe-inspiring views of the lake and dozens of parks, large and small, where one can stop to soak in the beauty or simply relax on a sandy beach, listening to the waves and occasionally catching a glimpse of majestic freighters plying the waters on their way to distant ports. The east shore is further blessed because the lakeshore's two main roads, M25 and US23, hug the shore virtually from beginning to end. And to make it even better these roads are enjoyable two-lane byways not high-speed highways or interstate expressways. In other words, they are a joy to ride, even in areas where development crowds out the pines.

To add to the abundant delight of this tour the points of interest along the route are almost too many to name. No matter a traveler's interests, from historic sites to freighter watching, geology to lighthouses, tall ships to old forts, there are attractions and events to meet one's desires.

We'll begin our ride at Port Huron, at the southern end of Lake Huron and the beginning of the St. Clair River. The city is a strategic player in international business with the Blue Water Bridge and railroad tunnels that connect Michigan and Canada located here. Port Huron was the boyhood home of Thomas Edison and the city celebrates this fact. The Thomas Edison depot museum, located on the south side of the blue water bridge, houses many Edison exhibits as well as being a historic railroad depot. The Edison museum is part of the Port Huron museum, an organization that has three distinct units. In addition to the Edison Museum they also oversee the Huron Lightship, a national historic landmark, in waterfront park. The retired coast guard cutter *Bramble* is another portion of the museum, also located on the waterfront.

Keep in mind that every ship traversing the great lakes, whether upbound or downbound, must pass by this point, making the St. Clair River one of the best places in the world to watch large ships from a close vantage point.

The Port Huron to Mackinac sailboat race—the largest freshwater sailing event in the world—is a weeklong event held each July that's been going on for over ninety years. Sailors from around the world come to compete in this very prestigious race. Associated with the race is the blue water fest; Port Huron's boat week. This is a busy and crowded week in this region and if you enjoy the crowds, music, boat displays and many other events then you will love this festival. If you're seeking a quieter place, however, you might want to avoid the period right after the 4th of July.

A fun diversion in Port Huron and a way to really take in the nautical theme of this area is to take a cruise on the *Huron Lady II*, a sightseeing boat that sails lower Lake Huron and the upper St. Clair river. Call (810) 984-1500 or go to huronlady.com for information and reservations. They offer daily sightseeing cruises, private charters, or nice dinner cruises.

North of Port Huron is The Thumb. The term "The Thumb" is a local colloquialism that brings blank stares when used in conversation with someone who doesn't live in Michigan. But Michiganders refer to "The Thumb" with the same assumptions of mutual understanding that people in Massachusetts refer to "The Cape" or San Franciscans talk about "The Bay." Every resident of Michigan is born with a map of the Lower Peninsula attached to their arm in the form of their right hand, and a map of the Upper Peninsula in the form of their left hand.

Our ride takes us north from Port Huron on state route 25. The scenic and cultural attractions of this state highway are well known but few are aware of its special credentials. Route 25 was the first officially declared scenic highway in Michigan. It was awarded this honor in 1940.

Fort Gratiot, just north of Port Huron, is the first suggested stop on the tour. The old fort was originally built in 1814 following the war of 1812 in recognition of the strategic importance of the waterway, and to serve the increasing marine commerce on the great lakes. It was completely closed down in 1895 though it hadn't been used in many years. The nearby Fort Gratiot Lighthouse is the oldest surviving lighthouse in Michigan, the original structure had its origins in 1825, making it the first lighthouse to be built in the state. That lighthouse was destroyed in a storm just three years later and was rebuilt in 1829. The current structure was built in 1861. The lighthouse is located off M25 on Omar Street near the Coast Guard base just north of Port Huron. The structure is open for climbing and tours during business hours.

North of Fort Gratiot things improve rapidly. State route M25 hugs the shoreline providing mile after mile of scenic vistas as one rides north. The road isn't the kind that gets kudos for its many curves and hills, but rather it is a fun biking road for more sublime qualities. It is a relaxing ride through small towns and open spaces, always with the beautiful blue waters of Lake Huron just a short distance to the right as we ride north. There are a number of local parks along the route that provide access to the lake. Three state parks in the Thumb also provide large blocks of public land, campsites and beach access. Lakeport state park is less than 10 miles north of Port Huron, and Port Crescent and Sleeper State Parks are located at the tip of the Thumb. All three are popular, so advanced camping reservations are recommended.

The village of Lexington, known by the catchy byline 'The First Resort North' with its 116-year-old general store, is a picturesque small town on the lake, as is Port Sanilac, 10 miles further north. Port Sanilac is a good spot to do a little walking around to view the historic lighthouse and explore the Sanilac County Museum and Historical Village. This village museum has seventeen historic buildings, ranging from log cabins to a Victorian mansion, on ten acres of land. It's located on the south side of Port Sanilac and is an educational and enjoyable stop and a chance to see what life was like in the Thumb in the late 1800s.

Just after crossing the Huron County line is the tiny village of White Rock. Before it was destroyed in an 1871 forest fire White Rock was one of the larger towns in Michigan. The community is named for a large white boulder located offshore in Lake Huron that was used as a boundary marker to define the territory, south of that location, ceded by Ottawa, Chippewa, Wyandot, and Pottawatomie tribes in the Treaty of Detroit in 1807. A small park and historic marker commemorate this event. This large boulder had special spiritual importance to Native Americans from that area and was a well-known feature. There is a lighthouse here but it's a private building and residence, not an official lighthouse. It was built to observe the village's history and a 19th century lighthouse that was destroyed along with the village in 1871. There is also a one-room schoolhouse museum at White Rock the reflects conditions one hundred years ago.

Smile are commonplace as M25's smooth pavement slips under you, seldom without a view of the lake. Unlike the Lake Michigan coast, the Lake Huron shoreline in the Thumb is less developed and makes for an enjoyable ride with less traffic and congestion. After Port Sanilac, the next town of any size is Harbor Beach, many miles north. It seems almost every place has some obscure claim to fame, and Harbor Beach's place in the record book is for the world's largest man-made freshwater harbor. There is also a nineteenth century lighthouse that is worth a stop to see. Two museums in Harbor Beach are interesting stops; the Frank Murphy House and Museum (former governor) and the Grice Museum, which includes agricultural equipment, an old schoolhouse and more.

Seven miles north of Harbor Beach is Port Hope, named in 1857 by two men who landed here after drifting in a boat. It became a lumber town shortly thereafter and the large Stafford and Haywood Sawmill was constructed in 1858. After fire destroyed the sawmill all that remained was the eighty-foot tall chimney, still in excellent condition in Stafford Park. The chimney is now a national historical site. Like dozens of Michigan lumber towns, the population of Port Hope grew rapidly in the late nineteenth century only to collapse after the surrounding forests had been cut over. In addition to the Stafford chimney there are three other reasons to stop in Port Hope. One is to explore lighthouse county park with its old light, next is the Depot Heritage Center and the third is to stop in at the Port Hope Hotel. This business doesn't have to pretend to be unique and filled with history, it has earned both titles the hard way, by being a landmark for many decades. The ambience has no semblance to fast food places but their claim to fame also includes their super-sized Leroy Burger. Nearby Whiskey Harbor was given that name because it was where whiskey was snuck in from Canada to avoid import duties. This remote shoreline was particularly busy during Prohibition when revenuers did battle with organized crime gangs from Detroit who largely ran the business of importing illegal alcoholic beverages from Ontario. The shoreline is a quiet and beautiful, if rocky, place today.

Leaving Port Hope M25 turns northwest and then west to the tip of the Thumb. The Pointe aux Barques lighthouse is six miles north of Port Hope and is the next suggested stop. This 89-foot tower is in Lighthouse County Park. It's a scenic and fun stop and camping is even allowed. While the lighthouse isn't normally open to the public for climbing, because it is located in a county park the exterior and lighthouse grounds are accessible. (It's an active navigational aid, and is open for climbing on summer holiday weekends and the town's festival, which is the first Saturday in August) There is also a shipwreck museum in the park with artifacts, pictures, and interesting information on the shipping history of this area.

Just a few miles further northwest is Huron City and its museum village; sites that are definitely worthy of some time. A large portion of Huron City is a designated historical district. The entire town burned during the great 1881 forest fire and was rebuilt. Those buildings are now protected for posterity in the living museum and make for a fascinating stop.

A short trip up the road from Huron City is Grindstone City, a small village that was once renowned for producing some of the finest grindstones in the world. In the 1830s early explorers discovered that the Marshall sandstone formation surfaced at the tip of the thumb. Marshall sandstone at this location is of an exceptionally high quality that makes superior sharpening and grinding stones. For nearly one hundred years Grindstone City was synonymous with high quality grinding stones that were shipped around the world. The demand for the stones ended in 1929 when artificial sharpening materials were produced. During the heyday of Grindstone City everything from small whetstones for sharpening knives to massive grinding stones weighing thousands of pounds were produced. Several of these large circular grindstones can still be seen as landscaping decorations in the vicinity.

Just prior to entering Grindstone City we leave M25 for a few miles and take the shoreline road. From M25 turn onto Old Lakeshore Road for a short distance, and then onto Bluff Road. Bluff Road takes you to Pointe aux Barques Road, which you'll stay on traveling west through the Grindstone City area.

Point aux Barques Road rejoins M25 a short distance west in down-town Port Austin. This is a good place to stop again for a great view of the lakeshore. There is a long breakwall that offers a splendid opportunity for a walk. Just west of town exposed sandstone bedrock creates a scenic lakeshore outcropping. The rock features are on private property and can't be visited by land but they can be viewed up close via water access. There are companies in town that rent kayaks or provide other means of getting, or being taken, to rock features such as Turnip Rock and the Thumbnail. It's an enjoyable though somewhat strenuous outing in a kayak so plan on at least a half day if this adventure is part of your plans.

West of Port Austin our road starts its curve to the southwest on the west side of the Thumb. The Garfield Inn Bed & Breakfast in Port Austin makes for a special stop should your lodging desires ever include a historic B&B that's been around for many generations. The "Garfield" in Garfield Inn refers to President Garfield, a frequent guest at this former luxurious home that dates from the 1830s.

West of Port Austin the road goes through about eight miles of mostly public lands, part of Sleeper State Park, Port Crescent State Park, and Rush Lake State Game Area. The two state parks offer nice camping facilities if you wanted to spend more time on the nearby shoreline. Port Crescent State Park is the location of the ghost town of the same name, which was developed at the mouth of the Pinnebog River in the 1850s. It was a major lumbering center and one of the two lumber mills in the town had a 120-foot brick chimney. The town and mills were abandoned when the forests were cut and following the great forest fire of 1881 that swept across the Thumb. A portion of the old chimney has been restored with original bricks and is part of the park entrance sign. A few miles beyond Sleeper State Park is the village of Caseville. This popular and fun summer destination has a large public park and excellent beach.

M25 continues southwest on the east shore of Saginaw Bay past places such as Wild Fowl Bay (check it out in the spring and fall for waterfowl migration activities) and towns of Bay Port, Sebewaing, Unionville and Quanicassee. This region has some of the best agricultural land in the state and the Bay City area is noted for specialty crops such as potatoes and sugar beets as well as more common beans and corn. Sebewaing, once a major Chippewa village, hosts the annual Sugar Festival each summer. Lake Huron also plays an important role in life in this area, whether it's sport fishing, boating, beaches, waterfowl hunting, or in the case of Bay Port – commercial fishing. To celebrate this long economic and cultural history Bay Port hosts the Fish Sandwich Festival every August, and has for over forty years. I've attended this event and it's a guaranteed good time. Events such as this are of course a fun summer ritual in small towns all across the Midwest. They celebrate those things that make them unique, be it asparagus, zucchinis, copper mines, old forts or a hundred other possibilities. Every town has a special history or activity to be proud of.

Follow M25 into Bay City, across the Saginaw River, to M13 / Euclid Avenue, turning right. Route M13 leads north along the west shore of Saginaw Bay to the town of Standish and route US23.

But before heading north there are a few things to do in Bay City and the west shore area. In Bay City a stop at the Saginaw Valley Naval Ship Museum is time well spent. It's home the *USS Edson DD-946*. This Vietnam era Forestt Sherman Class destroyer is one of two left in the United States. Virtually all of the ship is open to the public for viewing. The US Flag that was flying aboard the *USS Selfridge DD-357* when Pearl Harbor was attacked is displayed in the ship. To get there take Trumbull Street north from M25 on the east side of Bay City. Taking a tall ship cruise on Saginaw Bay is another possibility. BaySail / Appledore Tall Ships Company offers public cruises as well as educational, training and research outings. Check out their website and arrange a sail if you can park the bike that long. https://www.baysailbaycity.org/ Another company offers a different kind of sailing diversion. The Bay City Boat Lines company offers cruises on the historic Saginaw River. Check them out at www.baycityboatlines.com. Finally, just northwest of Bay City at 3582 State Park Drive is the Saginaw Bay Visitor Center. This is one of the oldest interpretive centers in the state. It's part of the Bay City State Recreation Area and the displays and rangers will answer any question you ever had about Saginaw Bay. A state park entry permit is required.

North of Bay City is the town of Pinconning. The unusual name is derived from Native American language and roughly translates to the place where wild potatoes grew. This makes some sense since the area is in a lake plain with fertile loose soil ideal for root or tuber crops.

For one hundred years Pinconning has been synonymous with cheese, however, not potatoes. In 1915 Mr. Dan Horn started the cheese variety that bears the town's name to this day. Pinconning is still nestled among dairy farms that provide milk for this unique style of Colby cheese. There are several cheese shops in Pinconning that are happy to sell you fresh Pinconning cheese to take with you on this coastal journey.

From Pinconning ride north on M13 to the bustling town of Standish where we pick up route US23, our host all the way to Mackinaw City at the end of this tour. A few miles further on US23 is the village of Omer, made famous because of suckers. Not gullible people, but fish. Every spring for generations suckers have run up the Rifle River from Saginaw Bay to spawn. Along the river, especially near the US23 bridge, were virtual encampments of spear and hook and line fishermen trying to catch a bag full of these fish, which are highly desired when smoked. The upper portion of the Rifle River is a popular canoeing stream and liveries in Omer cater to canoe enthusiasts.

Further northeast, located on the river of the same name and a couple of miles inland from Lake Huron's Saginaw Bay, is the village of Au Gres. As you might guess, Au Gres derived its name from early French explorers who described "gritty stones" in the area. Thus the descriptive French name. Today Au Gres is much more famous for fishing than the condition of its beach stones and is billed as the Perch capital of Michigan.

Au Gres is a tourist town primarily. Its location provides many opportunities for recreation, including charter boats on the big water for fishing, golf courses, canoe rental on the river, and several small parks and campgrounds nearby. It has a large marina at the river mouth and is definitely a water-oriented recreational town.

A few miles northeast of Au Gres US23 starts its northward journey at Point Lookout. This geographic feature is generally considered the boundary between Lake Huron and Saginaw Bay. The next point of interest is the village of Alabaster. A historical marker in Alabaster tells the story of what put this town on the map—gypsum. The U.S. Gypsum Company has mined the mineral here for well over a century. It was first discovered in 1837 by Douglass Houghton, a famous early geologist for the government, with actual mining of the material beginning in 1862. The large quarry located nearby is responsible for Michigan leading the nation in gypsum production, which today is used primarily in drywall. When in the village of Alabaster one definitely should stop to view the offshore gypsum loading facility. It's very impressive, though the rail tram is no longer used.

Heading north a short distance takes us to the twin cities of Tawas City and East Tawas. This locale is also a nautically-based recreation area. Tawas Point State Park and inviting beaches draw many vacationers to the area. The Tawas Point Lighthouse, standing 68-feet high and built in 1876, is a popular attraction. Nearby inland lakes and the Huron National Forest also attract outdoor recreationalists, ranging from snowmobilers to deer hunters. The Iosco County Historical Museum on West Bay Street in East Tawas tells the story of this area during its lumbering and railroad heydays of the last century and a half.

Heading farther north up the coast brings us to the small resort towns of Au Sable and Oscoda, located on opposite sides of the famous Au

Sable River's mouth. Both towns have their roots in the lumbering era, as does much of northern Michigan. The Au Sable River and Lake Huron are both famous for high quality fishing opportunities. Fishing guides and charters are available on either the river or the lake. A short diversion might be of interest at this point. The River Road begins in Oscoda and runs along the south shore of the Au Sable west for about 20 miles. It is a designated scenic drive that might be considered a worthwhile detour on this trip. The Lumberman's Monument is on this scenic drive. It was built to honor all those who worked in the lumbering heyday of Michigan in the late 19th and early 20th centuries. Besides an impressive monument there are a number of museum displays. Iargo Springs is a bit further west. These springs flow into the Au Sable River at the base of a high bluff. Stairs lead down to the river and springs.

North of Oscoda US23 becomes prettier and less developed. The motorcycling is fun and the landscape is picturesque. For the next hour you'll pass through some small towns, all pretty much dependent on tourism and Lake Huron for their source of revenue. Sturgeon Point Lighthouse, with its keeper's house transformed into a museum, is just north of Harrisville. Also at Sturgeon Point is Old Bailey School museum, one of very few log cabin one room schools from more than a hundred years ago that still survive in Michigan.

The village of Ossineke is ten miles south of Alpena. There are a couple of fun stops here, both on US23. The first is the dinosaur gardens prehistoric zoo. This unusual attraction has outdoor displays of cave men fighting dinosaurs, giant snakes, and sundry prehistoric beasts. Nearby, at the corner of Nicholson Road and US23, Paul Bunyan and his large sidekick Babe the blue ox stand guard. Always a good place for a photo op. Northern Michigan is Paul Bunyan country and this famed giant lumberjack can also be found in Alpena, but in a very different form. On the campus of Alpena Community College stands a 30-foot metal Bunyan, made in the 1960s out of various car parts.

Alpena is the only large city in this part of the tour, checking in at about 11,000 residents. It is located on Thunder Bay at the mouth of the Thunder River. Alpena is a small industrial town. It started out in lumber, but because of huge limestone deposits at the surface it quickly became a major cement production center and limestone quarry, continuing to this day. Several very large quarries, including what is allegedly the world's largest, are located nearby.

In addition to the usual maritime activities that can be found up and down this coast, Alpena offers something new. It is home base for the Thunder Bay National Marine Sanctuary and Underwater Preserve, a 448-square-mile area of shipwrecks protected from being disturbed but open for viewing by divers. Alpena has at least three different companies that cater to divers and tours of the preserve, including a glass bottom boat tour. (AlpenaShipwreckTours.com)

There are also many historic lighthouses in the northeast coastal area. Early each October Alpena hosts the Great Lakes Lighthouse Festival. Alpena is also home of the Jesse Besser Museum. This facility has a marvelous collection of attractions, including a planetarium, a museum with many exhibits ranging from local history, Native American history, and a historic village with buildings from bygone days. It is located on Johnson Street in town. Go to bessermuseum.org for more details.

Heading north on US23 out of Alpena takes you through what I consider to be the prettiest stretch of the road with its sweeping curves and forested hills. Though it is inland a couple of miles you are still treated to beautiful lake views because the road runs along the west shoreline of Grand Lake, a long narrow lake located midway between Alpena and Rogers City. The motorcycling charms in this part of the state are wonderful with open roads, great scenery, and a relaxing ambience that brings and keeps a smile on the rider's face.

If you wish to take a different route at this point, take a county road that runs up the east shore of Grand Lake and close to the Lake Huron. Leaving US23 about twelve miles north of Alpena, Rayburn Highway goes east along the south shore of Grand Lake to Grand Lake Road, which in turn runs north on the narrow strip of land between Lake Huron and Grand Lake. The road then returns to US23 on the north side of Grand Lake as Highway 638. This scenic and lightly traveled alternative also allows you to stop at the historic Presque Isle Lighthouse. Go ahead and climb the 138 spiraling steps to the top of Lake Huron's tallest lighthouse and earn the reward of a tremendous view.

Proceeding north from the Grand Lake area our next stop is Rogers City—known for good reason as the nautical city. Take time to wander the waterfront and marvel at the collection of large boats moored there. Rogers City is home to the world's largest limestone quarry, which is near town. The Great Lakes Lore Maritime Museum is on 3rd street in the downtown section, east of US23. This unusual museum focuses on people and events in Great Lakes maritime history as much as they do artifacts and antiques.

Continuing beyond Rogers City the highway hugs the coastline. Just north of town is Hoeft State Park, which has nice campground and beach facilities. Forty Mile Point Lighthouse, another historic structure that can be easily accessed is seven miles north of Rogers City.

It's marvelous open road and Lake Huron vistas for many miles until we get to the city of Cheboygan situated at the mouth of the Cheboygan

River. The riding is great. Like other cities on the northeast coast it has a nautical theme. In addition to Lake Huron attractions, the Cheboygan River is the eastern terminus of the inland waterway, a series of lakes and streams that cuts a 40-mile channel across the northern tip of Lower Michigan. A series of locks controls water levels and allows passage for pleasure boats from Lake Huron to Lake Michigan.

It's a mere fifteen miles from Cheboygan to Mackinaw City and the end of this tour. About midway between these cities is Mill Creek Historic State Park. This is a fascinating stop where you can view an operating water-powered sawmill that was first used in the 1790s. A collection of historic buildings and artifacts makes this park unique. In recent years a zip line attraction has been added allowing riders the option of gliding high above the valley and creek that provides the water necessary to run the mill. It's a highly recommended stop.

Mackinaw City is the end of our trip. There is so much to do in this small town that I can't begin to list all the attractions here. A ferry boat trip to Mackinac Island should be high on the priority list. Mackinac Island is largely a state park, and no motor vehicles are allowed on the island. You get around by walking, riding bicycles or by horse-drawn carriage. Historic Fort Mackinac on the island is an enlightening stop, and bicycle trips around the eight-mile perimeter of the island are also popular. Arch Rock, Skull Cave and many other attractions also await in this most historic place. And perhaps, above all, there is the fudge.

In Mackinaw City the authentically reconstructed Fort Michilimackinac is an interesting way to learn about the fascinating history of the straits area, harkening back to what I wrote at the beginning of this chapter regarding European interest in this region going back to the 1600s. There are dozens of stores to browse and a great shoreline on which to relax, watch the sailboats or just marvel at the sight of the Mackinac Bridge looming in the distance. You'll also want to explore Old Mackinac Point Lighthouse on the shoreline just east of the Bridge. And yes, Mackinaw / Mackinac really is spelled two ways but pronounced the same, with the 'aw' sound at the end.

I think that you will agree that Michigan's sunrise coast truly is an eye-opener and makes a delightful motorcycle outing.

4. Rocks, Classic Cars and a Grand River

SOUTHERN MICHIGAN bikers seem to have an inferiority complex when it comes to the topic of motorcycling roads. Most riders assume that one must go to northern Michigan for enjoyable motorcycling opportunities. Let me discredit that assumption here and now. The heavily populated southern portion of the Lower Peninsula does not have to take a back seat to anyone when it comes to fun and interesting places to ride.

I've long believed that the important thing to remember about motorcycling is that the enjoyment is in the riding. A person might make one or two long rides to great destinations over the course of a year, but that same rider will ride local roads on a regular basis. In my mind that makes nearby highways more important than popular destinations or roads that a person might ride once or twice each year. The goal is to get out on enjoyable motorcycling roads near home as much as possible. It is time to change that inferiority complex into a superior attitude and explore some of the roads and attractions in the southern farmlands portion of Michigan.

We'll begin this tour in the small charming town of Grand Ledge, just west of the state capital of Lansing. Grand Ledge is perhaps unique to a certain degree that though it has become a bedroom community for Lansing it definitely has not lost its identity in the process. It's still the kind of bustling small towns that were common in the past. Two landmarks make Grand Ledge well known as a destination spot – the Grand River and the impressive sandstone ledges along the river. The river is the longest in the state draining the largest watershed, ultimately draining into Lake Michigan at the city of Grand Haven. The dramatic sandstone ledges are unique in southern Michigan. There is a trail at the base of the ledges along the shore of the river, accessible in Fitzgerald Park on the west edge of town. Visiting the ledges is certainly a suggested stop before embarking on this ride.

Begin the trip by going north on M100 – the town's main street. The road loses its state highway designation at the I96 expressway two miles to the north. Continue on what is now Wright Road as it carries you first through some wooded lands and then into the serious farmlands of central Michigan. At Fowler turn left onto M21 and ride the short distance to the Ionia County line. It's easy to find because the road makes a sweeping curve to the south at that point. One half mile into Ionia County turn south onto Hubbardston Road and take it one mile south to Kimball Road, where a turn to the west gets you started on a scenic and fun river road; the river once again being the Grand River. Kimball Road began life centuries ago as one of several Native American trails that converged at present day Lyons, where the Maple River joins the Grand River. This was a major Indian village in the past.

About four miles after turning onto Kimball Road you will see a small park and scenic overlook on the south side of the road. This is a very nice stop. The small park is named in honor of Fred Green, a former Governor of Michigan, and is located atop a high bluff overlooking the Grand River. It's an especially pretty spot in the fall. From this point west the road follows the Grand River closely for about thirty miles as it meanders in a westerly direction toward Lake Michigan. And of course as all riders know, roads that mimic an adjacent river create enjoyable motorcycling opportunities.

Just a few miles west of Green Park is Lyons, a small town with an interesting history. Lyons was named in honor of Lucius Lyon, one of the earliest settlers in the Grand River valley, who later became a noted politician and judge. The site that was to become the town of Lyons was an open prairie of 1,100 acres, maintained by the local Indians. The natives referred to the site as Cocoosh, in honor of the Potawatomi chief who bore that Anglicized name. When the first settlers arrived in this area around 1830 the old men of Cocoosh Village told stories about a major battle fought here between Native American tribes long before they were born. The story had been handed down by oral tradition and told about a large tribe from near the Ohio River attacking. Old defensive earthworks and burial mounds discovered by early settlers, unfortunately long destroyed, bore some evidence that the story may have had some basis in fact.

The river road jogs south two blocks on the west side of Lyons and then continues west with the name Riverside Drive. This road too was an old Indian trail coming into the native village from the west. After crossing busy M66 about five miles west of Lyons continue west on Riverside. This stretch is very pretty with lots of curves and wooded land as it passes through the publicly owned Ionia State Recreation Area. About eight miles past M66 is the town of Saranac. The river road jogs three blocks south, continuing west on Summit Street which becomes Riverside Drive again west of town. The lightly traveled road in a mostly wooded setting curves in time with the river's meanderings and is an enjoyable ride.

West of Saranac the road the road name eventually changes to Grand River Drive, though no turn is necessary. Six miles west of Saranac the road makes another short southerly jog and then intersect with Segwun Avenue at a stop sign. Segwun Avenue to the north crosses the nearby Grand River and goes into the town of Lowell, but at this stop sign we're going to turn left / south.

Going south Segwun Avenue soon changes names to Alden Nash Avenue and goes through a couple mile wooded area and then crosses the

I-96 expressway. South of the highway our road turns into state highway M50. Enjoy the curves and jogs of M50 for eighteen miles through pleasant farm country to the village of Lake Odessa and then four more miles to M66 where we turn right.

Stay on Route 66 just a couple miles, turning right onto M43 to the city of Hastings, a small but active city that is the county seat for Barry County. The landscape in this part of the ride is mostly farmland with wooded stretches. It's a pleasant setting and relaxed riding.

Route 43 makes a westward turn in Hastings. Continue west through Hasting but on the west side of town, where 43 turns straight south again, we want to continue due west on M179 into the scenic Yankee Springs Recreation Area. The mark of the last glacier to cover this region is clear west of Hastings with forested glacial moraines being the primary landform. Like many other places in Michigan where moraines are present the landcover is usually second growth forests, because the rocky gravel and steep slopes of the moraines proved unfit for farming. Often these features have become public forests or recreation areas because landowners were unable to make a living on the poor quality land and sold it or the land reverted due to failure to pay property taxes. M179 is an enjoyable ride as it traverses the hills of this scenic region.

After about six miles on M179 you come to Yankee Springs Road. Turn left / south here and ride this fun road down to Delton Road, an enjoyable ten miles through rolling forest and fields. Go east on Delton Road two miles and we'll once again join route M43 at the village of Delton, turning right onto M43. This state road is our host for four miles as we ride south to Hickory Corners Road.

Turn east on Hickory Corners and after just two miles you come to the Gilmore Car Museum. This is a highly recommended stop on the tour. Gilmore is one of the nicest museums of its kind in the state, with loads of cars, motorcycles and associated motoring paraphernalia. Plan on a couple hours. A Vintage Motorcycle Show is held on the second weekend of June and it has evolved into one of the larger and most popular shows in the region.

Upon departing the museum travel east on Hickory Corners Road, through the namesake village and east all the way to M66. This is a very pleasant ride through pretty countryside. There is one important turn to make. Just after stopping at the M37 intersection Hickory Corners Road ends. A slight left jog is required at the T intersection of Hickory Corners and Hutchinson Road. At this T go left a very short distance then turn right and resume eastward travel on what's now Mud Lake Road. Take this entertaining pavement to M66 and turn left.

Route 66 guides us for about twelve miles as we travel back north. Two miles north of the village of Nashville is State Road – turn right here. State Road soon becomes Vermontville Road and brings us to the crossroads village of Vermontville. I suggest stopping in the center of Vermontville to do a little exploring. A local chainsaw carver has several of his works of art on display in and around town. There are a few historical markers around the main intersection and a veterans memorial in the park in town. There is also a tavern on Main Street that's a good lunch stop.

Not surprisingly this village was the idea of an immigrant from the state of Vermont. He arrived in 1836 at which time he named the soon-to-be-village, though it wasn't officially incorporated until 1867. As the name suggests the town has a Maple Syrup connection. In late April each year a festival draws many to the town for the festivities. Weather permitting, local riders and motorcycle clubs participate.

Our ride continues east from Vermontville. On the east edge of town the road splits; we want the right fork, which is still Vermontville Road. Ride this pavement east fourteen miles to Potterville. This is a pleasant stretch of road that makes for enjoyable riding through rolling farm country with a lot of wooded land.

One of the more famous places in Potterville is Joe's Gizzard City, on Main Street. If you are in a mood for food that you won't find at cookie cutter fast food joints give them a try.

Turn left on M100 in Potterville and in ten minutes you'll be back in Grand Ledge. This 180-mile ride provides proof to establish southern Michigan's motorcycling credentials.

5. Judge Dexter's Trail

AS I'VE NOTED elsewhere in this book there are very nice motorcycling roads in all parts of Midwestern states. Contrary to prevailing opinion that a person must go to remote corners of their respective state to find good roads and nice scenery, these features can be found even near the largest cities. This particular route is an excellent case in point.

Located between the large university and business centers of Lansing and Ann Arbor, this enjoyable ride carries bikers through scenic rolling lands made up of forests, farms, hills, and lakes on narrow twisting two-lane pavement that's as much fun as any found in the hinterlands. Unlike most of the tours detailed in this book, however, this ride has a destination, and for those unfamiliar with Michigan I should explain. Our destination is Hell. Yes, that's right. We're heading to the tiny burg near Ann Arbor that proudly carries the tag of Hell, Michigan. It's a popular motorcycling focal point not only because of its name but primarily due to the great roads that lead to it from any direction.

But this ride has a second fundamental reason for being included and that is the roads, in particular a historic road that had its beginning in the 1830s when a certain Judge Dexter led pioneers through the wilderness on a trail he cut through the forest that became known as the Dexter Trail. Much of his circuitous route still exists today, upgraded with asphalt but retaining its charms and enjoyable meanderings through pleasant southern Michigan scenery. No offense to the good judge, but we'll use his trail as our means of going to Hell.

Let's begin the 85-mile loop in Mason, the county seat of Ingham County. (Ingham County is also home to the state capital of Lansing and Michigan State University in East Lansing. Michigan is the only state in the nation in which the state capital is not also the county seat of the county it's located in.) Mason is named in honor of Michigan's first governor, Stevens T. Mason, the so-called boy governor who became territorial governor in 1834 at the ripe old age of twenty-two, and then became state governor in 1837 when Michigan was granted statehood.

Mason is home to Dart Container, the largest producer of foam cups and packaging in the world. The county courthouse, occupying an entire block in downtown Mason, is one of those old impressive buildings that are fun to view, admiring architecture that unfortunately isn't used in building design anymore. Construction began in 1902 and took two years. It's listed on both the state and national register of historic places. Mason hosts the annual Cruise the Courthouse Car Show each summer, usually

July 4th weekend. It's a large show that has been going on for thirty years and keeps getting bigger and better.

To start the ride head east on state route M36. A mile east of town, just east of the fairgrounds, Dexter Trail veers off heading southeast. Turn here and let the ride begin in earnest. The Trail gets gradually better as it progresses southeast. There is one easy to miss curve in the road and that is one mile east of Williamston Road. Dexter Trail makes a ninety-degree turn to the right but the pavement we're on continues straight ahead as Carter Road. So be on guard and make that right turn, there is a small sign, and stay on Dexter Trail, which angles southeast for several more miles and then turns straight east. It'll cross state route 52 and about four miles further east it will "T" at M36 just north of the village of Gregory. (yes, the same state route 36 that was in Mason, it too meanders southeast somewhat parallel to Dexter Trail.)

Turn right onto M36 taking it to Gregory and continue to follow this road as it turns directly east at the village. M36 travels through a region of lakes and gentle hills for roughly five miles to the town of Pinckney. On the west side of Pinckney turn right onto Howell Street, which becomes Toma Road outside of town. Take this easy to find road south just a mile to Patterson Lake Road and turn right. Patterson Lake Road will carry us into Hell after negotiating a few fun curves through a wooded landscape. The road to Hell is indeed paved and fun.

In Hell you will want to stop to take some pictures to prove that you have been to Hell and back. There is a tavern that's a popular gathering place, as well as a couple small shops that sell items ranging from ice cream cones to every type of Hell-related knick-knack one can imagine. There are a few tables for relaxing with an outside drink or treat. Hell actually got its name from Hell Creek which flows through 'town'. The history books are unsure as to how the creek received that notable appellation.

Continue the ride by going west on Patterson Lake Road through a hilly scenic publicly-owned landscape of forest and lakes on a very enjoyable road. Patterson Lake Road seamlessly turns to the west as Doyle Road. Less than two miles on Doyle turn left onto Unadilla Road. Just west of Unadilla Road is a small airport for gliders. If you pass this you know you've gone a couple hundred yards too far west.

Unadilla Road goes south through the tiny eponymous village and jogs east one block, continuing south as Hadley Road. The jog is obvious; no concerns about missing it. Hadley Road continues the southward ride through the same sort of scenic landscape and fun pavement. Continue straight south across Territorial Road, following the pavement south to state route M52. South of Territorial Road our pavement changes names twice but it's of no concern as the gray line route is obvious, as well as enjoyable.

Judge Dexter's trail also went through the Unadilla area, perhaps on this very stretch of road, though road names have changed and memories gone foggy. The town of Dexter, just to the south, was where the trail through the wilderness began.

Turn right onto M52 at the traffic circle and ride nearly ten miles north. At what looks like a fairly busy intersection with a large propane dealer and a farm grain facility turn left onto West Territorial Road. Follow this road, which combines with route M106 for less than two miles, and then further west on Territorial for four miles to Bunker Hill Road. Go north on Bunker Hill Road to the "T," jog left a couple blocks and then turn north onto Williamston Road. This road will carry us north through some scenic countryside, including a large block of managed wildlife land, and back to Dexter Trail. On this part of the ride I suggest continuing north on Williamston Road past Dexter Trail less than two miles to the village of Dansville. Check out the old fire barn on the south side of town. In Dansville turn left onto our old acquaintance M36 again for the short ride back to Mason. About midway between Dansville and Mason, on the south side of M36 near Meridian Road, is a small roadside park with a plaque that details the history of the first rural electrification efforts in 1927.

You won't be alone on this set of great motorcycling roads nor in the village of Hell. These roads and the unique destination are popular with motorcyclists from all parts of southern Michigan and northern Ohio and Indiana. Various clubs make the run and over the years an assortment of motorcycle events have been held at nearby Hell Campground.

6. *Porcupine Mountains to Brockway Mountain*

MICHIGAN'S LAKE SUPERIOR basin is one of the most geographically striking regions of the Midwest. It is a land of ancient mountains, dozens of tumbling waterfalls on wild streams, endless forests and scenic beauty. The legacy of a long cultural history remains in the form of old mine shafts and associated equipment and buildings, and even a dialect that reflects the native ancestry of many of the residents. It's also a land of marvelous roads that delightfully carry tourists of all kinds through this unique landscape. This ride explores the prominent geologic wonders of the Lake Superior shoreline in the western Upper Peninsula, with some of the oldest rocks on the planet, dating back a billion years, that we tread on today imagining what stories they could tell. The Porcupine Mountains and the Keweenaw Peninsula are the focus of the tour and besides fascinating natural wonders the expedition is filled with marvelous scenery, great riding roads, and fascinating historical and cultural wonders.

The Porcupine Mountains Wilderness State Park (better known simply as The Porkies) is a crown jewel in Michigan's wonderful state park system. At 59,000-acres it is the largest state park in the state as well as the most geologically dramatic. As its name suggests, it is also a wild land where people are the visitors and bears, wolves and eagles hold claim to the land. Native Ojibwe people gave the mountains their name because when viewed from canoes in Lake Superior the hills reminded them of a crouching porcupine.

While the central portion of the Upper Peninsula is the location of many iron ore mines, in the northwest region, including the Porkies and the Keweenaw Peninsula, it was copper that first brought people here long before the Europeans arrived on the scene. Copper has been extracted from countless shallow pits throughout the region, and on Isle Royale, for thousands of years. Gold and silver are also mined in the vicinity but not at the same intensity as copper and iron.

Begin the marvelous excursion in Silver City on the eastern border of the park. The first stop on the ride is perhaps one of the most beautiful scenes in Michigan, atop an ancient basalt mountain overlooking the Lake of the Clouds. To get to this piece of paradise ride scenic state route M107 west from Silver City into the park. The highway snakes its way up the hills along the Lake Superior coast with occasional stunning views of the shimmering steel blue waters in the distance and into the park, ending at the overlook. The view from the rocky escarpment high above the lake nestled in forested hills is stunning. There is a fenced viewing area for safety and plenty of rock ledges to provide places to sit and enjoy the scenery. There is often morning fog near the big lake so for the best pho-to-taking conditions mid-morning or later is recommended.

When finally ready and able to leave the beauty behind, depart on M107 back to Silver City and the adventure continues to the east. While still along the shore of Lake Superior gather up your nerve and try a dip in the cold water. Even if just wading up to your knees the shock of the cold Lake Superior water will give you a renewed respect for those who make their living on the Lake. It also makes for bragging points after the trip.

Ride along M64 east to Ontonagon, where you may want to spend a little time. The Ontonagon Lighthouse is a nice destination. The existing 40-foot high light tower and associated keeper's house were built in 1866 and are listed with the National Registry of Historic Places. For an actual tour of the lighthouse stop in at the Ontonagon County Museum at 422 River Street, or contact them at ontonagonmuseum.org/lighthouse. The brown sandstone courthouse is also an impressive building to take a gander at. Though everyone agrees that this town's unusual name came from Native American languages, no one is quite sure which language or the original meaning.

In Ontonagon turn right onto M38. After about twelve miles signs for the Adventure Copper Mine site in Greenland appear—another inter-esting stop. They offer four different underground tours and if a person wishes they can even try their hand at rappelling down a shaft on a rope. The mine operated from 1850 to1920. Check them out at adventuremine-tours.com/.

Just east of Greenland turn north onto route M26 and enjoy its charms thirty-seven miles to the city of Houghton. Along the way we ride through one mostly abandoned town after another whose economic lifeblood dis-appeared after the local mines closed. But it's also a scenic and enjoyable ride through forests and small clearings of farmlands. This is one of rel-atively few places in America where the population today is significantly lower than it was a century ago. Forests have replaced much of the land where farming had been attempted in the poor rocky soil.

Houghton is the largest city in Houghton County and its county seat. It is named in honor of Douglass Houghton, early Michigan explorer, geologist, and physician. As part of an official geological survey team Houghton was largely responsible for getting the word out about the mineral resources of this region.

Ride 26 / 41 across the canal into Hancock and the fabulous Keween-aw Peninsula. There is much to explore and see, including ghost towns, old mine sites, waterfalls, lighthouses, lonely shorelines, and fabulous motorcycling roads to tie it all together. There is still a strong Finnish and

Cornish influence here due to the many immigrants who came here 150 years ago to work the mines.

This ride includes both coasts of the Keweenaw, not just a ride up US41 in the center of the peninsula. Once across the canal stay on M-26 to Lake Linden. While in Lake Linden it is an excellent opportunity to check out the Houghton County Historical Museum. It includes the Copper Country Railroad museum and much more. And it's right on highway M26. In Lake Linden Bootjack Road goes east off 26. Take this road a short distance and Traprock Valley Road heads off to the north. Take Traprock Valley Road a little less than two miles to Gay Road; turn right and follow it through the forests to the village of Gay. This nearly abandoned village has seen busier days. A century ago it was a major copper processing facility built by the Mohawk Mining Company in 1898. The village is named after a founder of Mohawk Mining; Joseph E. Gay. The huge chimney, part of the old stamping mill, still stands. Ironically, one of the worst pollution problems in western Lake Superior today is caused by the millions of tons of stamping 'sands' that resulted from the copper processing done a century ago at Gay. This waste has made its way into the water and currents have moved it around, covering vital spawning reefs and also releasing toxins such as arsenic and other metals into the water.

The Gay Bar is a popular place to stop for a break or to take a picture by the sign. If you can time it right, each July4th tiny Gay has a sizable and fun parade. Proceed on scenic Gay Road north along the water's edge almost twenty miles to the small town of Lac La Belle. This picturesque and fun route will have smiles on your face for sure. It's a great example of wonderful motorcycling roads connecting the many attractions of the region. Turning left on Lac La Belle Road takes you to US41 near the town of Delaware, and the Delaware Copper Mine site. This underground mine as in operation from 1847–1887 and guided or self-guided tours of the mine are available. The mine is an interesting place to visit. In addition to the well-lit mine tunnels they also have a display of antique machinery and engines. The mine is located on route US41 and is open 7 days per week from June–October.

When done touring the mine head north on 41 to Copper Harbor and the tip of the Keweenaw Peninsula (meaning "portage" in Native American language). One of the Michigan roads that always gets mentioned by out-of-state writers is US41 in the Keweenaw. It is definitely worthy of the acclaim as it twists and curves its way to Copper Harbor and the end of the road. North of Delaware mine US41 is a wonderful motorcycling road.

The village of Copper Harbor, Michigan's northernmost, is a small outpost but there are a few things to see and do. Just beyond Copper Harbor at the road's end is Fort Wilkins State Park, a restored fort from

Michigan's early history. Copper Harbor is also where you can access the Isle Royale Ferry for a trip across Lake Superior to Isle Royale National Park. Isle Royale is a wilderness park, America's least visited, and not a place where one finds plush accommodations. Visitors live off, and in, whatever they carry in their backpack. There are a few shops in town selling local crafts and agates.

From Copper Harbor we ride route M-26 along the shoreline back south on the west side of the Keweenaw. This superb stretch of road carries you along the scenic shoreline through Eagle Harbor and Eagle River.

But first Brockway Mountain Drive is on the agenda. This ridge top byway offers wonderful views of the stony hills, lakes, and forests near Copper Harbor. Gain access to the Drive just west of Copper Harbor. A large sign identifies the location. At the present time the condition of Brockway Mountain Drive has deteriorated and the pavement is quite rough in places. The severe winters have not been kind to this byway. It is passable and still offers the same marvelous views, but take it slow, after all it's not a road as much as it is a lengthy viewing platform. Brockway Mountain Drive is the highest byway between the Alleghenies and the Rocky Mountains.

Two options on the BMD. You can take the Drive to its south end and connect with M26 at that point, or go back to route 26 via the same Copper Harbor entry point that you used to get on the Drive. I recommend this latter option because it allows you to see the entire stretch of the peninsula on the western side, beginning at Copper Harbor.

Route 26 sticks close to the shoreline along the peninsula's northern and western shore for many miles. It's a wonderful stretch of road with great scenery and fun pavement. It carries us to the coastal towns of Eagle Harbor and Eagle River where there are attractions and views unique to this region. Just south of Eagle Harbor you might want to stop at the Jampot, a small roadside bakery operated by monks. They make arguably the best breads, pastries and preserves to be found anywhere.

The nearby Eagle Harbor lighthouse and museum is first rate and is a wonderful place to stop not only for the lighthouse but to see the lake up close and watch the waves crash on the rocks. Eagle Harbor is a small harbor town today but was a boom town a century or more ago because of several active nearby copper mines. The lighthouse is at the rocky entrance to the harbor and is a working light. It still guides boats of all size across the northern side of the Keweenaw Peninsula. The original lighthouse was built in 1851 but had to be replaced in 1871. The lighthouse is furnished with period furnishings and open to the public from mid-June to early October. Three museums are open at the same time. There is a small admission charge to the Light Station complex. If the buildings are closed visitors are welcome to walk around the grounds.

Though ancient igneous rocks and stone hills make up much of the Keweenaw there is a stretch of M26 between Eagle Harbor and Eagle River that is called Sand Dunes Drive due to the sudden appearance of small sand dunes in this part of the Keweenaw shore. At Eagle River the coast turns mostly rocky again and this is a popular place to hunt for agates and colorful stones, even bits of copper. There are many wonderful things to see in Copper Harbor, Eagle River and Eagle Harbor so don't be in too much of a hurry. Follow scenic and fun 26 south until it joins with 41 again and turn southbound onto US41 at the village of Phoenix.

Ride US41 south through several old mining communities for fourteen miles. When you see the signs for Calumet and route M-203 it's time to turn so we can explore the southwest corner of the peninsula. In Calumet a recommend stop is at the old Fire Station, also called the Red Jacket Fire Station. This exceptional building, built in 1899, is typical of much of the wonderful architecture in this region. The towns and citizens had some wealth a century ago and they used it to build impressive and long-lasting buildings. The structure is on the National Register of Historic Places and is part of the Keweenaw National Historic Park. Today it houses the Upper Peninsula Firefighters Memorial Museum. It's on 6th Street just one block south of M-203.

Continue west on 203 to take in the southwest corner of the Keweenaw. There are two highlights in this corner of the peninsula; McClain State Park and the Portage Canal. McClain Park has a good beach and is famous for sunsets. It faces west across the vastness of Lake Superior and sunsets are legendary. If you're into camping you can't do much better than this location.

Just south of the park 203 turns east along the canal. At the west end of the waterway you get a good view at the Keweenaw Waterway Upper Entrance Lighthouse. From this point east to Hancock 203 hugs the north shore of the canal and offers a bounty of grand views and vistas.

Route 203 carries us all the way back to Hancock and the Portage Canal Life Bridge and the end of this marvelous 200-mile ride through Upper Michigan's Copper Country and renowned mountains.

7. A Yooper Chemistry Lesson: Iron, Copper, Wood and Water

THIS TOUR IN THE western portion of the Upper Peninsula conveys travelers through a magical land of waterfalls, old mines, countless acres of forests, hills, sparkling trout streams, and historic cultural sites that beckon exploration. The roads are smooth, traffic is light, and the riding is good; in fact, it's great. This circular ride can of course be joined at any point along its path but I'll start in the attractive city of Crystal Falls, the county seat for Iron County. Located on the Paint River, Crystal Falls' history is based on both iron and timber.

Iron County was established in 1885 when it was split from Marquette County. As was the case with several newly-formed counties in Michigan there was a serious dispute among the citizenry in the formative days as to where the seat of county government was to be located. At the time of Iron County's creation Iron River was the only incorporated village in the county and was the county seat by default. After Crystal Falls was settled a somewhat heated dispute over the location of county buildings immediately arose between the east side of the county, whose residents wanted Crystal Falls as the county seat, and west siders who favored Iron River. It even got to the point where county records were 'stolen' and moved from one town to the other. It was eventually decided to hold a county-wide vote on the issue where the seat of county government would be. A vote was held in 1888 and Crystal Falls won by only 5 votes. In 1889 the issue was again put on the ballot and this time Crystal Falls was chosen by almost one hundred votes.

I mention this incident because as a result of the voters' decision a beautiful courthouse was built in Crystal Falls in 1892, which today is on the state and federal lists of Historic Buildings. I recommend spending a few minutes to view this structure. It was built when the local economy was strong because of lumber and iron, and when citizens were proud to show their community pride by investing in inspiring and dignified public buildings. It's proudly located at the main intersection in downtown Crystal Falls.

Just east of the courthouse, on Superior Avenue / M69 is the Harbour House Museum where the history of Crystal Falls can be examined. The manmade history of this area is relatively recent compared to some unique natural history. This city is famous for something that most folks wouldn't think of as the basis for bragging rights; fungus. Crystal Falls received international attention in 1992 due to the discovery of a giant fungus in nearby forestland. The fungus covered an area of more than

30 acres and had a total mass estimated at 100 tons. At the time it was believed to be the oldest living organism on earth as well as one of the largest. Crystal Falls adopted it as a tourist attraction and holds a "Humungus Fungus Fest" every August.

From Crystal Falls state route M69 carries us eastbound to begin the ride. Unlike highway US2, which dips south into Wisconsin for a bit, state route M69 goes pretty much straight east from town and, more importantly, is not only a scenic highway but also has less traffic overall and fewer trucks than US2.

About five miles after leaving Crystal Falls there is an optional short side trip to see a site where unfortunate history was made. The location today consists only of a marker and small church, but the quiet location is where the worst mining disaster in Michigan's history occurred. It's the site of the former Mansfield Mine in a geologic area called the Menominee Iron Range. The mine was dug several layers deep under the Michigamme River and in 1893 the mine caved in under the river, which came roaring into the mine killing twenty-seven miners. If you wish to go to the location turn left onto the Mansfield Cutoff Road / aka Old 69. After 7 miles on the old pavement Stream Road goes north one mile to the location. Stream Road is gravel so riders of heavy baggers will want to check the weather before going off the pavement. The road is fine if it's been dry but can be inadvisable following rain events.

M-69 transports us 13 miles to the village of Sagola and route M-95, onto which we make a left turn and ride north. A couple miles after our northward turn is a Louisiana-Pacific lumber mill where local conifers are chipped into small pieces and made into the Oriented Strand Board that is so common in the construction industry today.

Ninety five is a relaxing ride as it meanders lazily through the Copper Country State Forest in the heart of the Upper Peninsula. Because of the ethnic background of many local residents M95 is officially known as the Leif Erickson Memorial Highway. It's an enjoyable and relaxing ride – no roadside cliffs or hairpin curves, just gentle meanders on mostly level ground. About midway through this north / south stretch of road we move from the Central to the Eastern Time Zone upon crossing the Marquette County line.

Eventually 95 intersects with US-41 where a left turn eventually delivers us to the town of Champion, which calls itself the horse pulling capital of the U.P. The town hosts horse pulling competition events through the summer. These are fun events that include other entertainment and social activities. If you're into this particular unique pastime check out their schedule of the town's web site.

West of Champion we'll ride through the rugged Michigamme watershed, which consists of rocky outcroppings and many lakes, all surrounded by miles of beautiful forestland that somehow not only survives but thrives in this rocky, infertile, and very cold, soil. There are moose and wolves, as well as ubiquitous deer, in this neighborhood so keep a close watch on the roadsides. There is a museum in the village of Michigamme that has displays relative to the mining and logging eras, as well as a 1900 steam fire engine.

This part of Michigan is in the Lake Superior snow belt and winters here are extreme. In the high and wild region north of 41 snowfalls in excess of 300 inches are common. The record year was the winter of 1977 / 1978 when 390 inches fell near the village of Herman – that's almost 33 feet of snow in one winter!

We stay on route US-41 as it curves to the north to the village of Alberta. This small town has a fascinating history and is more testimony to the impact Henry Ford had on the western Upper Peninsula in the 1920s and 1930s. It was a company town built out of the wilderness by Mr. Ford and the Ford Motor Company in 1935. Ford at one time had huge holdings in the Upper Peninsula, in the range of 500,000 acres. Ford wanted a dependable supply of the right kind of timber for his automobiles, which in the 1920s and 1930s had a significant amount of wood in them. Ford built several large sawmills in the UP, and in fact in the town of Kingsford at one time 8,000 people worked in his various plants and mills. He also had built a network of railroads connecting his various forestlands, mills, and factories.

Ford wanted his workers to live near the land and to work on the land. As a former farm boy Henry Ford never lost his love of the land and of his belief that working the land was one of mankind's highest callings. Alberta was built out of the forests with comfortable homes for the workers and a state-of-the-art sawmill. In the 1950s, when wood was no longer utilized in cars or trucks, Ford Motor Company donated the town and 2,000 acres of surrounding land to Michigan Technological University for use as a forestry research and education center. There is a sawmill museum in Alberta that tells the fascinating story of Alberta and Henry Ford.

A few miles north of Alberta is the small town of L'Anse, the county seat for Baraga County, and situated on the southern end of Keweenaw Bay. With 2,000 residents it is certainly one of Michigan's smallest county seats. The French named this location in the late 1600s when they first explored the southern shore of Lake Superior. L'Anse roughly means 'the cove', which makes sense given its location at the base of the bay.

Ride 41 around the south end of this picturesque bay and you soon come into Baraga, named after Bishop Baraga, aka The Snowshoe Priest, who ministered to the local Indians in the 1830s. Check out the impressive monument to the snowshoe priest just south of town perched atop what are known as the Red Rock Bluffs. In Baraga there are a few other places that might catch your interest, including the Sand Point Lighthouse (closed to the public but photographs from the outside are welcome), the Baraga County Historical Museum, and the Ojibwa Casino and restaurant.

In Baraga turn onto M-38 and ride it 30 miles west across the base of the Keweenaw Peninsula to its junction with highway M26. We'll go left / south on 26 a few miles to its end at its junction with route US45, where a left turn onto 45 will continue our southerly direction, all the way to Bruce Crossing and highway M28.

The town with this unusual name was originally called Bruce's Crossing when its post office opened in 1888. It got its name from the first postmaster, Donald Bruce, who also owned the local store. It was shortened to Bruce Crossing in 1891.

From Bruce Crossing M28 delivers us across the wild and rugged southern portion of Ontonagon County to Bergland on the northern tip of majestic Lake Gogebic. About midway between Bruce Crossing and Bergland is another typical small UP town with an interesting history. The town is called Matchwood and was a company town built and given its name by the Diamond Match Company, which owned the local forests in the late 1800s. The Bergland Cultural and Heritage Center on the west edge of the village is the perfect place to take a break and learn about the fascinating history of this region.

Just west of Bergland turn south onto route M64 and follow this scenic and enjoyable pavement for many miles along the west shore of Lake Gogebic. This is the UP's largest inland lake and a beautiful one at that. State route 64 takes us all the way to US2 at the south end of this fabled fishing and resort lake. At US2 turn left, heading east toward the town of Watersmeet. The stretch of US2 between M64 and Watersmeet is what many people imagine when thoughts of this part of the country come to mind; a wild mix of forests and lakes creating a scenic tableau worthy of the local appellation as God's Country. It's a beautiful area and after 30 delightful miles we arrive at the small outdoor-oriented town of Watersmeet, nestled in the Ottawa National Forest.

I suggest stopping at the Forest's Visitor Center, located at the intersection of US2 and US45. The center has a good mix of displays and does a great job informing and entertaining the public as to this region. A unique part of the national forest lays just southwest of Watersmeet. The Sylvania Wilderness is 19,000 acres of water and forest, with more wolves and bears than humans. A century ago it was the private domain of a group of wealthy industrialists who saved it from the lumberjacks' axes. The last surviving member of the club sold the land to the U.S. Forest Service in 1967. The Forest Service removed lodges and other 'improvements', reverting the land to the same wilderness it was over 100 years ago, except that now it belongs to you and I.

Unlike many places in the UP, Watersmeet's name isn't derived from Native Americans or early French explorers. Instead, it's very simple. This literally is where the waters meet. From this immediate area the Ontonagon River begins and flows north into Lake Superior, the Paint River flows east to Lake Michigan, and not far to the south the Wisconsin River begins its passage southwest to the Mississippi River.

Riding east on route US2 through this rolling forested region one can immediately begin to sense what a special place this is. Highway US2 itself is a unique part of the larger story. Starting a century ago the dirt trail that morphed into the smooth pavement we enjoy today served as a vital interstate, and even international, transportation link. During the named highways period, 1914 – 1925, it was part of the Theodore Roosevelt International Highway, and locally it was called the Cloverland Highway. The word 'Cloverland' is still in wide use today in this part of the state. That word came into use about a century ago after the UP had been stripped of its trees following the lumbering era of roughly 1880 – 1920. What was left was barren acres of stumps and burned desolation. Landowners, businessmen and civic leaders in the southern portion of the Upper Peninsula began to look for other ways to profitably put the land to use. Since the land is less rocky and the weather more amenable to agriculture in this area than in the immediate Lake Superior region they came up with the idea of selling it to immigrants and easterners as prime cleared farmland. They came up with the word 'Cloverland' to describe the region from roughly Escanaba to Crystal Falls and south to Menominee. What better name than that when trying to sell land to would-be farmers.

The Theodore Roosevelt Highway got its international status because this road connected Maine and Washington, with a portion between Vermont and Michigan that went through Canada. But we returned the favor. Before 1960 there was no road around Lake Superior. Therefore the old US2, which ran from the international border at Sault Ste. Marie to St. Ignace and then west, was a link in Canada's Kings Highway, which went from coast to coast in Canada (mostly). Fascinating stuff.

The thirty miles between Watersmeet and Iron River is more of the same scenic laid back riding experience we've been enjoying. Iron River is a good place to do a little exploring. As its name suggests, the mining of iron ore played a major part in the city's history. Ore was found in sufficient quantities to justify removal around 1870 and mining was an economic cornerstone of this region until the Depression, when most mines closed down due to lack of profit. The mines were reopened during World War Two to satisfy the nation's demand for iron, but closed again after the war.

There are several recommended places in Iron River to investigate. First is the restored depot if you are a fan of railroad history. Also, if you are a fan of rodeo, time your visit for the annual professional rodeo event held in July. You might also want to tour the Pentoga Park Indian Burial Grounds on the south end of Chicagon Lake just east of Iron River. Another recommended diversion is the Iron County Historical Museum. It is the largest locally-owned museum in the UP. It consists of 26 buildings on a ten acre former mine site. The complex is two miles south of US2, in the adjacent town of Caspian. To get there go south on M189 from Iron River, then left onto county road 424 a short distance, left onto Museum Drive to Brady Street, and the complex is to the right. Can't miss it.

Resuming our travels east on US2 brings us back to Crystal Falls and this marvelous 255-mile trip becomes a memory and stories that you will love to share with others. I appreciate that it's easy to ride this number of miles in one day, but it would be a serious injustice to yourself and this part of the state to simply ride without frequent stops to take in the sights, meet the people, and to explore the many welcoming attractions.

8. Pictured Rocks and Historic Bays

THE UPPER PENINSULA of Michigan is a land where superlatives apply. Words such as 'great' and 'wonderful' are overused today and have lost some of their meaning. But the UP offers a splendid grammar lesson in the use of these adjectives. It's a land of great roads, marvelous scenery, fabulous motorcycling, and smile producing fun. Unspoiled nature still prevails with the power to elicit exclamations of "Wow" from admirers. There is the unique geography and geology to consider, the history, the culture, and the interesting people. While much of America has become homogenized in recent decades, and many local cultural personalities around the country have been assimilated into the larger look-alike package that franchise businesses and restaurants and expressways have created, the UP is still exceptional. It's a delightful suite and the "Welcome to the UP" sign that greets visitors crossing the Mackinac Bridge means just that.

This central UP tour runs coast to coast; from the northern shore of Lake Michigan to the southern rocky beachhead of Lake Superior. The route takes us to two of the primary cities in northern Michigan, Escanaba and Marquette, as well as to fascinating and history filled lesser visited places such as the tiny towns of Big Bay and Seney. In between we'll ride scenic roads through the heart of the peninsula and along the way witness what has made this part of the state tick for nearly two centuries; mines, shipping, timber, and amazing natural wonders that have attracted tourists for generations.

Begin the excursion in Escanaba, on the west shore of Little Bay De Noc. Across the water from Escanaba the Stonington Peninsula juts into Lake Michigan creating two bays, Little Bay De Noc on the west, and Big Bay De Noc on the east side of Stonington. These bays derived their names hundreds of years ago by early French explorers and missionaries. An Indian tribe called the Noquet lived in this area and the French named the bays after them, calling them the Bays of the Noquet, or Bays De Noc.

Escanaba is a good starting point because it offers all the amenities needed by travelers, including a wide range of lodging options, as well as motorcycle shops, car repair facilities, and any other needed services or recreational desires.

The city has long been an important port for shipping ore, lumber, and various other goods and resources produced nearby. The town has much to offer and it's worth spending some time here to explore the many offerings. Beautiful Ludington Park is on the waterfront. Within the boundary of the park is the Sand Point Lighthouse, open Memorial Day to Labor Day for tours. It was constructed in 1867 when shipping of iron ore, copper, and lumber made this city a busy port. Behind the lighthouse if the Delta County Historical Museum.

In the downtown section is one of the most famous buildings in the region, the House of Ludington Hotel. This iconic structure, built in 1864, was the home of lumberman Nelson Ludington. The Bonifas Arts Center on South 1ˢᵗ Avenue offers varied displays of art and artifacts, and there are some delightful microbreweries that you won't want to miss if craft beers are your idea of how thirst should be slaked. Escanaba is also home to the Upper Peninsula State Fair every August – a large and fun event. And if racing is your thing then a trip to the UP International Raceway at nearby Bark River will satisfy that craving.

When ready to depart, go north on US2 / US41 a short distance to route M35. Turn left onto 35 and ride towards Gwinn. This is one of the more unique roads in Michigan because it traverses the four major landscapes in the state; urban, agricultural, forestry, and mining at the northern end. Route 35 connects the city of Menominee at the southern border to Marquette in the north. Upon leaving the urban landscape of Escanaba and driving north the road first passes through a mostly agricultural region (this is the banana belt portion of the UP, after all) but the landscape quickly transitions to typical northern forestland.

For a number of miles the landscape is mostly trees with a couple very small crossroads villages thrown in to add some variety. Gwinn is the first town of any size that'll be encountered. It owes its existence to the Cleveland-Cliffs Iron Company, which owned mines in the area a century ago. The manager of CCI at that location thought a company town to house miners would be a good thing, so a town was platted on paper and then completed in 1910 according to an urban designer's plans.

North of Gwinn is where the road and the scenery really get interesting. What look like small mountains loom over the treetops. But they're not mountains, they're massive piles of rock from local mines. The Empire Mine near Palmer is huge; there is just no other way to describe it. Though vehicular traffic is quite light in the vicinity of Palmer it's wise to slow down and be extra cautious due to some tight curves and the possibility of trucks. Rocks and gravel can also appear on the road.

In order to better appreciate the role and impact of iron mining you might want to visit the nearby Michigan Iron Industry Museum in Negaunee. A couple miles south of Negaunee a sign provides directions. Turn onto Maas Road / CR492 and it takes you west to Forge Road and the museum.

Route 35 ends at Negaunee, where a right turn onto M28 / US 41 carries us into Marquette, the second major UP town on the route. Marquette is the Upper Peninsula's largest city and an important port. US41 makes a

90-degree turn to the southeast on the east side of town and just prior to this curve you'll see Lakeshore Road to the left. Turn onto it and casually cruise this street along the beautiful waterfront for many blocks. Take in the park, the maritime museum, the ore docks, and ultimately popular Presque Isle Park. On the north side of town, past the Coast Guard station, you will see Hawley Street going west. Turn onto this and it turns into Big Bay Road outside of town.

Shortly after turning onto Big Bay Road you'll see a sign for Sugarloaf Mountain on the right. If you're up for a bit of a workout this is a very nice stop and climb to the top for views well worth the effort. Steps have been placed to help traverse the steepest sections of the rocky mount.

Once underway again on Big Bay Road kick back and cruise the roughly 25-miles northwest along the Lake Superior coast to the tiny burg of the same name on the shore of Lake Independence. The village of Big Bay is on the north shore of Lake Independence, situated on a narrow strip of land between this inland lake and Lake Superior's Big Bay to the north. Despite seemingly being so far away from civilization the town of Big Bay is actually a busy place. There is much to do here, especially in the outdoor recreation arena. Big Bay is one the edge of Michigan's most remote wilderness area and offers solitude and natural beauty for those who travel here to get away from the hustle and bustle of modern life. The Huron Mountains lay just to the west, and many rural trails carve through this beautiful region. If you're on the right kind of bike be prepared for some fun times.

If Big Bay and the Lake Independence are hopping today, it's nothing compared to eighty years ago. Back in the 1930s Ford Motor Company had a plant here and Henry Ford himself was a frequent visitor. The presence of this facility resulted in many people living nearby to work at the plant. It also resulted in Ford executives living here as well as frequent visitors from Ford's Dearborn headquarters. These managers ate and stayed at Thunder Bay Inn, which is still here, with essentially the same ambience as it had all those years ago. The Inn is a favorite stopping point today for photos and food.

An interesting historical side story involves Mr. Ford and the Michigan Highway Department in the late 1920s. When state route M35 was originally platted it was going to stretch from Menominee all the way northwest to the Lake Superior shore and the towns of L'Anse and Baraga. This would have meant carving the highway through the wilderness of the beautiful Huron Mountains highlands and along the wild Superior shoreline, including lands near the Huron Mountain Club, a large wilderness area owned by some of the wealthiest industrialists of the day; but Henry was not yet a member. Club members and Henry

Ford didn't want to see the beauty of the area spoiled by a main road and they learned that if enough landowners in the area where the road was to be built signed a petition against it, the road could be legally blocked. Ford owned many large parcels in the region, which he used to guarantee a supply of quality hardwoods for manufacture of his cars. In cooperation with the Huron Mountain Club he agreed to formally oppose the road and used his significant influence to that effect. The petition was successful, the road wasn't built, and by 1929 Mr. Ford was a club member.

Though Ford Motor Company was a major actor it wasn't that company alone that put the town of Big Bay on the map. During and immediately after World War Two the Army had a small base here, using the land at the lighthouse, which is perched on a high cliff, to help protect the country's northern border. Anti-aircraft artillery was installed and soldiers not only manned the base but also came here for training on the 90-mm guns. In 1952 one of the most famous murders in Michigan's history occurred here when an army officer killed a local bartender. It seems that the officer's wife unfairly charged the bartender with assault after she came home late and somewhat intoxicated. A book was written about the incident, which in turn resulted in a movie – *Anatomy of a Murder*. Much of the filming occurred in Big Bay and the Thunder Bay Inn, as well as in the Marquette County Courthouse (a beautiful building that is worth a tour) Jimmy Stewart and Lee Remick starred in the movie. The lighthouse that once guided ships away from rocks, and then stood nearby as anti-aircraft artillery gunners practiced by firing rounds over Lake Superior, still stands today. Times have changed, however, and today the lighthouse is the Big Bay Lighthouse Bed & Breakfast. I have stayed there and highly recommend spending time at this unique B&B.

Because there is no better alternative route we're going to return to Marquette the same way we left it. This is a good thing because riding Big Bay Road once is fun, but riding it twice is double the fun. One suggestion, if you didn't make the one mile side trip to the Thomas Rock Scenic Overlook, two miles south of Big Bay on CR510, you might want to stop on the way back south. The vista north toward town and Lake Superior are quite nice.

Go back to US41 again on the east side of Marquette and head east. We'll once again be on US41 / M28 for a short distance. The federal highway turns back south and we continue our ride on state route M28 east to Munising, one of my favorite roads and places in the entire state. The 45-miles between Marquette and Munising are a delight to ride with abundant scenery and many nearby attractions of the natural kind. Depending on a person's interests and desires activities such as waterfall hikes to simply sitting on the beach listening to the waves pounding on the shore and staring at the northern water horizon are options.

Once in Munising plan to spend some time because this delightful town has so much to see and do. It's easy to spend a full day right here, enjoying waterfall excursions, boat cruises, and much more.

Munising is perched on the shore of beautiful Munising Bay and is surrounded by high lands that give it a unique and rugged look. Grand Island materializes just offshore in the morning fog and the sea cliffs that make up the Pictured Rocks are visible in the distance. There are a dozen waterfalls within ten miles of Munising where streams can be seen tumbling and dancing their way down the forested sandstone bluffs toward the big lake. Several of them are easily accessible with a short walk or even no walking at all – some are visible from the road. This is truly a place of natural delights. I encourage anyone visiting this town to take in all that it offers, including a sightseeing boat trip out to the pictured rocks. Lunch at the Dogpatch Restaurant is a memorable event if the timing is right.

Munising of course has a long maritime history given its location. This central coast of Lake Superior is especially treacherous. Trout Bay and the Munising harbor, protected by Grand Island, provided the only refuge for seafarers for many miles. Native Americans long used the sheltered bay where present day Munising is located. They referred to the spot as *kitchi minissing* or the great island. Grand Island is indeed a great island and a ferry delivers adventurers to the island for day hikes or longer excursions. Today it is protected as a National Recreation Area. The best known tourist attraction in Munising is the Pictured Rocks boat tours. And these excursions are definitely recommended as the best way to see the seaside cliffs. There are many other interesting things to do out of Munising besides the boat tours. Airplane rides over the lakeshore for a dramatic view of the sea cliffs and Grand Island are a fun option. You can also take a glass-bottom boat on the bay to view shipwrecks. This and so much more. Check out the options on Munising's web site - http://www.munising.org/.

When the tourist in you has been satisfied and you're ready to move on follow the signs east from downtown Munising on route H-58 to H-13 (Miners Castle Road) and turn left. An enjoyable ride through dense forests north to the road's end at the Lake Superior headlands delivers grinning riders to the rock walls that are the basis for the Pictured Rocks National Lakeshore. A pleasant 20-minute walk to Miners Falls is a recommended option while traversing Miners Castle Road en-route to the lakeshore. The Miners River plunges forty feet into a rocky gorge and the sight and sound of the waterfall are well worth the easy hike on a hard-packed trail from the parking lot. Once at the Lake Superior shore things get even better with a stunning bird's eye view from atop the cliffs, and the iconic and much photographed rock formation called Miners Castle. (The natural erosion process caused half of the Miners Castle structure to tumble into the lake several years ago, but the remaining formation is still most impressive.)

Motor south back to route H-58 and ride this marvelous pavement east through the beautiful Pictured Rocks Lakeshore as it twists, dips, and weaves its way to the village of Grand Marais at the east end of the park. The years-long paving project for Route H-58 was finished just a few years ago and the road quickly became a motorcycling destination for Midwest riders. It definitely won't disappoint. It is an opportunity to scrub some of the rubber off your sidewalls, but beware of other drivers or riders doing the same. I clearly recall trips down the old rough and rocky version of H58 when it would rattle the lugnuts off a car's tires.

There are several scenic attractions along the way, especially the impressive and totally unexpected Grand Sable Sand Dunes tucked between Lake Superior and Grand Sable Lake. Miles of sea cliffs to the west suddenly give way to some of the largest freshwater sand dunes in the world. I challenge you to park your bike and hike to the top of the dunes! The park's visitor center and Sable Falls are also just west of Grand Marais near the dunes and are both recommended stops.

Once into the small outpost of Grand Marais we head south on state route M-77 to M-28 and the village of Seney. But prior to leaving this small end of the road village, head north a couple blocks to the shoreline to do some exploring along the town's lakeshore. Though tiny, the town is lively. There is a seaplane event in June, a July 4th festival, a kayaking event in late July, and a Music and Arts event in August. There are three museums that will be of interest to a wide range of folks. They are the Lighthouse Keepers Museum on the Coast Guard Road, the Old Post Office Museum on Lake Avenue, which tells the story of this town over the past three centuries, and the Pickle Barrel House Museum, also on Lake Avenue. This is a 16-foot high house built in 1926 in the shape of a large barrel.

When ready to depart the outpost of Grand Marais head south on M-77 to M-28 and the village of Seney. Though a quiet wide spot in the road today Seney was once a rip-roaring town whose population was largely lumberjacks and people whose mission in life was to separate lumberjacks from their hard-earned money. Formed in the 1880s when logging of the local virgin forests began it quickly turned into a raucous town that had 21 saloons and one church. It's where lumberjacks from local camps came to have some fun and perhaps earn a knife in their back in the process. This is also Ernest Hemingway country. It's where his Nick Adams character gets off the train after a devastating forest fire swept the area, and hikes to what Hemingway wrote to be the Big Two Hearted River to camp and fish, and try to forget his own memories of World War One.

Make a very short jog west and then follow M-77 south again. Just south of Seney you pass the headquarters of the Seney National Wildlife Refuge, a 95,500-acre wilderness area. There is a visitor center to browse and if you're up to it walking tours through part of the refuge are available. There is also a seven-mile self-guided tour for motorized vehicles but use your own best judgment as to taking a large motorcycle on the tour.

This part of the UP is quite flat and is a mixture of old farmlands and sparse forests. M77 delivers us south to US2, passing through the villages of Germfask and Blaney Park along the way.

Turn west onto highway US2 and you'll quite soon be in Gulliver. A left turn at the caution light in Gulliver leads to the Seul Choix Point lighthouse if in the mood for a diversion. If not, US2 soon arrives in Manistique, which offers several options for food, service, or lodging.

Along the highway west of Manistique signs appear for two state parks. The first, 12 miles west of town, is for Palms Book SP and Kitchiti-kipi (Big Spring). The park is about ten miles north of US2 but well worth the detour. Taking a glass boat out onto the crystal clear 40-foot deep pond, with 10,000 gallons of water per minute bubbling upward, is quite an experience.

The next suggested side trip is on state route M183 south on the Garden Peninsula to the Fayette State Park – a restored iron smelter town on the east shore of Big Bay de Noc.

Continuing west on US2 a short distance west of M183 takes us to a road that few tourists drive on, heading down to the harbor town of Nahma on the north shore of Big Bay De Noc. The road, Ee25 follows the waterfront south to Nahma. An old gas station at the intersection of US2 and our side road helps locate it. Ride Ee25 along the shoreline and eventually you'll end up in Nahma, a tiny town formed in 1881 by the Bay De Noquet Lumber Company.

An unexpected surprise in Nahma is the Nahma Inn. It offers great food, spirits, and lodging in a building that's over 100-years old. Once finished exploring this small harbor town head straight north on Gg / River Road. It basically goes north from Nahma but in an exceptionally enjoyable manner as it follows the meandering Sturgeon River. The landscape from Nahma north to US-2 is heavily wooded and Gg Road makes the best of it with its serpentine twists and turns. It's a good one. After a few miles we'll find ourselves at US2 again at the crossroads called Nahma Junction. Turn westward onto US2 and in a few miles yet another possible interesting diversion presents itself – County Road 513 heading south to the southern tip of the Stonington Peninsula and the Stonington Lighthouse. The last couple miles of the road to the lighthouse are hard packed stone, so decide accordingly. I've never found it a problem but if it's been raining heavily recently you might want to reconsider.

West of Stonington Peninsula it's a short drive around the northern tip of Little Bay de Noc through Rapid River and Gladstone, back to Escanaba and the end of this marvelous 380-mile ride. (Please note that the 380-mile length is point-to-point to the various places as described in this ride. The several side trips I suggest (e.g. Big Springs, Fayette, Stonington lighthouse etc.) easily lengthen the trip by more than fifty miles.

North Star Delights

I find it fascinating that the states of the Midwest are all comprised of two or more distinct geographic regions. Southeastern Ohio's Appalachian foothills' region is a very different place than the Maumee River valley of northwestern Ohio. The rich farmlands of southern Michigan share virtually no similarity with the iron and copper mining areas of the Upper Peninsula and the Canadian Shield bedrock that defines that region. And southern Indiana and Illinois are culturally and geologically different than the northern halves of those two states. This variety is a fascinating underpinning of the Midwest's diversity and strengths.

Minnesota does nothing to break this pattern. As with other areas of the heartland a person can easily experience different economic, political, historic, and geological zones in the same state on the same day. Minnesota has three broadly defined regions, based on landforms. These are the Superior Uplands in the north, the Drift and Till Plains in the south central and southwest part of the state, and the Driftless area of the southeast corner of the state. I mention this not just as a curious fact but because these regions and their native landscapes have a very real impact on Minnesota's motorcycling opportunities. As with other states I will identify prime biking roads in each region because every region has its strengths and charms.

The Superior Upland covers much of the northern half of the state including of course the Lake Superior basin and the so-called Arrowhead region north of the big lake. The region is mostly composed of surface rock making it unsuitable for largescale agriculture. Minnesota's highest point, The Superior Upland region is the most rugged area of the state and includes thick forests and thousands of lakes and rivers. It's where Minnesota's iron ore deposits are found and its highest point, Eagle Mountain at 2,301 feet, is located in the region.

The Drift and Till Plains region is agricultural. Deep rich soil is the byproduct of ancient glacial action. It's relatively flat, with most geographic relief being from glacial moraines or, especially in the southwest quarter, resulting from valleys that were eroded down into the ground from glacial outwash.

The Driftless area of the southeast presents a landscape unlike the rest of the state. This area was not affected by the leveling or bulldozing action of the last glacier. The ancient hills and rock bluffs and river valleys that have been there for eons are still present today. The beauty of this area is enhanced by the presence of the Mississippi River which bisects the Driftless zone. Over the millennia the Mississippi River has carved its way through the ancient bedrock hills with the result being bluffs with stone cliff faces looming on both sides of the river. The fact that shoreline roads follow the meanderings of this and other rivers in Minnesota means miles of fabulous motorcycling. The more than 400,000 licensed motorcyclists in Minnesota are happily aware of the great motorcycling opportunities in their state, now it's time for other riders to also enjoy the North Star State's hospitality, beauty and roads.

- Great River Road National Site: https://www.fhwa.dot.gov/byways/byways/2279/maps
- Minnesota Great River Road site: http://www.mnmississippiriver.com/
- State Parks: https://www.dnr.state.mn.us/state_parks/
- Campground reservations: 866-857-2757 / https://www.dnr.state.mn.us/state_parks/reservations
- Tourism Information: https://www.exploreminnesota.com/index.aspx
- Lake Superior Scenic Byways: https://www.superiorbyways.com/
- Minnesota Scenic Byways Site: https://www.dot.state.mn.us/scenicbyways/.

1. *Superior National Forest Scenic Loop*

THIS ENJOYABLE 175-mile loop explores the wilderness north of Lake Superior on three of the region's renowned scenic roads. Beginning our tour in Two Harbors on the Lake Superior coast, route 61 is legendary for its scenery and motorcycling charms as it carries us five miles beyond Silver Bay to Tettegouche State Park and Route 1 heading north into the woods. This well-known scenic byway from the Lake Superior shore inland to the wilderness outpost of Ely is a favorite for bikers who like to venture off main roads while still enjoying the qualities of lightly traveled pavement. Route 2, aka Forest Service Road 15 connecting Ely and Two Harbors finishes this picturesque adventure into the woods and lakes of northern Minnesota.

The town of Two Harbors is typical of northern Minnesota and Great Lakes communities, being both a 'working' northern and lakes city as well as a tourist center. There are a few things to check out here prior to putting kickstands up. If railroading history is of interest is the Duluth and Iron Range Railroad Museum on South Avenue near the lakeshore and railroad tracks. The Castle Danger Brewery is nearby as is the Two Harbors Lighthouse. As we ride east the 1,400-foot-long Silver Creek Tunnel makes for an interesting experience and sight. The tunnel eliminated a dangerous narrow strip of pavement that had perilously clung to a roadside cliff.

In fairly quick succession Gooseberry Falls and Split Rock Lighthouse State Parks arrive. There is a visitor center in the Gooseberry Falls park and of course walking trails. Split Rock Lighthouse is located at the easterly end of that park and can be seen from the highway at a distance or via park road up close. Even when viewed at a distance from the road this lighthouse, perched atop a cliff and partially shrouded in the fog that often blankets the shoreline, presents a dramatic image. The lighthouse location is fairly easy to miss if not watching for signs. It's also easy to not be attentive for directional signs because the scenery is so fabulous and the road so enjoyable.

Route 1 heads north at the east edge of Tettegouche State Park. The state has labeled it a scenic route and the road lives up to its designation. The first several miles have a bit of low density development but after the village of Finland the landscape becomes more and more wooded as we traverse the Finland State Forest. At Isabella the road makes a lengthy westerly run, then angling northwest for the last stretch into Ely. With 3,500 year-round residents, and a higher population in summer months, Ely seems like a bustling town after experiencing the wide open spaces of the surrounding forests. It is of course an outdoors related center with several outfitters and businesses catering to canoers, fishers, campers, and hikers. There are two fascinating wildlife facilities here. On the east side of town is the International Wolf Center and just west of town on route 169, just off highway 1, is an educational and research facility called the North American Bear Center. Both are open to the public. In town route 1 is Sheridan Street which is lined with stores, tourist shops, restaurants and lodging facilities to meet the needs of travelers or shoppers of souvenirs.

To complete the loop we ride back south on route 1 for about 27 miles (depending on your actual 'starting' point) to route 2 / aka US Forest Service Highway 15. This quiet two-laner accompanies us southeast through similar countryside all the way back to Two Harbors. Though certainly not arrow straight this road is less meandering than route 1 but that doesn't mean it's not a joy to ride. The scenery is typical northern woods with lots of lakes and streams in a forested setting. There are some mines nearby so occasional truck traffic is present. It's also appropriate to issue an advisory for wildlife. There are many large critters in this region; deer, bears, wolves and more. Be on guard for them. It's a thrill to see them at a distance but keep an eye out for those who are crossing the road to get to the greener grass on the other side.

About midway on our return trip route 2 makes a westward jog of about a half-mile where it meets route 11 to cross railroad tracks. Eleven continues to the west and our road turn south just west of the tracks. The train tracks handle the needs of some mines to the north near the town of Babbit, straight south of Ely.

In the last few miles north of Two Harbors our road straightens out and even passes through a bit of farmland before entering town. Think of it as decompression, the same step that a diver must take upon ending an extended submersion. This is a wonderful day ride though it could easily be made a two-day loop with overnight reservations in Ely. There are opportunities to see and do things along the way that add on fun-filled hours.

2. Fergus Falls To International Falls

THIS ENJOYABLE lengthy ride takes in much of what Minnesota has to offer; rolling farmlands, the prairie pothole region, lakes and rivers, and northern forestlands. It also includes much of the west central part of the state frequently overlooked by non-local riders unless they're westbound on I-94 to distant locations. The ride begins in Fergus Falls, a town of about 13,000 that serves as the county seat of Otter Tail County and is on the demarcation line between the lake and forest country to the east and the prairies to the west. The town is on the Otter Tail River so given its connection to this marine mammal it only makes sense that there would be a giant Otto the Otter monument in Grotto Park, located in the southeast part of town. It's one of those 'mandatory' photo op stops.

North Union Avenue, aka Old route 59, is the main north / south street in Fergus Falls and we'll ride it north out of the city. Union Avenue T's at Fir Avenue at the north edge of town. Take Fir Avenue west and then north as it curves and becomes county road 88 at the Fergus Falls Wildlife Area. Route 88 loosely parallels I-94 northwesterly (and keep us off the expressway!) until it intersects with US59 – the enjoyable road that carries us the 41 remaining miles to Detroit Lakes. Fifty nine enters the lakes region very quickly after departing Fergus Falls. The town of Detroit Lakes is situated on the shore of a large lake called Detroit Lake.

Like Fergus Falls the Detroit Lakes area is somewhat schizophrenic. Immediately east is the resort lake region where thousands of people flock each summer to cottages and lake recreation. Travel west on US10 just a few miles and one enters the prairie farmland. This makes the town's economy dependent on each source of business. In early August each year the WEfest is held in Detroit Falls. This is a large country music event that attracts some of the best in the business. The Classic and Antique Boat Show is also held in August.

On the north side of town state route 34 heads east, that's our road. This is a really nice motorcycling byway that transports us the fun forty miles to Park Rapids through a rolling landscape of forest, fields and lakes. An interesting phenomenon takes place in the last ten miles of this leg of the trip. The landscape suddenly changes from lakes and woods to irrigated farmlands, with circular irrigation patterns the norm. Park Rapids continues the agriculture / lakes and forest split personality. It is the county seat of Hubbard County and a museum of the same name in town does a nice job detailing the history of the area.

We leave Park Rapids by taking county road 4 north to where it joins highway US71. To get on CR4 go to the east edge of town, two miles east of the bridge. CR4 is a more enjoyable and lesser traveled parallel route to US71 in this stretch as it meanders between the many lakes in the area. As we approach Lake George, and US71 again to the north, the landscape has lost most vestiges of agriculture and is mainly north woods motif. We will be on US71 only a short distance (11 miles) in order to once again forsake busy highways in favor of scenic byways. We'll leave 71 behind and follow county road 16 east across 12 miles of a pleasant montage of broken forest to route 371. Turn left and take it the short distance to US2 and the town of Cass Lake, a small town located within the Leech Lake Indian Reservation.

Go east on US2 across the isthmus for a bit less than five miles total. Turn left onto Cass County Highway 10 and ride it north into the woods. It soon seamlessly becomes Scenic Highway and then county road 39; no turns necessary. This scenic and lightly traveled pavement carves through the forest and lake landscape in a very enjoyable fashion and leads us ultimately to US71 again at the town of Blackduck. Turn right onto 71 and take this wonderful stretch of motorcycling nirvana in the large block of state forest, through the twin cities of Big Falls and Great Falls, and ultimately to International Falls. This 250-mile trip can be done in a day but one has to question why. As with all good motorcycling routes there are attractions, events and facilities along the way that add a great deal to the enjoyment of any ride. Plan to stop and smell the many flowers along the route and make it an enjoyable relaxing, and even educational, two day outing.

3. Minnesota Driftless Region Tour

THIS SWEET RIDE of 140 wonderful miles takes in the best of the south-eastern Minnesota driftless area on winding roads through scenic hills and even presents an opportunity to explore a couple caves – a rare treat in the North Star state. Begin the ride in La Crescent following route 16 south along the big river for a short distance and then inland among the forested hills where the road enjoyably meanders for more than forty delightful miles accompanying the winding path of the Root River. The first half of this ride is not only great fun it's also easy, just stay on route 16 all the way to Preston and three miles beyond. In the Preston area route 16 briefly combines with US52 and continues west.

Three miles west of Preston on route 16 look for county road 11 going south. Turn onto eleven for one mile then turn right onto county road 118 and the fun begins anew as we enter a large block of forest lands containing the restored village of historic Forestville, operated by the Minnesota Historical Society, and Forestville Mystery Cave State Park. Route 118 goes directly to the historic village site but watch for signs for access to the state park and mystery cave. There is a charge for entry to the village museum complex and of course normal state park fees apply for park entrance.

Take CR118 through the woodlands. West of the park CR118 "T's" at county road 5. Turn left and head south five miles to route 44. Turn left / east onto 44 and ride its smooth straight pavement 14 miles to route 139. Two miles before reaching route 139 is 295th Avenue. If a person wishes to explore a second cave turn right here and follow it two miles south to Niag-ara Cave. This is a private operation on county highway 30 just east of 295th Avenue. Hour long tours take explorers deep into the cave, which includes a small underground waterfall. I've never been there but have seen some positive comments about the experience and the facility's overall operation.

Once on route 139 go north the very short distance to Harmony and turn right on US52. Highway 52 continues southeast three-and-a-half miles and then turn south into Iowa. But where it turns south state route 44 continues due east – that's our road. Route 44 is our riding partner all the way back to the village of Hokah where it rejoins route 16 and the short ride back to La Crescent. The segment of this tour on 44 between US51 and Hokah is delightful, as most rides in this unique geologic area are. It's a wonderful mix of tree covered hills, neat hillside farms with their hallmark contoured fields, and mile after mile of curves and smiles. This is also apple and orchard country and neatly manicured orchards add a special scenic quality to the ride.

The village of Caledonia is encountered on this last stretch. It's characterized as the Wild Turkey Capital of Minnesota and it's the county seat of Houston County. The county courthouse is an attractive stone building that deserves a close look. Beaver Creek Valley State Park, an excellent example of southeastern Minnesota's exceptional bluff lands is just 4 miles west of Caledonia on route 1. It's a good place to explore the ancient bedrock geology up close.

4. The Superior Shoreline

THE ARROWHEAD COUNTRY of Minnesota is nothing short of spectacular in every aspect that is applicable to motorcycling. The roads are fabulous, the scenery is incredible, the numerous and varied attractions and stops along the way are marvelous and the overall experience is as enjoyable as can be found anywhere. This 175-mile tour (including the Duluth Skyline Drive) focuses on what is perhaps the pinnacle route in the Arrowhead – the Lake Superior Shoreline between Duluth and the Ontario border. It is one of the most awe-inspiring and enjoyable rides in America. Add to the long list of positive features the fact that it is easy to follow. All one need do is get on Old 61 (stay off the new highway 61 expressway which 'official' routes directs you to!) and head northeast with the remarkable vista of Lake Superior on your right and forest-covered cliffs and hills on the left, broken by occasional waterfalls, lighthouse and other wonderful diversions.

The ride begins in Duluth. But prior to heading out we should spend a couple hours exploring this unique port city. It's not often that a major international waterfront port is located in the middle of a continent. Duluth has more than its share of fun and interesting places to discover prior to hitting the road. One of the quickest ways to learn about this area and its history is a stop at The Depot. Technically it's the St. Louis County Heritage and Arts Center Historic Union Depot. You can understand why it's known locally simply as The Depot. The original depot once served seven different rail lines and 5,000 people per day walked through its doors. This fascinating museum houses everything from old railroad cars and locomotives to historical and cultural artifacts and displays that span two centuries. The Lake Superior Railroad Museum is also at this same facility. The museum has seven steam, 14 diesel, and two electric locomotives, and more than 40 other pieces of rolling stock. The frosting on the cake is that the Railroad Museum also operates the Lake Superior Scenic Railroad – a person can take a train trip along the lakeshore between Duluth and Two Harbors. It just doesn't get any better.

The Lake Superior Maritime Museum is another point of interest that will captivate those who love the nautical history of the region. It's run by the Army Corps of Engineers and is located at the north end of the aerial lift bridge. And finally, the *SS William A. Irvin*, a Great Lakes freighter museum ship is anchored in Canal Park, ready for your boarding and inspection.

And of course when a rider happens is in Duluth he or she might want to stop at Aerostich / RiderWearhouse. What Bass Pro Shops or

Cabela's is to outdoors folks Aerostich is to bikers. If it involves a motorcycle or rider, they've got it. A rider can even call ahead to set up an appointment to get properly fitted for riding gear. No need to buy things that end up not fitting correctly. They're at 8 South 18th Avenue West, or GPS coordinates N 46° 46.190 W 92° 07.175.

When our tour of discovery in Duluth is complete, our trip into Arrowhead Country is going to begin on the Duluth Skyline Drive, a 20-mile long semicircle around Duluth on the high lands on the outer edge of town. The byway is situated atop a cliff hundreds of feet above the city and the lake with remarkable views of both features. And it ends at Old 61 so we can proceed on the Lake Superior shoreline ride without worrying about tricky navigation.

The Skyway begins on the west side of town, west of the zoo, where South Boundary Avenue hits the US35 expressway. The Skyline is on the north side of 35 immediately adjacent to it for a short time, then it angles off. It's marked along the way as Skyline Parkway and is quite easy to follow. At the University of Minnesota campus it begins following actual streets until the byway ends at University Park and route 61. The Drive is quite well signed along the entire route.

Old 61 begins as Congdon Boulevard then county route 61 and eventually, appropriately enough, Scenic Highway beyond Knife River. Our entertaining road eventually morphs into state route 61 and the waterfront fun continues uninterrupted. At no point is it necessary to get on the new Route 61 four-lane divided highway that runs between Duluth and Two Harbors.

The attractions on this route are too numerous to write about them all. Be willing to take the time to explore sites as you pass them on the road and I guarantee you won't regret the pauses in riding. The only way you'll be disappointed is if you just keep riding (which is tempting because the riding is so great!) and don't stop to enjoy the natural beauty and sights.

Once under way on Congdon Boulevard the city soon ends and the wild side of Minnesota begins. Just beyond Knife River there is a small unusual stop in the form of the Buchanan Historical Marker. It was once an elaborate stone roadside rest area from circa 1940 that also marked the old settlement of Buchanan. It's a 'ghost rest area' now but much of the interesting old stone work remains. The town of Two Harbors is next and a suggested stop if railroading history is of interest is the Duluth and Iron Range Railroad Museum on South Avenue near the lakeshore and railroad tracks. The Castle Danger Brewery is nearby. Further east the 1,400-foot-long Silver Creek Tunnel is perhaps an unexpected surprise for travelers. This tunnel opened in 1994 and eliminated a dangerous narrow strip of pavement that had perilously clung to a roadside cliff. This section of the road has countless spectacular views of the lake as the pavement hugs the shoreline

In fairly quick succession Gooseberry Falls and Split Rock Lighthouse State Parks arrive. There is a visitor center in the Gooseberry Falls park and of course walking trails. The impressive lighthouse is located at the easterly end of that park and can be seen from the highway at a distance or via park road up close. When viewed from a distance from the road this lighthouse has an eerily remarkable look to it, perched atop a cliff shrouded in the fog that often blankets the shoreline, especially in the morning. It's fairly easy to miss if not watching for signs. It's also easy to not be attentive for directional signs because the scenery is so fabulous and the road so enjoyable.

At the Cross River there is a waterfall, small historical museum and at the river mouth a historical marker for French missionary Father Baraga. The marker requires taking a side road to the lakeshore. Further along the tiny burg of Tofte hosts the North Shore Commercial Fishing Museum. Between here and the town of Grand Marais are several opportunities to view waterfalls. We'll go through the town of Lutsen, located in the Sawtooth Mountains. Lutsen Mountain Ski Area offers the longest and tallest ski runs in the Midwest and the gondola on Moose Mountain or the chairlift on nearby Eagle Mountain offer rides to the top in the summer for spectacular views of the surrounding area. Grand Marais is the largest city on the route east of Duluth. The towns of Lutsen and Grand Marais are located within the Superior National Forest and wilderness soon returns once beyond the city limits. As we approach the Ontario border the road enters the large Grand Portage Reservation. The Grand Portage National Monument is a recommended stop. This facility has many interesting displays and buildings that recreate the important role that this locale played in trade, transportation, and the early settlement period of this region. Near the border signs for the High Falls of the Pigeon River provide notice of this must see attraction.. These 120-foot cascades, the state's highest, are marvelous and crowds will not be an issue. Grand Portage State Park is also nearby.

Though this road traverses a region that retains much of its wilderness look and feel there are many places for overnight accommodations, ranging from rustic campgrounds to motels and B&Bs. During summer motorcycling months advance reservations are recommended to be on the safe side.

One final note is that it is important to keep local weather conditions in mind. Morning fog is common. It's often best to wait until mid-morning to ride to allow the fog to burn off. This makes riding more comfortable but also enhances scenic viewing capabilities. Also keep local weather conditions in mind. It might be 80-degrees just a few miles inland but 60-degrees on the lakeshore. This vast cold lake creates its own weather systems and fog and cold mist is a fairly common reality. Come prepared accordingly. Chances are good that your cool weather or rain gear can remain in the saddlebag but if they're needed and you don't have this gear you'll be in for a long cool and potentially damp ride.

With that advice in mind, enjoy. This is truly one of America's premier motorcycling adventures.

5. Grand Rapids and International Falls Ride

THIS 120-MILE RIDE is set in the heart of northern Minnesota's forest and lakes region. As the roads make their way north they meander around countless lakes and through large blocks of state and national forestlands. The riding is great and the scenery delightful.

Begin the ride in Grand Rapids, on the upper Mississippi River and the county seat for Itasca County. The city earned its name because prior to lumbering days there were major rapids on a three-mile stretch of the river at this site. Those rapids lie under the impoundments that now line that stretch of river. The community was formed as a lumber town and turned into a major lumbering center. Today it's a busy city of about 12,000 people, more in the summer as seasonal residents return to their cottages. It's surrounded by a thousand lakes and endless outdoor opportunities. There are a couple items that might be of interest near Grand Rapids. On the southwest corner, on the Paper Mill Reservoir of the Mississippi River is the Forest History Center. It's only logical that such a museum would be found in this town, set as it is in the heart of lumbering country. The museum has a replica logging camp and lots of historical items related to that industry and time period. Continuing the lumbering theme, the Tall Timber Days Festival is an annual summer event with lots of forestry and logging related exhibits and skills competition and demonstrations. Unrelated to forests and logging in every way, for movie buffs this of course is the birthplace of famed actress Judy Garland. Her museum is on the south side.

Begin the ride to the northern border from downtown Grand Rapid's main street which is US2 / aka 4th Street. At 3rd Avenue / state route 38 point the front tire to the north and the fun begins. Almost immediately the road curves around McKinney Lake and then literally dozens of lakes in quick succession, setting the theme for the entire tour.

North of the village of Big Fork the countryside temporarily opens up a bit and we leave most of the lakes behind. The designation of our road as route 38 ends at Effie, after 46 marvelous miles, where it intersects with route 1. My scenic route has us continuing straight north on the same alignment onto what is now county road 5. We could take route 1 to the west and then route 6 north again but the CR5 alternative is much more enjoyable as it follows the winding Big Fork River. Road 5 angles northeasterly for about seven miles and then begins a roughly seven mile curvy route along the river west to route 6 where it T's. Turn right onto 6 and continue the northward ride.

Route 6 joins US71 at the twin towns of Big Falls and Grand Falls, on opposite sides of the Big Ford River. This area mixes agriculture in with forestry and the land is a bit more open especially as we ride northeast on US71 out of the state forest and to the town of Littlefork. US71 turns north at this point following the Little Fork River north to the Canadian border and then east on 71/11 to the famous town of International Falls on the Rainy River.

There are several fun things to do here in the brief summer period. International Falls is called the icebox of the nation for good reason. For an average of 110 days each year the temperature does not get above freezing. That's a good point to keep in mind when planning any northern Great Lakes region ride, be it northern Michigan, Wisconsin or Minnesota. The Lake Superior region stays cold late into the spring and turns cold again early in the fall. I've had some cold Memorial Day rides in the north so I normally wait until mid-June to be on the safe side. International Falls used to have a very large thermometer in recognition of their "icebox" reputation. The thermometer broke and was removed a few years ago.

Smokey Bear Park, with its giant 26-foot statue of Smokey, could be considered a must stop photo op. There are also two museums in the park of interest. The Koochiching Museum presents the cultural and historical story of this region and the second, the Bronko Nagurski Museum, tells the story of this well-known Chicago Bears player who is from International Falls. The park is on US71 just west of the bridge to Canada. The park and museums are a fine place to end the ride.

Since this is a major resort area and border crossing site there are many places providing services such as lodging and restaurants. It's a busy place and reservations are recommended.

6. Mississippi River Bluffs Ride

MINNESOTA'S PORTION of the Great River Road National Scenic Byway is 565-miles in length, stretching from the river's headwaters to the Iowa border in the southeast corner of the state. But not all of the byway presents great motorcycling opportunities and the upper portion can be hard to follow; especially if trying to describe the route in print. My favorite segment is the bluffs region of southeastern Minnesota, from the Iowa border 115-miles north to Red Wing. The road and scenery that make up this portion are both extraordinary. There are also countless attractions along this road, too many to mention, ranging from lock & dam facilities to a variety of museums, tour boats, scenic overlooks and Native American mounds.

Let's start at the south end of this route. I'm sure the good folks of Iowa will allow us to gather in St. Albin on the border and adjacent to a large wildlife management area comprised of the bottomlands along the river. Waterfowl and other wildlife thrive in the habitat provided by these productive swamp lands.

As we begin the ride north in Minnesota we'll be on route 26 for many enjoyable and scenic miles until we intersect with route 16 just south of La Crescent (across the river from La Crosse, WI) Route 26 literally hugs the shoreline for much of the distance between the state line and La Crescent. Route 16 soon joins with US14 into and through La Crescent. La Crescent is the official apple capital of Minnesota and every year in mid-September the Apple Fest is a guaranteed good time. It seems that most towns along the river road have developed local parks with scenic overlooks. That's no surprise because there is no shortage of high bluffs along the river. In La Crescent Eagles Bluff Park fulfills that duty. It's on the north side of town and on the west side of our road.

One of the realities of major river systems is that large towns get built along them. The La Crescent / La Crosse area is the first sizable urban area along this ride and because it's also the point where I-90 crosses there is some unfortunate traffic congestion. The easiest option is to follow US14 through town and get on the expressway when the two roads merge for a short distance. When 90 turns west take the exit and follow US14 northward along the river. For a long stretch routes 14 and 61 share the pavement.

The town of Winona presents another urban area, though smaller and easier to manage than La Crescent. Our road skirts around on the west side of town and then bends back to the river once past the busyness. There are some suggested places to check out in Winona. One is Garvin Heights City Park, on the left side of route 61 as one is riding along the west shore of Lake Winona. The overlook on the high hill in the park provides another wonderful view of the bluffs, especially the highest hills that are in this vicinity. Even if you don't consider yourself an art aficionado you will enjoy going to the Minnesota Marine Art Museum. It's meant for art lud-dites like me. It's on the river just north of the bridge at 800 Riverview. And there's the Winona Tour Boat offering cruises on the river. They're located just south of the bridge, very near the Island City Brewing Company.

North of Minnesota City the scenery and road character improve again. There are a number of parks and wildlife areas along this stretch of road, one of the nicer ones being the Wabasha Overlook on 61 just south of the town of Wabasha. The road continues to please as we ride north along the riverfront in Lake City and on to Red Wing where this particular ride ends. But because the bike is parked doesn't mean it's the end of things to do. There are several attractions in Red Wing that help a person soak in what this river ride is all about, plus some other unique things that aren't found elsewhere.

Coming into town Barn Bluff (called that because it's shaped like an old style barn) is between route 61 and the river, just south of the bridge. It's a bit of a hike but the view from the top is incredible, well worth the walk. Sorin's Bluff in Memorial Park is another overlook that offers amaz-ing views of the town and river. The Aliveo Military Museum, at 321 Bush Street, is a small museum with a broad collection of memorabilia dating back as far as the American Civil War, though mostly WW2. The town is of course famous for Red Wing brand boots and shoes. The Red Wing Shoe Store and Museum at 315 Main Street is definitely something that you won't find anywhere else. A photo standing next to the giant boot makes an interesting Facebook status update photo.

Best of the Buckeye State

O hio is a wonderful place to explore on a motorcycle. And it is best seen from back roads and in overlooked small towns to be fully appreciated. By riding the premier roads in this book about the best of the best a thoughtful rider enhances his or her appreciation of the history of this fascinating state while having a wonderful time motoring down hundreds of miles of great biking roads.

This book is of course meant to be more than typical tour guides that simply provide routes and destinations. In this book it's all about the journey; a destination is optional. It's also about telling the stories of the places you're riding through so that the land and the people who shaped it come alive. Each enticing mile of pavement we ride leaves impressions of enjoyment and discovery. Likewise, every small town we explore opens the possibility of discovering places and events that can amaze. They've always been there but perhaps our paths just haven't crossed yet.

I believe that the motorcycling experience can be enhanced if a rider delves into the history and events that accompany the roads we explore. I want to tell readers about the Ohio that most people don't see because they're rushing by the real stories on busy highways oblivious to all the interesting things around them. Far too many opinions about what the Midwest has to offer in the way of enjoyable roads and picturesque landscapes are formed by folks spending too much time on major expressways such as I-80 or I-75. Serious motorcyclists know that the real Ohio and Midwest are found miles removed from these superslabs, not on or along them. As popular as attractions such as the Hocking Hills are the fact remains that most people have not seen their beauty and can't appreciate what the presence of places such as these mean to society. That is, until they take the time and make the effort to explore them, and the countless other places of equal beauty or cultural and historic importance that exist across the length and breadth of this marvelous state.

Though many roads make enjoyable motorcycling experiences, there are certain traits that make a road more appealing and keep us coming back for more. These traits are usually geographic in nature. Ohio is blessed with four basic geographic and cultural zones: the Lake Erie region, the Ohio River valley, the farmlands and forests, and the Appalachian hills of the east and southeast. This book discusses the best riding opportunities that take advantage of all four of these regions.

* Ohio State Parks web site: http://parks.ohiodnr.gov/
* Camping or lodging reservations: https://ohiostateparks.reserveamerica.com/welcome.do
* Ohio River Scenic Byway Site: https://www.fhwa.dot.gov/byways/byways/2286
* Ohio Tourism Board: http://ohio.org/
* Ohio Scenic Byways Program: http://www.dot.state.oh.us/OhioByways/Pages/

1. The Hocking Hills and So Much More

THIS LONG 220-MILE ride is one of my favorites in Ohio. With all the flowers to smell along the way it should certainly be given due deference and be ridden over the course of two days, not rushed through in one. The roads that make up the excursion take a rider through the best of Ohio's natural regions, from the Ohio River on the south, through the forested hills, waterfalls and caves of the Hocking Hills region, and a delightful rolling mix of farms and forests for mile after enjoyable mile. The hard part of the ride is having the discipline to touch the brakes occasionally to visit the many scenic and historic attractions along the way.

The outing begins at the history-filled village of Middleport, on Route 7 along the Ohio River. Middleport was founded in 1798 in large part by Revolutionary War veterans. The old Pioneer Cemetery is actually an interesting stop if old headstones and monuments more than two hundred years old are of interest to you.

Prior to the Civil War Middleport was an important stop on the Underground Railroad. During the Civil War citizens stopped John Morgan's Confederate raiders from entering the town in a battle on Middleport Hill. Amazingly, the village boasts three Medal of Honor winners. The first shot fired by an American in World War II was by command from a man from Middleport.

If you are a railroad fan visit the Hobson Railroad Yard roundhouse and repair facility. There is also the town's streetcar line. This short history bio of Middleport just proves something I've believed for years; that small town America is filled with remarkable people and places and stories. We just have to take the time to explore them.

Depart Middleport by going east / north on route 7 a couple miles to route 124. The fun begins immediately as we ride this scenic two-laner through the forest all the way to Wellston.

One twenty four is a wonderful road that'll have you singing its praises every time you and your buddies share stories about great rides. As you get near Wellston you'll see signs for the Buckeye Furnace State Memorial. This site is worth the 6-mile round trip detour. Buckeye Furnace is a charcoal-fired iron blast furnace of the kind that were common throughout southern Ohio in the mid-to late 1800s. This furnace was built in 1852 and was in use until 1894. It's all there – the casting shed, the original stack, the charging loft where the raw materials of limestone, iron ore and charcoal were loaded into the furnace, and the engine house which housed a steam-powered compressor. The park itself is open year-round, though the museum is open only during the normal warm weather tourist season.

Continue west on route 124 until you arrive at route 327 just south of Wellston. Head right on 327 taking it through town. Route 327 is our guide northwest to route US50. Go right / east on US 50 almost eight miles to the village of Allensville and Goosecreek Road / county road 18, turning left onto Goosecreek Road. (To help find this intersection – there's a small car dealer on the northwest corner and a school on the southwest corner.) Just a half-mile after turning onto Goosecreek Road the pavement forks – Goosecreek Road is the right fork) This fun county road wanders northerly many enjoyable miles to the town of South Bloomingville and route 56. Turn right on 56 and follow its many curves east to Hocking Hills State Park and state route 374, which takes us north into the main portion of the park. Please note that the Ash Cave attraction is on 56 just before reaching route 374.

Once in the park you have a smorgasbord of delights to choose from. Watch the signs for the various attractions or stop at the park headquarters to get brochures – whichever you choose I certainly wouldn't be in too much of a hurry in this beautiful piece of God's Country. I think you'll agree that The Hocking Hills deserve all the praise that is bestowed on this unique region by two and four wheeled tourists alike. I suspect you'll agree that if there are motorcycling roads in Heaven they'll look amazingly similar to these.

Ash Cave, the beautiful Cedar Falls, Old Man's Cave, spectacular Conkles Hollow – these and many more marvelous sites are here for your enjoyment. There are plenty of camping and other lodging possibilities in this area should you want to extend your fun another day.

When finally ready to leave this beautiful area continue north on 374 and enjoy its indirect ways to route 33. Almost all the attractions in this area are along route 374. At one point it joins route 180 for a while and then continues on alone backtracking westerly for a bit (past Cantwell Cliffs) and then north to route 33, which we'll ride east to the town of Logan.

Once in Logan take route 93 north across the Logan River and then several miles north of town to route 668 on which we turn left / north. Route 668 guides us all the way north to Somerset, carrying us across more picturesque countryside and offering many miles of great motorcycling along the way. The road loses its curves for the last few miles to Somerset but a series of enjoyable and scenic roller-coaster hills more than make up for the straight alignment. Somerset is small but prosperous-looking town that shows its age well. In the traffic circle in the center of town is a marvelous monument to Civil War hero General Sheridan, and the stately 1829 courthouse. Several other fine old brick buildings are also in Somerset. In town follow the jog east on US22 for almost a mile and 668 departs northward again.

Remain on route 668 many more miles north of Somerset. For the entire stretch 668 is a collection of high hills, tight curves and grand scenery. You'll love it! SR668 terminates in Brownsville at US40 just north of I-70. At this point jog two blocks west / left and proceed north again on Brownsville Road / County Road-668, following the signs to Flint Ridge.

This ancient flint quarry is three miles north of US40 and is a recommended stop. Taking the short walk on the trail that winds through pits dug over the past 10,000 years is truly thought provoking. The many small quarries aren't much to see by today's standards but a person has to use their imagination to truly understand that they are the result of thousands of people digging with their hands and stone tools for the last one hundred centuries. The flint found in this part of Ohio is of a particularly high quality and made excellent knives, spear points and arrowheads. Aboriginal peoples came from long distances to quarry flint at this site and the items they formed from the flint were used as barter in trade. As a result the flint mined at Flint Ridge can be found at archeological digs around the country.

Continue six miles north on CR668 upon leaving Flint Ridge and just prior to crossing the Licking River is Brush Creek Road. If you go down this road a very short distance there is a parking lot for the west end of the Black Hand Gorge Nature Reserve. The area east of here has the deepest gorge in Ohio. The famous 'black hand' was a petroglyph on the river cliffs which was long ago destroyed by engineers digging a canal. There is a lengthy walking trail (five miles) along the south side of the river that goes from the west parking lot to the east lot, located near the village of Toboso.

To continue the ride go north past Brush Creek Road to state route16 and turn right. Even though this is a divided 4-lane highway it is quite scenic with hillside escarpments resulting from blasting through the hills during construction. Four miles after you turn east on SR16 you'll see the exit for SR146. If you take this exit and follow the signs about two miles to the southeast you'll come to the headquarters of the Black Hand Gorge area and the east parking lot.

If you choose to pass up the gorge you might want to exit here anyway to top off your gas tank; it'll be the last gas station you see until Loudonville, which is about 55 miles away.

To continue the ride get off at the next exit and proceed north on route 586. This is where the tour really gets fun; and that's saying a lot based on the great riding experienced in the last fifty miles. Take 586 north to SR79, turn right, and continue north on 79 all the way to the tiny village of Nellie. In Nellie we'll go right on US36 for maybe one hundred yards. Immediately after crossing the creek make a tight turn onto SR715 for perhaps one of the ten best riding roads in Ohio. SR715 twists and turns in a westerly direction and then goes over the levee of the Mohawk Dam on the Walhonding River. This stretch on and near the levee is breathtaking in my humble opinion. Continue on 715 through the village of Walhonding and turn north onto SR206. Two-O-Six takes you to US62 and a stop sign. Though 206 ends here right straight across from you County Road 25 continues due north – and so do we. After a mile CR25 makes a ninety degree right turn. Another road goes straight at this point so you have to be sure to follow the traffic sign and turn right. (There is also a warning sign at this rural intersection saying 'dangerous intersection'. I suspect that the folks taking the road that goes straight ahead assume they have the right-of-way, rather than drivers coming around the curve on CR25). Once you make the right turn CR25 meanders northeast and north into the village of Glenmont, turning into Clifton Street in Glenmont. This last stretch is very enjoyable although it passes through countryside that now has more farms and less wooded land. In Glenmont go left two blocks and proceed north again on Monroe Street, which turns into CR52. Fifty Two is a fun ride that goes north to Nashville on state routes 39 & 60.

Leave Nashville via 39/60 west bound. This is a fairly main road but it is still fun with its many dips, curves and hills. Eventually it'll arrive in Loudonville and gas stations once again. Loudonville, in the Mohican River valley resort area, is a fine town to stop and stretch your legs. On our trip we're going to go south on SR3 for just a bit and then west on SR97 through Mohican State Park and State Forest. This is a beautiful area and I definitely recommend going into the park to the Clear Fork Gorge overlook, and a bit further west on Mohican Forest Road 51 to the orange fire tower, which is open for climbing by the public. The climb is truly 'breathtaking' and the view from the top is fantastic.

If you wish, before turning onto SR97 from SR3, continue south just a short distance to a neat old grist mill.

Take SR97 with all its twists and turns and enjoyable pavement to Lexington. This marks the end of this fabulous ride through the heart of Ohio. The main attraction at Lexington is the Mid-Ohio Sports Car Course. Mid-Ohio is the venue for the annual Vintage Motorcycle Days sponsored by AMA. This event is a feast for those who ride, own or just love to look at old bikes.

The race track is just west of Lexington and south of SR97 where it passes the Clear Fork Reservoir. Many thousands of us have camped on the shore of Clear Fork Reservoir while attending races and other events at Mid-Ohio.

I think anyone who takes this ride through the picturesque Ohio countryside will agree that the Midwest has scenic delights that take a back seat to no one and that the motorcycling opportunities here are also second to none.

2. Ancient Treasures

I LOVE IT WHEN great riding roads happen to also be routes along which are fascinating places to visit. This ride meets both criteria – fun roads and attractions that'll leave a person filled with wonder. This 150-mile trip takes us to seven fabulous earthen structures built by the hands of ancients for reasons we still don't completely fathom.

Earthworks such as Fort Ancient and the Serpent Effigy Mound weren't built by a wandering tribe of hunter-gatherers that happened to stay put for a few weeks. These civilizations were sophisticated residents of this land for centuries, from before the birth of Christ to about 1750. What I find amazing is that artifacts found in some of the mounds include copper from Isle Royale in Lake Superior to Conch shells and fossil shark teeth from the oceans. This evidence of long distance commerce confirms that Native Americans were wide-ranging travelers who traded across immense distances much like modern-day Americans.

Commence this two-wheeled exploration of Ohio's native peoples in Lancaster. This attractive town is located on the western edge of the eastern Ohio hill country. The surrounding countryside is scenic and that attribute makes it a fun biking region. If you happen to be in Lancaster in early June be sure to attend the large antique car and motorcycle show. It's been a fixture at the Fairfield County Fairgrounds for over 40 years. Later each June is the Earth Angel Super Cruise-In – an annual event featuring old and unusual cars, motorcycles and more, along with major entertainers and singing groups. For more information check out the Angel Foundation at www.earthangelfoundation.org/. It's all about helping sick children get a new lease on life. Lancaster was also the childhood home of General William Tecumseh Sherman, the Civil War general whose famous, or infamous, 1864 March to the Sea guaranteed his place in history. The Sherman House Museum is located at 307 Main Street and is open afternoons during the warm months.

Proceed west on US 22, then taking state route 159 southwest when it splits off from route 22. This stretch of road is pleasant, but we're saving the best for later. Our first stop on the tour is at the village of Tarlton. Turn right onto Redding Street (at the intersection with the old brick building). Just a mile north of Tarlton is the earthworks called the Tarlton Cross, because of its shape. It's located in a small park open to the public. You have to cross scenic Salt Creek on a foot bridge and then climb a hill in a picturesque setting to get to the earthwork, but it's well worth the walk. The mound looks amazingly similar to a Celtic cross in my mind, with a round circle where the two arms cross. This is the only cross-shaped mound known to exist and interestingly the arms are oriented north / south and east / west. There are also some conical mounds, and a very unusual stone mound, located in the 17-acre park.

From Tarlton we continue southwest on 159 to just north of the town of Kingston where we turn right onto route 361. We'll be on 361 just a short distance, but just prior to reaching US 23 – when the road heads straight west and just after crossing a stream – is a small park with several monuments for several noteworthy Indians and whites of the late 18th century. At this location in 1774 a huge Elm tree existed, called the Logan Elm, under which Chief Logan of the Mingo tribe gave his eloquent speech seeking peaceful relations between the natives and white settlers who were beginning to encroach on the Indian's hunting lands. The Elm tree survived until 1964 when it finally succumbed to Dutch Elm disease, which killed millions of Elm trees across America in the 1950s and 1960s. Its measurements made it one of the largest known Elm trees in America.

Continue west on 361 to US 23, go south on 23 about a mile, then veer off to the right taking Orr Road south a couple miles, turning right onto Kellenberger Road / CR 278, heading west. Kellenberger Road carries you over the Scioto River and its wide flood plain to state route 104 where we head south towards Chillicothe. Coming into town you'll see the Mound City Group National Monument and the Hopewell Culture National Historical Park. I hope you'll stop to check out this amazing park and museum. It offers insight into the lives and contributions of these remarkable people. Seeing these magnificent mounds and earthworks, and the handmade artifacts they contain, is a humbling experience.

A bit further south on 104 is the Adena Mansion Historic Site. It's an interesting stop and there's even a pull-off on the winding narrow road going up to the hilltop mansion that offers a dramatic view east to Mt. Logan – the picture memorialized on the Great Seal of Ohio. The mansion and extensive gardens were recently restored. The mansion appears now in the same manner it did when originally built in 1807.

From Chillicothe we head west on US 50. The first few miles west of Chillicothe on 50 are typical urban sprawl ugliness. Be patient because after SR 28 splits off US 50 becomes a very nice road west through the Paint Valley all the way to the village of Bainbridge. Two miles east of Bainbridge, immediately west of the Paint Valley High School is the Seip Mound, earthworks built well over a thousand years ago. Clearing and farming damaged several of the geometric formations on site but the main central mound and an earthen wall remain, and it's impressive. The mound is 240 feet long, 130 feet wide and 30 feet high. Posts on site mark the locations of ancient buildings that once existed within the earthworks.

This is another cool site that will have you asking yourself how, and why, did they do this?

We haven't discussed motorcycling conditions much yet but believe me they get better as we go along. They're certainly not bad in the area leading to Bainbridge but when we turn south on SR 41 just west of Bainbridge, and proceed through a wonderfully hilly mix of forest and farmlands, it keeps a smile on your face. This area is remarkably scenic and the roads are custom-made for motorcycling with a mixture of sweeping curves that allow high speed, coupled with tight dips and curves that'll satisfy peg scrapers.

Our next stop on this Native American heritage ride is at the Fort Hill State Memorial, a mile off of route 41 just south of where state route 753 intersects our road. It's difficult coming up with the right words to give proper dues to this earthwork. The Fort Hill structure contains one of the best preserved hilltop earthen enclosures in the country. The earthworks are a very impressive mile-and-a-half long loop that encloses 48-acres! And it's at the top of a high series of hills, not on flat ground like some other ancient structures. The whole site is set in a scenic area and is a great place to take a walk to stretch your legs. You don't want to pass it by.

Leaving Fort Hill continue south on 41 until you intersect state route 73 at the village of Locust Grove. Go west on 73 and very soon you'll encounter what is perhaps the most famous Indian earthworks of them all – Serpent Mound, which is protected in the Serpent Mound State Memorial. This is the largest of all effigy mounds in America. This quarter-mile long serpentine embankment is on a bluff top high above Brush Creek. The mound is almost as high as a person and averages twenty feet wide at the base. It is truly an impressive structure. A viewing stand allows a person to view the mound from above, giving a much more striking perspective of just how large and finely sculptured this earthwork is. A large museum is also located at the site though it's open only during the summer.

Interestingly this structure means many things to different people. It has been interpreted as representing everything from the biblical snake that tempted Eve with the apple (an egg-shaped object at the serpent's mouth adds to this theory) to new age ideas about alien civilizations and lost races. I think it's great that we'll never really know. The builders are probably still chuckling as to the unsolvable enigma they left behind. The fact that all ancient civilizations such Egypt, Ireland, Britain, Africa, Central America, South America, Asia, and North America built various huge labor intensive structures meant to last for millennia is amazing.

Back on the road, continue west on route 73 to the burg of Belfast. At this point 73 makes a hard turn to the north but we want to turn left and go south onto 785, taking it south and continuing with it as it curves west over to Fairfax. This road becomes County Road 3 / Ridge Road after you cross route 247 at Fairfax.

I think that you'll agree that 73 is a delightful motorcycling road and the county roads that we're going to take to get us up to US 50 west of Hillsboro certainly continue that fine tradition. Follow Ridge Road west to Sugar Tree Ridge and route 136. Go north about a mile on 136 and then turn left on Sorg Road – which is still CR 3. County Road 3 / Sorg Road goes west, then turn northwesterly with the name changing to Danville Road as you approach route 138 and the village of Danville. In Danville we have to turn right on 138 for just a couple of blocks and then turn left again on Danville Road, which is CR 6 west of the village. This road goes west a very short distance then turns straight north, taking us to US 50.

Go nine miles west on US 50 to state route 251 and turn right. Go north on 251 less than three miles, through the village of St. Martin, to route 123 and turn left. Route 123 takes you northwest through the town of Blanchester and then all the way to US 22. Route 123 continually amazes you with its fun biking antics. Just when you think it's about to mellow out up jump more tight curves and hills. Make a left turn onto route 22 / 123 following it into Morrow, where 123 continues north over the Little Miami River with its busy canoe liveries. About three miles north of Morrow route 123 swings west but we want to continue right straight ahead (north) to route 350. There is a white barn with a metal roof at the corner where route 123 swings west and we proceed straight north.

Go east on 350 just about three miles when we'll cross the Little Miami River again, and just beyond the river is the fabulous Fort Ancient earthworks and museum. But what an amazing three miles this is! Almost immediately after turning east onto 350 you'll see a sign stating in so many words that unless you're driving a standard-sized vehicle don't proceed any further. Route 350 descends down a long steep hill with hairpin curves that'll have your knuckles white and your brakes cooking. This is a fabulous run but one where speed is not a wise choice.

I've used up my supply of adequate words and therefore am at a loss when trying to describe Fort Ancient. The Fort Ancient earthworks, a National Historic Landmark, has 18,000 feet of high earthen walls and is perched on a hillside above a gorge on the Little Miami River overlooking the surrounding lands. The role of Fort Ancient in the lives of the builders seems obvious. Perched three hundred feet above the river and protected on three sides by ravines, with a series of parallel berms and what appear to have been moats likely filled with water, it has all the markings of a well thought out defensive fortification. What makes this series of structures unique is that stone piles are included that go beyond traditional burial mounds. One of the stone piles has been shown to serve as the base point for taking celestial readings. When viewed from this spot sunlight coming through gaps in the earthen wall line up exactly for major seasonal events such as the equinoxes and solstices. This celestial calendar information was no doubt used by the ancients for things such as planting of crops and ceremonies. The museum has 9,000 square feet of display space for artifacts and interactive exhibits that documents 15,000 years of native peoples and their cultures, lifestyles and tools. The museum is open Wednesday – Sunday during summer months.

This marks the end of this tour along the path of Ohio's ancient peoples. The riding has been great but appreciation for the accomplishments of those who lived on these lands before us is even greater.

3. From the Fort to the Port – Old Route 24

USUALLY PROGRESS screws up perfectly fine motorcycling roads by con-
verting scenic and curvy two-lane byways into four lanes of straight and
flat boredom. But sometimes progress comes in the form of a totally new
road parallel to the original. This means not only leaving the original road
in its old enjoyable condition but actually making it even better by moving
the worst of the traffic, especially trucks, to the new highway. That's what
has happened along the Maumee River.

Route 24 has always been a busy road connecting Fort Wayne and
Toledo, or the Fort to the Port, as the old-timers used to say. At the same
time it was a favorite of motorcyclists and Sunday afternoon car drivers
looking for an enjoyable road trip through pleasant river scenery and to
unique historical sites that are part of the Erie Canal that borders the road
between the towns of Maumee and Defiance. But traffic increased to the
point that it was neither an efficient mover of commerce nor an enjoyable
afternoon ride anymore. For the sake of safety and efficiency something
had to give. That something was a new parallel divided highway, a su-
persized US24.

That leaves the rest of us able to enjoy Old 24 and it is a day trip that
deserves to be in this book of the best.

Let's start this 120-mile ride on the east side of Fort Wayne at the I-469
beltway. Old 24 is south of the Maumee River and immediately north of
the new US24 highway. Construction of the 469 and US24 expressways
made it difficult to access Old 24 at this point. Our road is a dead end on
the east side of 469 with no nearby access from the highways. The best
way to get on Old 24 is from Lincoln Highway / Dawkins Road just to
the south of the Xway. Take the Lincoln Highway east from 469 and turn
north onto Doyle Road about a half-mile east of 469. Doyle T's at Old 24
near its terminus. Turn right onto 24 and we're on our way.

Proceeding east into Ohio the road becomes County Road 424 and
carries the 424 county road label all the way to beyond Napoleon. The
first portion of this ride from Fort Wayne to Defiance gets progressively
nicer as farmland turns more wooded and the road more closely accompanies the river. Our road crosses under the new US24 just west of Defiance and continues into town as Holgate Avenue then 3rd Street. County
road 424 is called the Maumee Valley Scenic Byway in this stretch.

In the city of Defiance 424 crosses the river as Clinton Street, so turn
left onto Clinton from 3rd. CR424 commences east tight on the north
shore; turn right immediately after crossing the river. Scenic tree-lined
sweeping curves are the norm for most of the next part of this ride and

the scenery is especially nice in this central part of the ride as the river and road are more closely connected. Continue following 424 through Napoleon all the way to the town of Waterville. On the southwest edge of Waterville, by the quarry, veer right onto River Road. This two-lane street runs tight along the river between Waterville and Maumee and is much more pleasant than the main road at this point.

There is much to see in this final stretch. Check out the Battle of Fallen Timbers monument and then cross to the south side of the river in Maumee on Conant Street. On the south side turn right in just two blocks onto route 65 / West River Road. A stop at the Fort Meigs site just a couple blocks to the west is definitely suggested. After about two miles of suburban riding the road leaves the city behind and becomes its normal pleasant self as we ride west to Napoleon and the end of this southern leg. West of Grand Rapids route 65 turns to the south but route 110 continues straight ahead. Just continue straight on 110 along the river.

Following the south side of the river opens new opportunities for things to see and do as well as add scenic and fun miles to the outing. If we want to enjoy this route to the maximum degree and take advantage of the several things to do along the way I suggest doing both parts of the route.

If a person wants to skip the busy Maumee section of this outing, skipping the Battle of Fallen Timbers and Fort Meigs sites, then cross the river in Waterville on the Waterville Swanton Road / route 64 instead and turn west on the south shore at the roundabout on route 65.

The river and the adjacent roads between Maumee and Fort Wayne are the main reason for the ride, but the historic Miami & Erie Canal that parallels the road and river is also an integral part. There are many places along the road between Defiance and Maumee where one can pull over and immerse themselves in the story of this historic canal. A fun option is a packet boat ride at Providence Park. Experience a mule-pulled ride on the small cargo boats that traversed this canal for many decades and were a critical part of the economy of Ohio.

In the town of Defiance a person can spend a couple hours stopping at historic points of interest on both sides of the river. I suggest a stop at the Old Fort Defiance Park at the confluence of the Auglaize and Maumee Rivers, and Chief Pontiac Park on the north shore of the Maumee immediately after turning right onto 424. There are also other attractions in Defiance (originally called Fort Defiance by General 'Mad Anthony' Wayne) involving Indian Wars and War of 1812 sites and canal history.

4. The Triple Nickel

OHIO'S ROAD numbering system makes sense. If you're in a hurry and just want to go from point A to point B then take a busy single or double-digit state route. But it's the triple digit routes that motorcyclists love. Many of these routes, especially in the southern and southeast portion of the state are legendary. They're often narrow, twisting, hilly and scenic. These roads conform to the landscape rather than bulldoze through it. They go over hills and follow the curves of rivers and valleys. They haven't been 'improved' by making them flat and straight. And because of the narrow pavement large vehicles often aren't welcome on these roads, making them even more enjoyable for two-wheelers.

One of the most celebrated triple digit roads is Route 555 – the Triple Nickel. It's a destination road for bikers from much of eastern America.

Describing the route is easy. Get on route 555 about five miles south of Zanesville where it begins at the Muskingum River and state route 60. Then head south. This magical road seems to just keep getting better as it winds its wonderful way 63-miles to route 7 on the Ohio River southwest of Marietta.

But prior to making this fun ride I suggest spending a couple hours in the city of Zanesville to check out some interesting points of interest. The old National Road runs through town. The 'Y' Bridge is of course always a curiosity to check out. There are steamboat excursion rides, southwest of town is the Zanesville and Western Scenic Railroad (some great riding roads to get there) and ten miles east of town is the National Road / Zane Grey Museum.

There are some interesting stops along the route in the form of old general stores and gas stations that'll transport you back about 60 years. These are fun places to stop to chat or take a break. You likely won't be the only biker there.

I have commented many times that if the Ohio Department of Transportation decommissioned route 555 and eliminated traffic on it, turning it into a closed road course, motorcyclists would be happy to pay money to ride its magical asphalt without having to worry about other vehicles interrupting or endangering their fun. This could be a major money maker for the state.

A word of caution should be interjected about this renowned ride. This road is not to be trifled with. Its motorcycling qualities are best exploited by experienced riders. It is narrow, comprised of many decreasing radius curves, and there are unexpected blind turns at the top of hills. The good news is that the entire stretch of 555 is rural countryside. This not only enhances the scenic qualities of the road but also reduces the number of cars competing for space on the curves.

Enjoy the ride but don't let imprudent exuberance turn the Triple Nickel into a wooden nickel.

5. Ohio's Dragon

THIS 95-MILE RIDE in southeastern Ohio's famed Appalachian foothills might be short but it is nothing short of fabulous. It's curves and scenic appeal makes one think of its more famous mountain cousin in Tennessee and North Carolina. For sheer nearby fun it can't be beat. If rolling curvy roads, beautiful scenery, light traffic and mile after mile of motorcycling delight interest you, then you will love this ride.

Begin in the capital city of southeastern Ohio – Marietta. This is fitting because Marietta's story reflects the history and culture of this entire region. It's a marvelous town that will keep a person busy for hours prior to or after the ride checking out the many attractions. They range from visiting a historic cemetery where Revolutionary War veterans are buried to Native American Mounds, the Ohio River Museum, the *Valley Gem* for steamboat rides, the *W.P. Snyder* Museum sternwheeler, the Campus Martius Museum and more. If a rider isn't from this immediate area I suggest spending the day before or the day after the ride here to explore all the charms of this town.

The first portion of this tour is on route 26. This road is officially labeled as the National Forest Covered Bridge Scenic Byway between Marietta and Woodsfield. There are four covered bridges that are quite close to route 26 including two that can be seen from 26. They are, in order toward Woodsfield: The Hills Covered Bridge on route 333 near Marietta with a small parking area accessible by motorcycles, followed by the Hune, Rinard and Knowlton. Some are an easy walk while others are a bit further from the main road. A fifth bridge, the Foraker is the furthest north located three miles east of Graysville. It's quite easily accessible, just take county road 12 / Greenbriar Road in the village of Graysville east to county road 40 and turn left for the short distance to the river and bridge.

To begin the ride motor east on route 26 from Marietta. The fun begins almost as quickly as you turn off of route 7 onto 26. There isn't much more that I can say about route 26 except that it is a wonderful biking road that weaves and turns in every direction as it makes it way northeast through the Wayne National Forest, mimicking the twisting behavior of the Little Muskingum River. This road isn't your typical laid-back motorcycle ride. Like the Triple Nickle and some others it's a somewhat demanding road that requires full attention if ridden aggressively. You'll earn those grins as you work the clutch and brake on the many tight curves. Twenty-Six eventually joins with route 800 just south of Woodsfield but our ride continues into the town.

Woodsfield is situated at the northern boundary of the national forest. Despite its small size it is the county seat for Monroe County. The old county courthouse in town is worth a look; very impressive old architecture. In town turn west on route 78, taking it seven miles to route 145 at the small burg of Lewisville. Nothing changes but the number assigned to the roads. It's the same enjoyable meandering asphalt through the hills and forests. One Forty Five continues the fun all the way south to the town of Lower Salem where we pick up state route 821 to carry us back to Marietta. Though still a pleasing road route 821 can be viewed as providing the necessary decompression before coming to a stop at a Marietta watering hole.

6. *Nirvana in Eastern Ohio*

EAST CENTRAL OHIO has some fabulous routes for motorcycling. Located at the northern edge of the Appalachian foothills, with hundreds of small streams carving downhill to join the Ohio River, results in a landscape of small hills and valleys. And since the original roads were built a couple centuries ago to follow the lay of the land they twist and turn and dip and climb in a manner that is ideal for exhilarating two-wheeled touring. This 180-mile motorcycling getaway takes advantage of the local geology to the fullest. It's a loop beginning and ending at the small town of Beach City south of Massillon.

From Beach City we'll ride east towards the state line then loop south and west again to just west of Newcomerstown. Then a fun ride north on state route 93 delivers us back to Beach City. It's a ride comprised of some of the very best motorcycling roads in the state but it's also filled with fascinating historical places and entertaining things to see and do.

Begin by riding east on State Route 212. With its many curves and hills 212 quickly grabs your attention and let you know that a fun ride awaits. Enjoy the ride on 212 east to Tuscarawas County and the town of Bolivar – the first recommended stop. Bolivar is a canal town, being the west terminus of the short-lived Sandy & Beaver Canal, which ran from Bolivar to Glasgow, PA. The town is named after famous South American General and freedom fighter Simon Bolivar. We have to put ourselves in the minds of folks alive in the early 1800s. From the period of 1810 to 1824 Simon Bolivar defeated the Spanish colonial masters in what are now Venezuela, Columbia, Bolivia and Ecuador. The same year Bolivar, Ohio was formed, the name of the country of Bolivia – previously called Upper Peru – was changed to its current name in honor of Bolivar. The young country of America, having won its own revolution not long be-fore, admired such men.

Besides the canal history, the main attraction in Bolivar is the site of Fort Lauren, the only Revolutionary War fort built in Ohio. This fort was built in 1778 by General McIntosh as part of George Washington's plan to take the war to the British in the frontier. For decades the British had held Fort Detroit and they were encouraging Indian attacks on settlers throughout the frontier.

The placement of a fort in the middle of enemy territory certainly got the attention of the British and their Native allies. It was repeatedly attacked and twenty-some American soldiers were killed and buried in the fort cemetery. The Tomb of the Unknown Patriot of the American Revolution is located at the Fort Laurens museum.

From the fort go back to SR212 and take it southeast to the town of Zoar. The history of Zoar is also a fascinating one. In 1817 a group of Germans seeking religious freedom bought five-thousand acres at what is now the town of Zoar. They believed strongly in the separation of church and state. Once in America they formed a communal society in 1819 called The Society of Separatists of Zoar. The commune prospered until the late 1800s and was disbanded in 1898 with assets divided among members. The many old buildings of the commune still exist.

To resume the trip turn east / left on 2nd Street, at the Zoar Hotel, go over the narrow bridge and continue east on what becomes Mineral City–Zoar Road beyond the city limits. Take MC-ZR east to SR800, turning north / left on 800 two miles to SR183 where we turn right, taking it through the village of Magnolia and on to Waynesburg. At Waynesburg get on SR171, taking it cross-country through the rolling woods and farmlands of Carroll County. SR171 ends at SR9 but Cobbler Road / CR71 continues straight ahead – take it. This whole stretch is wonderful riding and beautiful countryside. Cobbler Road runs into SR39, where we turn left and continue east to the town of Salineville just across the Columbiana County line. On the east side of Salineville you want to get on SR164 southbound. At this corner there is a brown sign pointing south to "Brush Creek Area". This is a short but very fun road south to Monroeville, and the Monroeville-Irondale Road, on which you turn east / left. I'm sounding redundant, but Monroeville-Irondale Road is another great biking road as it winds over the hills and through the woods to Irondale. It's the kind of road that makes you and your bike feel like you are dance partners, moving to the beat created by machine and road.

The last couple of miles into Irondale are especially nice as you wind down the steep hills to the river valley below. As you enter Irondale you will see a blue iron bridge straight ahead of you, and a road immediately before the bridge. Turn right on this road, called Creek Street / CR 56 and take it back to Hammondsville. This short stretch of road is very cool! It has high cliffs on one side and the river on the other as it winds south.

From Hammondsville take State Route 213 south through the beautiful hills and valleys of that make up this entire region of the state. Tag along with SR213 to the crossroads of Knoxville and pick up SR152 and follow it southwest. I guarantee you'll love this part of the tour, and it only gets better. Just beyond the village of Richmond turn right / west on SR646 and follows its wonderful curves over hill and through dale into Harrison County and the town of Scio. Shortly before arriving at Scio you'll pass through the tiny burg of New Rumley. This town's claim to fame is that it was the birth place of General George Armstrong Custer, of Civil War and western Indian Wars fame.

Route 646 deserves to be nominated for the motorcycling roads hall of fame. It is that wonderful. In fact if at any time on this tour you lose the grin on your face it's because you've been pulled over for speeding. There is no other rational explanation. These roads are wonderful.

Depart Scio to the south on SR 646 / Tappan-Scio Road to US250 and Lake Tappan. Take US250 left / east along the shoreline less than two miles and turn right to drive over the lake on Deersville Road, following it as it curves around eventually reaching the small village of Deersville. At the stop sign in Deersville turn left / south onto Mallarnee Road, which becomes SR799 a few miles south. Route 799 is a designated scenic highway and as you follow it along the rugged shoreline of Clendening Lake you'll understand why. The scenery is fabulous. Enjoy route 799's charms all the way to SR800 and then follow 800 a short distance to the left into the village of Freeport.

From Freeport we work our way west for quite a distance on route 342 which shortly joins forces with SR258. I'm sorry if I'm again sounding redundant but this road continues to amaze and please you with its wonderful scenery, hills, curves and just plain great motorcycling character. These magical qualities aren't lost until just prior to arriving at Newcomerstown, located just west of I-77.

The name of Newcomerstown almost certainly brings a puzzled look to many faces when they first hear it. You're no doubt guessing that there's a story behind the name, and you'd be correct. If the town had retained its original Indian name – Gekelemukpechuk – there would really be a lot of pained expressions as people tried to pronounce it.

Gekelemukpechuk was the capital of the Delaware Indian nation. When the white folks first arrived in the 1770s they found a prosperous and peace loving village of a hundred log cabins ruled by Chief Netawatwes, a name that was pronounced Newcomer by the whites. Chief Netawatwes maintained peace during the Revolutionary and Indian Wars. Chief Newcomer's town had always been a large and important village, but it began to grow substantially when the canal arrived in 1827. Newcomerstown has always been strategically located; in the past it was the canal, two railroad lines and a stagecoach road that crossed here. Today it's two major highways. The town has stories to tell beyond those I've mentioned. Cy Young and Woody Hayes were both native sons. A couple of interesting places to visit here are the Temperance Tavern Museum, housed in an 1841 inn, and the USS Radford National Naval Museum located next door.

Coming into Newcomerstown from the southeast on route 258 you'll want to turn left onto State Street, taking it several blocks west to College Street where you'll turn right. Going north on College Street takes you to

US 36, but just prior to reaching route 36 you'll pass Cy Young Park on your right. There's a monument to this baseball superhero in this park that's kind of nice to see.

Leave Newcomerstown via State Street, which becomes county road 9 west of town. Follow this to state route 751 and continue into West Lafayette. In town, at the Train Wreck Memorial, turn north onto Kirk Street / state route 93. Route 93 will be our entertaining riding partner north all the way back to Beach City.

The Train Wreck Memorial in West Lafayette is there for a tragic reason. In September 1950 the popular passenger train Spirit of St. Louis collided with another train carrying 600 men of the 109th Field Artillery Battalion of the Pennsylvania National Guard, killing 33. The memorial was placed near the site of the accident in 1990. A 105mm howitzer is also at the memorial to commemorate the manufacture of 105mm shells at the nearby Moore Enameling Company during World War Two. West Lafayette was once known as the Enamel Center of the World. So many small towns have such fascinating stories to tell!

Route Ninety three is a meandering road that winds through a pleasant mix of farm and forest. Only near Sugarcreek is there a stretch of straight road through open countryside. It's an enjoyable ride all the way. Lots of Amish folks in the area so beware of horse-pulled carts on the road. At the north end we have to get on US250 for a short ride into Beach City.

7. The Ohio River Ride

THERE'S SOMETHING special about riding along a river. The roads are generally scenic because of the tree-lined nature of rivers and floodplains, and the meanderings of streams make adjacent roads enjoyable with lots of twists and turns. Rivers don't flow in straight lines and neither do the roads that accompany them. Often there are riverside bluffs or rock walls that add scenic value. And of course there are the sights and sounds of a river, especially a large working river like the Ohio. Watching barges, freighters and other large boats ply the waters is always impressive.

When a rider follows a large river they are almost always also on the pathways of history. Early America was explored and settled by means of its waterways. Large or small, rivers were the early highways used by Native Americans, early explorers and settlers alike. Much drama was played out over the centuries on the rivers that we are fortunate enough to ride alongside on smooth winding highways today. The Ohio River in particular is truly impressive. It is a muscle-bound river making its way through a ruggedly beautiful landscape. This is the namesake river for this state – the river that the Iroquois called Ohiiyo – which meant Good River!

This 375-mile ride follows the Mighty Ohio from Wellsville in the northeast to New Richmond just east of Cincinnati at the southwest end. Get ready for a very pleasant two or three-day ride during which you will not only enjoy the biking qualities of this route, which after all is what this book is all about, but you'll also marvel at the historical and other unique attractions along the water.

I'm starting the tour at Wellsville rather than at the state line because there is too much congestion and not enough riding pleasure on the river road in the East Liverpool urban area. The Wellsville region once was home to a large pottery industry. A fascinating remnant of that history exists in Wellsville in the form of the Bottle Kiln. This impressive fire kiln is a 41-foot high brick structure that is amazingly well preserved given its age and exposure to the elements. It's maintained by the Wellsville Historical Society and can be found at the corner of 3rd and Lisbon in Wellsville.

Start the ride by turning onto route 7 and letting the fun begin. From the beginning of the tour the road is cut into hills resulting in towering cliffs on the inland side and of course the river itself hugging the east side of the road. Route 7 is an enjoyable and interesting ride as it travels through various small river towns. You get quite a patchwork effect while following the river. One minute you'll be surrounded by beauty with the river on one side and marvelous hills and bedrock cliffs on the other, and then around a curve is a large power plant or steel mill. The towns along the river all seem congested. When you have only a small amount of flat land between the water and the cliffs you have to squeeze everything into a small space.

The first large town encountered is Steubenville – the City of Murals and birthplace of Dino Paul Crocetti – better known to most folks as crooner and comedian Dean Martin. It's worth a ride through downtown to see 25 murals painted on various buildings. Each mural tells the story of an important event in this historic city. A stop at reconstructed Fort Steuben is also recommended. The fort was originally built in 1786 when the Continental Congress sent the First American Regiment to the Ohio frontier to guard surveyors as they began mapping the newly-won lands west of the river, and to prevent illegal squatters from taking possession of lands not yet conveyed by treaty. The fortress was named in honor of Friedrich Wilhelm von Steuben, a Prussian officer who aided the American cause in the recently-ended war of independence. The fort burned a few years later and the town of Steubenville was eventually formed on the same site.

One of the more amazing sights in Steubenville is looking across the river at the very impressive bare rock cliffs that line the river on the West Virginia side of the river.

Further southwest past Bridgeport and the National Road is the small town of Bellaire. At Bellaire one can admire the fabulous Stone Bridge / B&O Railroad Viaduct if they wish. This amazing piece of work was built between 1867 and 1871 largely by Irish stone masons, and its 43 stone arches span one-and-a-half curving miles leading to a bridge across the river!

About ten miles south of Bellaire Route 7 becomes more scenic and enjoyable as it traverses through lightly developed countryside. Less than thirty miles from Bellaire is the small town of Hannibal, and the Hannibal Locks and dam. This is a great place to stop and explore the impressive navigation system on the river by means of a viewing platform and visitor center at the locks. Also at Hannibal is Kiedaish Point Park – an overlook that perches seven hundred feet above the river valley and provides for a fabulous view of the river and the broad valley it has carved over the millennia.

Upon leaving Hannibal kick back and relax as you ride along with the river on one side and the Wayne National Forest on the other. At the village of Fly you may want to stop briefly to consider that the Fly-Sistersville Ferry has been carrying people and freight across the river at that spot since 1817. You'll no doubt notice the ferry fighting the mighty Ohio River current as it struggles to reach the opposite shore.

Marietta is next on the menu and a recommended stop. Marietta was founded in 1788 and named in honor of Marie Antoinette, then the sitting queen of France. Marietta is filled with history – from the haunting ancient Native American Conus Mound in Mound Cemetery to its Historic District – where fifty-three historic sites are to be found on a walking tour. Interestingly, more Revolutionary War officers are buried in Marietta than anywhere else in the country. Marietta is also home to Campus Martius, site of the Northwest Territory Museum and the nearby Ohio River Museum where the only steam powered sternwheeler towboat, the *W. P. Snyder*, is located. Campus Martius had its beginnings as a stockade built in 1788 to protect the seat of government of the Northwest Territory, as well as to protect settlers that were starting to come to the new town. By 1795 it was no longer needed. Call 740.373.3750 for more information and museum hours. These two recommended stops are located off SR7 at the point where the highway bridge crosses the Muskingum River.

Marietta claims a footnote in history as being the first city in the Northwest Territory. Well, this is technically true; it was after all formed just one year after the Northwest Ordinance of 1787 by which congress created the Northwest Territory. Prior to that sovereignty of the land where it sits was claimed by France and Great Britain – and let's not forget the claim of Native Americans who possessed the land for millennia. Three other cities located in what was to become the Northwest Territory - Detroit, St. Ignace and Sault Ste. Marie - all predate Marietta by a hundred years or more, and Vincennes by over fifty years, however. Not to diminish Marietta's importance, it did serve as the first capital of the Northwest Territory from which Governor Arthur St. Clair presided over this vast new part of the nation during a period of great danger and upheaval on the frontier.

While driving through Marietta Route 7 joins company with SR60 for a short time. When heading north through town on 7/60 I recommend a very short side trip to view what's locally called The Castle. This beautiful Victorian Era home is open for tours during the summer months, but it is fun to just ride by and admire the wonderful architecture and style of this stately home. Turn right on Scammel Street and go two blocks to Fourth Street. The Castle is on Fourth Street just north of Scammel.

A more time consuming attraction in Marietta is the Valley Gem Sternwheeler riverboat. Take an old-fashioned riverboat trip down the Ohio River to really see it up close. Call 740.373.7862 for reservations. They operate Monday – Saturday.

When ready to move on continue southwest on Ohio Route 7 to the town of Belpre. Just as you enter town SR7 makes a ninety-degree turn west and US50 is straight ahead – take US50 south and just before crossing the bridge to West Virginia you'll see State Route 618 (Washington Boulevard) going west along the shoreline. This is the road you want, not only because it hugs the shore but it also takes you past Blennerhassett Island Historic

Park – an island in the river that stands in tragic testimony to the extent that some folks will go when tempted by greed, power and ambition.

Harman Blennerhassett was a wealthy aristocrat who had a mansion built on this wilderness island in 1798. No expense was spared. Try to imagine bringing the finest furniture, oil paintings, carvings, silver doors, French porcelain, and all supplies and craftmen necessary to build such a mansion down the Ohio on flat boats – this in an area where settlers were being massacred and conditions for the vast majority of people bordered on bare survival.

With a beautiful wife and a house filled with servants most of us would say that Mr. B had it made. A chance meeting with Aaron Burr - who is perhaps most famous for killing Alexander Hamilton in a duel – abruptly changed Blennerhassett's idyllic lifestyle.

Unfortunately Blennerhassett got caught up in Burr's territorial ambitions and joined him in a scheme to possess an empire of their own comprising what are now Texas and other parts of the southwest. Burr and Blennerhassett conspired to create a country of their own west of the Mississippi, but when President Jefferson caught wind of the conspiracy he ordered the men arrested for treason. Blennerhassett fled to the very western lands he hoped to rule some day but was captured nonetheless. He served a spell in a Virginia prison and upon release his Camelot-like life was ruined. The mansion was flooded while he was gone and then burned to the ground in 1811. It has been beautifully restored based on what could still be found of the foundation and other evidence of its original size and shape.

The park is actually on the West Virginia side of the river, but can be viewed from the Ohio shore. It is easily accessible by taking US 50 across the river in Belpre.

For you railroading buffs there is a small railroad museum in Belpre's Depot Park that might be of interest. When you've seen all you want to see in Belpre proceed west on SR618, which joins SR7/US50 just west of the Island. We'll take 7/50 for just a couple of miles at which point we leave it again to stay by the river as 7 and 50 head inland. Just prior to entering the small town of Little Hocking SR124 angles off to the left – that's the road you want. SR124 follows the river about as closely as you can without getting water in your gas through the small towns of Hockingport, Reedsville, and finally the tiny town of Portland. This stretch of 124 is just great. It's often right on the water's edge with high cliffs of rock equally close on the opposite side. There are occasional caution signs in this stretch warning of rough pavement. They're not referring to the traditional pothole variety of roughness, rather the kind that occurs on many of southern Ohio's roads when the land under the road slips downhill.

The tiny town of Portland is where the Battle of Buffington Island was fought (the battle itself wasn't actually fought on the island, but rather on the Ohio shore of the river). A four-acre park preserves a small portion of the battlefield and two monuments honor the event. One of the memorials is in memory of Daniel McCook, a lawyer from Carrollton, Ohio who died in the battle. The story of "The Fighting McCooks" is an incredible one. In addition to Daniel and his eight sons, Daniel's brother John and his five sons all fought for the Union. Three of Daniel McCook's sons were killed. An impressive Conus Indian Mound is also in this park.

Shortly after leaving Portland SR124 turns inland but SR338 goes straight ahead along the river, so we just keep heading south, following the water. After tag-teaming the river SR338 eventually turns back north and meets route 124 again in the town of Racine. At the south end of a peninsula formed by the curving river the landscape changes greatly. There is a large fertile flood plain in this area where specialty crops such as tomatoes and other vegetables are grown. It's also an area of large gravel mining operations.

Ride SR124 all the way to the city of Pomeroy where Ohio Route 7 reappears. SR7 actually skirts Pomeroy to the north, so we want 7-Bypass, which tightly shadows the shoreline through town. Take a few minutes in Pomeroy to see the Meigs County Courthouse. This impressive structure is made even more unique because it is built into the side of a cliff, making all three stories accessible from ground level. Pomeroy is typical of several river towns struggling economically ever since King Coal was dethroned by mines in West Virginia and Wyoming. Ohio's high sulfur coal lost favor in the late 1900s due to high pollution emissions when burned. Pomeroy is undergoing revitalization and like many towns along the river it's capitalizing on its waterfront location for its resurgence.

The route 7-Bypass follows the riverfront through Pomeroy and Middleport, joining up with SR 7 a couple of miles west of Middleport. Take SR 7 through Cheshire and Addison, then through the busy US35 intersection, and on into Gallipolis – our next stop. The City of the Gauls was settled in 1790 by a large group of French settlers. The late eighteenth century was a period of great unrest and danger in France. The French Revolution was just beginning making it a dangerous place to live, especially for aristocrats and the educated class. This fact, plus highly exaggerated stories and claims by unscrupulous land developers led a number of French to invest in land on the Ohio River. Upon arrival the immigrants found the land deeds worthless. Congress eventually helped them acquire land and the next battle for these urban French was facing harsh and alien conditions in the wilderness in a place that was named in honor of their home country. Over time Gallipolis has lost its French flavor. An interesting stop in Gallipolis is the Our House Museum. It was built in 1819 as a tavern and served that purpose for many decades. The three-story brick building is located at First Avenue and State Street in town. A nice park on the river can be found at the south end of town. Gallipolis is a fun place to be every July 4th when the Gallipolis River Recreation Festival celebrates the holiday with four days of fun and games in the city park. It's been going on for over forty years, and always ends with an amazing fireworks show.

Upon leaving Gallipolis stay on SR7 as it winds through a lightly-developed area with the river on one side and Wayne National Forest on the other. It makes for very enjoyable motorcycling and sightseeing. Across the river from the large West Virginia city of Huntington some congestion is encountered again and at this point we'll pick up US-52 – our host for the next portion of the trip. Route 52 is a four-lane highway at this point and is easy sailing.

US52 steers us northwest at this point to Ironton, at one time the pig iron capital of the world. Early Welsh immigrants to this area found many minerals that were easily mined, including coal and iron ore. Ironton was a company town formed by the Ohio Iron and Coal Company in 1848. It grew very rapidly and from 1850 to the 1870s it was the center of the iron mining and steel production region. Many charcoal blast furnaces dotted the countryside (remnants of many still remain). This region of south central Ohio and northern Kentucky is known as the Hanging Rock Region – named after a high sandstone bluff on the river just west of Ironton – and easily mined iron ore was abundant. It wasn't until the 1870s when high quality ore was discovered in the Lake Superior region that the iron and steel-making fortunes of this region declined. Several of the palatial homes built by men who became very wealthy during the iron and coal heyday still remain in town. A number of large (14 x 40 feet) murals that were painted between 1991 and 2002 on various city buildings also grace the Ironton cityscape. I recommend getting off the main highway to take business 52 through Ironton.

Portsmouth, a city of 21,000 people located at the juncture of the Scioto and Ohio Rivers, is the next large town on the route. One of Portsmouth's most notable attractions today is the 2000 years of history painted in murals along 2000 feet of twenty-foot high floodwall. It's an amazing sight! One of the murals includes a fabulous motorcycle scene including an inset painting of the 1913 Portsmouth Motorcycle Club. To get to the murals follow the signs for south US 23. Mural signs direct you the rest of the way. Upon leaving the west end the murals you'll run into the Portsmouth Brewing Company restaurant. It's in an old red brick building and is a popular brewpub and eatery.

There are two Indian Mounds in Portsmouth. One – the Tremper Mound – is a couple of miles north off of SR104, but the other is just three blocks north of US52, about three-quarters of a mile east of US23. Before you reach US23 in Portsmouth watch for Hutchins Street, and take it north off US52 to Mound Park. When you think of Indians of course you think of Roy Rogers. Portsmouth was hometown to this western hero and a museum, open by appointment only, houses memorabilia about this TV and movie star and his famous horse Trigger.

The Portsmouth area is fairly congested for a small city, with US-52 and US-23 intersecting there as well as two busy bridges over the river but once past the local congestion US52 turns into a really nice ride west of the Scioto River where it passes just south of the Shawnee State Forest. In fact it's an award winning ride all the way from Portsmouth to near Cincinnati with mile after mile of open space, forest-covered hills, and frequent views of The River.

About midway between Portsmouth and Cincinnati are three small historic towns. The first is Manchester – the first town incorporated in the Virginia Military District. A little further west on route 52 is Aberdeen – the southern terminus of Zane's Trace – the trail built through the Ohio wilderness in the 1790s from Wheeling, WV.

The other historic town is Ripley. Being literally the dividing line between slave and free states, the Ohio River witnessed the human struggle for freedom up close and personal. Southern Ohio was the front line for the Abolitionists and Ripley was a well-known point on the Underground Railroad for escaping slaves. Many residents took an active role in making the Underground Railroad work. One man did more than most and this was The Reverend John Rankin - whose house atop Liberty Hill was a safe haven for many of the 2,000 fugitive slaves who escaped through Ripley. The Rankin House, built in 1825 by the Reverend, is today a National Historic Landmark and museum, is open for tours. It's located in the northwest portion of Ripley just off US 52. A sign points the way. Rankin House sits on the highest point of land around and it's a fun ride on a bike up to the house, as if you needed any more reason to go see it. The nearby Signal House, at the bottom of the hill near the waterfront, where Reverend Rankin signaled waiting slaves to let them know the way was clear, is now a Bed & Breakfast.

There are several locations along the Ohio River where Indian Mounds are present. Just watch for the signs. One such site is in Stivers Memorial Park in Ripley and another – the Eddington Mound – is near Chilo alongside the highway.

Proceeding west you'll pass the beginning of the Bullskin Trace (roughly today's SR133). Near Chilo there are two stops that are interesting and where you can learn a great deal about the river's locks and dam systems. The first is at the Lock 34 Museum and park, and just down the road are the massive Meldahl locks – they're impressive structures! A bit further west you'll cross the Grant Memorial Bridge and immediately across the bridge is President Ulysses S. Grant's birthplace and museum in Point Pleasant, where Big Indian Creek joins the Ohio River.

Ride the final five pleasant miles to New Richmond (America's Cardboard Boat Racing Capital) where this premier ride ends because of the impact of the Cincinnati urban area west of here. One of the more implausible places to visit on this ride is the Cardboard Boat Museum in New Richmond. The International Cardboard Boat Regatta is held in this town and the museum hosts the local organizer's work.

There are still a lot of interesting things to see along the river but this book is about quality of rides, not urban exploration. I believe that anyone who completes this ride end to end will agree that it deserves recognition as one of the best in the Midwest while at the same time serving as an amazing open air two-wheeled classroom of American history.

The Badger State's Best

Wisconsin is truly a land of motorcycling opportunities because of its unique geology and marvelous roads. Geography dictates and motorcyclists benefit. Mother Nature has provided several distinct geologic regions in Wisconsin that affect our two-wheeling prospects. Because of hills and ravines, and thousands of lakes and countless miles of rivers throughout the state, road builders had no choice but to make allowance for these obstructions and to largely abandon desires of straight and flat for winding and hilly.

This is most obvious in the scenic coulee landscape of southwestern Wisconsin. The land in this so-called driftless region was carved down from above when glacial melt water from the surrounding ice cap caused the region's rivers to erode deep valleys in the high plateau that originally covered this region, resulting in a dramatic landscape for our viewing and riding pleasure.

In the southeast quarter of the state the Eastern Ridges and Lowlands region provides the geologic backdrop. This unique district includes not only the Lake Michigan shoreline area, but also fascinating remnants left behind by the retreating glacier. These geologic features include hills, lakes, and rivers created as the ice melted. Winding roads wend through these features in places like the Kettle Moraine State Forest.

The Central Plain has stunning rock outcroppings and river valleys carved out of bedrock that delight us with their beauty and recreational opportunities. Features such as the Wisconsin Dells and stone arches are a part of this landscape. Castellated crags rising above the trees make for fantasy settings in stone that are a delight to behold.

The Northern Highlands is part of a great geologic feature called the Canadian Shield that stretches from northern Wisconsin all the way to the Arctic region of Canada. This is a landscape of ancient bedrock and poor soils more suitable to forestry than crops, thus it is the province of the Big Woods; a wild land where wolves and black bear wander freely. The region is interspersed with hills that are nearly 2,000 feet in elevation. Timm's Hill, located in Price County, is the highest point in the state at 1,952 feet above sea level.

The last geologic region in Wisconsin is called the Lake Superior Lowlands. This is a narrow strip along the shoreline of this majestic lake that is a world unto itself. Here you will find the rugged water's edge where bedrock cliffs meet crashing waves, and where majestic waterfalls and white water rivers tumble through rocky canyons in a rush to join the cold waters of Lake Superior.

In addition to the regional geologic differences, being surrounded by water on three sides by the Great Lakes and the mighty Mississippi River delivers a large slice of maritime geography and culture to enjoy.

This state also has a riding resource that locals know well and take advantage of at every opportunity—that is, its county primary road system, usually simply called the alphabet roads. These roads often provide better motorcycling enjoyment than state highways.

* Great River Road National Site: https://www.fhwa.dot.gov/byways/byways/2279/maps
* Wisconsin State Parks: https://dnr.wi.gov/topic/parks/
* Wisconsin State Parks Camping Reservations: https://wisconsin.goingtocamp.com/home
* Apostle Islands National Lakeshore: https://www.nps.gov/apis/index.htm
* Scenic Byways: https://wisconsindot.gov/Pages/travel/road/scenic-ways/byways.aspx
* Wisconsin Tourism Board: https://www.travelwisconsin.com/

1. Following the Kickapoo

ANY DISCUSSION about the best motorcycling in Wisconsin must include a ride through the heart of the so-called driftless area – the southwest corner of the state that escaped the negative leveling effects of glaciation. The geography of this corner of the state is custom made for fun biking with its dramatic hills and river valleys and the resulting winding roads that carve through the landscape.

Our 120-miles of great riding begins in the town of Tomah on the northern edge of the unglaciated area. Ride south on route 131, cross the I-90 expressway, and almost immediately the fun begins. About six miles south of Tomah the Kickapoo River begins shadowing our road and the two do a merry dance for many miles and endless smiles.

At the village of Ontario turn left onto route 33 and in one mile it enters Wildcat Mountain State Park. What had been merely a fun road becomes fabulous. The narrow pavement twists and turns and dips and climbs through the densely wooded landscape. It is the kind of road where many of us have been known to turn around and run it two or three times just because it is so enjoyable. If you like hairpin curves you will love this portion of route 33. Just as the road starts to calm down a bit, county road F goes to the right. Turn onto F, a very nice two-wheeling road in its own right, and ride it back west two miles to rejoin route 131 and continue the ride south.

For several miles 131 remains within the boundaries of Wildcat Mountain Park, exiting the scenic public land just north of the small town of La Farge. South of La Farge the entertainment continues unabated. It's a ride through remarkable countryside on a road that one couldn't be blamed for thinking was made primarily for the sport of motorcycling as it closely follows the meanderings of the nearby Kickapoo River. The Kickapoo is a beautiful and rugged river that winds in its deep valley through forested hillsides as it has for millennia. It remains one of the state's most scenic and popular canoeing rivers with whitewater rapids flowing with enthusiasm through ramparts of rock. The Kickapoo received its name from the Indian tribe of the same name that occupied this part of Wisconsin prior to European settlement. Some folks wanted to domesticate this wild river several decades ago with a dam. Public outcry fortunately prevailed and this beautiful stream was spared being forever tamed and silenced by concrete.

This delightful road is our riding partner south to Readstown where we meet route US61; and you won't find a disappointing mile between here and there. What with the curves, hills, great scenery, light traffic and wonderful overall ambience of the road, all one need do is kick back and enjoy a wonderful ride for many miles.

Route 131 and US61 share the pavement between Readstown and the approximately four miles south to Soldiers Grove. Here they split and we leave the heavier traffic of 61 and stay on 131 as it heads to the southwest. In Soldiers Grove a historical marker explains that this site was an encampment for soldiers pursuing Chief Black Hawk in 1832 and that the name of the town was changed in 1867 to reflect this history.

The enjoyment continues as we ride mile after fantastic mile south on 131, all the way to route 60. Go left / east on 60 about ten miles to US61. Route Sixty is another enjoyable road as it carves through the woodlands bordering the Wisconsin River. Turn right onto US61 and it carries us across the river and immediately entering the town of Boscobel—also known as the wild turkey hunting capital of Wisconsin. The Depot Museum, at 800 Wisconsin Street, is an interesting stop to get a glimpse at the history of this area.

Continue through Boscobel on 61 and on the south side of town Wisconsin route 133 intersects. Turn right onto 133 and the fun begins anew. We're going to stay on the state route for only about five curvy miles. Two miles west of the tiny burg of Woodman route 133 makes a southerly turn, as do we. A half-mile past that turn County Road K heads to the east and then south. Turn left on this lightly traveled scenic county road. It follows the meanderings of the Big Green River southward as it carves through the heart of the unglaciated beauty all the way to Lancaster, the end of this marvelous ride, where we can finally stop and catch our breath.

2. Stone Bridges and Blue Mounds

THIS WONDERFUL outing is in south central Wisconsin in the eastern edge of the Western Uplands region, a land of mesas, forested hills and dramatic bedrock formations. It's a region of splendid scenic beauty where enjoyable strips of asphalt wind among the bluffs and rivers. To top it all off there are attractions along the way that will make even the most tenacious rider stop to take a look.

This adventure in the hills begins in Dodgeville, whose history begins with southwest Wisconsin's lead mining boom of the late 1820s. Colonel Henry Dodge, who was to become the first governor of the Wisconsin Territory in 1836, led a group of miners and their families here in 1827 and started the settlement. The town grew rapidly until the late 1840s when miners left for the California gold rush. Dodgeville became the county seat for Iowa County. I mention this because the courthouse that was proudly built in 1859 is still in use, making it the longest serving such building in the state. The downtown historic district has several wonderful examples of impressive 19th-century architecture.

There are some entertaining things to do in town. In mid-July the Blues Fest is held rain or shine in a large tent on the courthouse grounds. Check them at dodgevillebluesfest.com. The Dodge Mining Cabin, built in 1827 is located on Fountain Street (take route 23 south a few blocks from route 18 and follow the signs). Dodge State Park is just north of town with a scenic waterfall, camping, fishing or just plain walking through the woods.

Put kickstands up and head north on route 23. The motorcycling fun begins almost immediately and rarely lets up for the entire 45-mile ride to Reedsburg. There are some things to check out along the way, including the famous House on the Rock and the Frank Lloyd Wright Taliesin Museum. After crossing the Wisconsin River the town of Spring Green and a couple miles of flat flood plain separate the south half of the trip from the north portion. Route 23 resumes north of Spring Green and the enjoyable riding also quickly returns.

Our road joins with route 33 on the west side of Reedsburg and continues east through town. Reedsburg sits exactly on the 90th degree of west longitude, which along with its historic downtown section is one of the things that makes it unique. It is also on the scenic Baraboo River. One of the most unique places to visit on this tour is a hotel conference center. But not just any run of the mill hotel lobby. The Voyageur Inn, at 200 Viking Drive in Reedsburg has an amazing collection of Normal Rockwell American folklore paintings on display, for free. It's a truly remarkable exhibition of American history from World War 1 to the 1970s by America's most famous folk artist.

Continue east on route 23 / 33 and on the east edge of town turn right onto route 136. One thirty six carries on the duty of assuring an enjoyable and gorgeous ride across a landscape that showcases the rugged beauty of this region. We are passing through the North Range, a series of geologically unique hills. These hills are formed of a particularly hard and resistant form of Quartzite that has resisted erosion for the last 350 million years. Just southeast of Reedsburg are hills that make up what's called the South Range. Together they form the Baraboo Range which about a billion years ago were as tall as the Rocky Mountains. They're no less picturesque today in their shorter forest-covered beauty.

The Baraboo River has carved a channel through the South Range at Rock Springs—a pathway also followed by route 136 all the way to US12. Before we arrive at US12 there is a highly recommended attraction that you may wish to see. Two miles east of Rock Springs is County Road I. If you turn right onto this road it will lead to the very impressive Mid-Continent Railway Museum just a bit more than one mile to the south of 136. If you visit only one railroad museum in the state it should probably be this one. It has an outstanding exhibit of a variety of rolling stock that is accessible for up close viewing. Train rides of approximately one hour round trip are available in cars from circa 1900.

Back on route 136 continue east to US12. Turn right and go one mile then turn right again onto county road W. Ride this lightly traveled scenic road about seven miles west as it meanders through the beautiful countryside. The South Range hills are just off to the left the entire stretch.

At about the seven mile point CR-W goes straight west and County Road PF angles off to the left – CR-PF is the road we want. Enjoy the charms of this magical road twelve miles through the woods and rolling fields to county road C, near the tiny town of Leland. You will go past 'southbound' C and a very short distance come to 'eastbound' CR-C. Turn left onto 'eastbound' C and ride east less than two miles to Natural Bridge State Park, our next stop. You will likely be the only visitor. It's a pleasant walk on a path in the woods from the parking area to the imposing stone arch formation and well worth it. The site has a long history, with thousands of years of human activity having taken place there. Just seeing the ancient arcing stone overhead is quite a thrill even if one ignores the archeological record of the place. It's definitely worth the short diversion from our road.

When leaving the park to continue the ride backtrack to CR-PF and backtrack the very short distance to 'southbound' CR-C. This fun road carries us many miles south, all the way to state route 60. At one point

CR-C "T's" at county road B. A one-half mile jog to the west on B is necessary, at which point CR-C continues its southward progression to state route 60.

Turn left / east on 60 and the magical ride continues unabated as the pavement meanders alongside the beautiful tree-lined Wisconsin River. Route 60 eventually joins with US12, carrying us into Sauk City. Ride US12 across the river and once on the south side quickly turn right onto route 78 and the amazing excursion continues as we ride 78 through the hills to Black Earth. It joins US14 for the last short stretch into Black Earth.

Along route 78 there are some points of interest that are worth a closer look. The first is just a couple miles south of Sauk City; the site of the 1832 Battle of Wisconsin Heights. This skirmish in the Black Hawk War is listed on the National Register of Historic Places. It is also managed and protected as part of the state's Lower Wisconsin State Riverway reserve. A series of trails take hikers through the battlefield to several sites where the fighting actually occurred. Finally, upon arriving at US14 the town of Mazomanie is just one mile to the west. Though it's not on our route, if a person is interested in the idea of a museum dedicated to post-World War Two microcars, mopeds and various related accessories, then a stop at the Midwest Microcar Museum might be of interest. There is no other quite like it. And it's only a mile away. Go west into Mazomanie, turn north on Cramer Street (the second street upon entering town) for four blocks then left onto Crescent Street. They don't have regular hours but check their web site for days they are open and for special tours. http://www.midwestmicrocarmuseum.com/

Continuing south on 78 delivers us to the village of Black Earth. (In town route 78 doubles as Mills Street) Six blocks south of the railroad tracks in Black Earth on 78 / Mills turn right onto Madison Street / CR-KP. Go west one mile on KP and turn left onto CR-F, also known as Blue Mounds Trail. This very enjoyable road takes us south to Blue Mounds State Park and Cave of the Mounds. The Little Norway Norwegian Living Museum complex is a mile east of Blue Mounds on county road-JG. It's an enjoyable and educational stop.

The Blue Mounds are a series of spectacular tree-covered hills located west of Mt. Horeb. Blue Mound State Park's 1,153 acres protects the mounds, among which is the highest hill in southern Wisconsin, rising to a height of 1,716 feet above sea level. Two forty foot high towers perched on the hill offer a marvelous panoramic view of the stunning landscape in this region. The Cave of the Mounds is located just east of the park and offers an underground tour of a cave accidentally discovered in 1939 during an explosion to remove rock in a limestone quarry. The million year old cave's presence was made known when the blast removed a wall of stone, and as they say, the rest is history. The cave is open for tours every day between Memorial Day and Labor Day. The constant 50-degree temperature in the cave is welcome relief on hot and muggy summer days.

When finished enjoying the unique attractions in the Blue Mounds area ride south a mile to US151 and follow this road west to Dodgeville. Though a main highway it traverses a pleasing landscape and the smiles continue all the way back to Dodgeville.

I think all will agree that this 140-mile blissful ride is one of the best that is found in this beautiful part of the state.

3. The Northwoods Superior Tour

THE NORTHWOODS and Lake Superior region of Wisconsin must be included in any book that extols motorcycling opportunities in the Badger State. Large blocks of state and national forests and thousands of lakes and miles of crystal-clear streams make this region a must see for any rider. And when hundreds of miles of two-lane asphalt curving through the hills and forests and along the magnificent Lake Superior shoreline are added into the montage, the deal is sealed.

There are countless options for fun riding in the northern portion of Wisconsin but roads in the northwest quarter allow access to both uplands and lakeshore. Our entertaining 215-mile northern ride begins at the resort town of Hayward, in the heart of the forest and lake country. The outdoors heritage of this region is made clear with the town's most famous attraction – the 40-foot high 140-foot long giant Musky at the National Fresh Water Fishing Hall of Fame and museum. Having your picture taken in the jaws of the monster Musky is worth the price of admission, though there is much more to see than just this iconic structure. The museum has many fascinating displays of interest if you have even a rudimentary level of curiosity in the outdoors or fishing. The Sawyer County Historical Society museum is a wonderful place to see artifacts that bring the history of northern Wisconsin to life. Hayward is also the site of the Lumberjack World Championships, where the best lumberjacks on the planet come to compete. Fittingly, it is the home of America's only licensed chainsaw carving school—the Wisconsin School of Chainsaw Carving. A car show and much more are part of the Musky Fest which makes for an enjoyable time if you are here in late-June. There are many motels, resorts and campgrounds nearby for lodging or camping.

In Hayward pick up Wisconsin route 27 and ride it north many miles, all the way to the village of Brule on US2. Go left on 2 for just two blocks to pick up CR-H, which we'll ride north through the Brule River State Forest to fabled route 13, the Lake Superior Scenic Byway. Go east on thirteen and the enjoyment quotient gets even higher.

Ride 13 through the Bayfield Peninsula and ultimately back south along the shores of Chequamegon (pronounced she-wa'-ma-gon) Bay to Ashland. This loop is nearly a hundred enjoyable miles, so unwind and savor the ride and the scenery. A cautionary note here; route 13 is obviously close to Lake Superior. Experienced riders know that while the temperature might be a balmy eighty degrees inland, there very well could be cold fog and drizzle near the lake. Be prepared with proper cool weather clothing and rain gear, just in case. Maybe it is just my bad luck, but I have encountered cold, foggy, and wet weather along the Lake Superior shoreline almost as often as not.

Near the northeast tip of the peninsula is the popular tourist destination town of Bayfield. You may want to park your bike here and walk around town and the waterfront. It is an interesting and enjoyable place to explore, and if you happen to be there during one of the many events the town hosts the fun meter points even higher. In Bayfield you can take a narrated cruise through the Apostle Islands National Lakeshore on a large cruise ship (highly recommended, plan on at least a half-day), take a sailing excursion in the bay or through the Apostle Islands archipelago, visit a local maritime museum, or simply walk, talk and gawk. The Chicago Tribune once called Bayfield the best small town in the Midwest, and it is easy to see why.

In the late 1800s, brownstone, a highly popular building material at the time, was mined on several of the Apostle Islands, especially on Basswood Island. Cities across the country utilized this attractive and distinctive brown sandstone to make striking buildings ranging from courthouses to row houses—especially in the east and Midwest. Many brownstone buildings in Chicago had their origins in Apostle Island quarries.

Riding south on route 13 is great fun, with the road near the water for the most part. Thirteen eventually takes us to U.S.2 and the Ashland area. At US2 I recommend making a right turn and going the short distance to the Northern Great Lakes Visitor Center. This marvelous facility is operated in partnership with several governmental and private organizations. It offers many exhibits and programs highlighting the natural and cultural history of the Lake Superior region.

Ashland is our next destination, as we ride east on US2. There are several things worthy of your time in this port city. As we enter town the most striking shoreline feature is the massive ore dock; so massive in fact that they are the largest docks of their type in the world! Chequamegon Bay stretches to the north from Ashland. This Ojibwa word is frequently used throughout northern Wisconsin by many places and organizations. It originally specifically referred to this Lake Superior bay, however, and it means 'place of shallow water' in the native tongue. It marked the location where Indians gathered to harvest fish in the shallows. The eastern and southern sections of the bay are shallow for significant distances out, creating excellent fish habitat and spawning areas, as well as making it easier to harvest those fish at certain times of the year.

Many commercial buildings in Ashland along Main Street and Chapple Street have large murals painted on their otherwise unappealing blank walls, depicting a variety of historic or cultural scenes. The 4th of July is always a good time to get away, and if you are in Ashland over this holiday be sure to check out the Bay Area Rod and Custom Car Show.

Departing Ashland on 2 sees us through the Bad River Indian Reservation for nearly twenty miles. Just two miles after crossing into Iron County we'll turn right onto route 169. This delightful lightly traveled road will twist and turn many miles southwest to route 13 and the town of Mellen. Just before reaching the small backwoods community of Mellen you'll ride through a portion of the large and highly recommended Copper Falls State Park. The Brownstone Falls and Copper Falls are worth the time and effort (and cost of the park permit) to view.

At route 13 turn left for about a half mile. Turn right onto Hillcrest Drive, and in two blocks turn off Hillcrest onto Wilderness Drive / County Road-GG. CR-GG is a wonderful riding road that carries us many miles southwest through the heart of the wild and beautiful Chequamegon Nicolet National Forest. This is a delightful ride through a land of lakes, streams and forest. This is an example of taking advantage of scenic lightly traveled county roads rather than using busier state routes to get to the same destination.

CR-GG delivers us to Route 77 at Clam Lake. Turn right / west on 77 and enjoy mile after wonderful riding mile as this scenic road takes us through the magical northern Wisconsin beauty all the way back to Hayward. A word of caution, and wonderful opportunity – the Clam Lake and route77 vicinity is Elk Country. Be alert and you may well see one of these majestic animals near the road.

4. Wisconsin's Thumb – The Door Peninsula

A GUIDE TO THE best motorcycling in Wisconsin would be conspicuously lacking if it didn't include the Door Peninsula. It's a unique part of the state in several perspectives; land cover, agricultural specialty crops, geology, the fact it is a peninsula, tourism sites and its maritime flavor and history; Wisconsin's Thumb is distinctive. We'll kick off this 220-mile peninsular quest from the Lake Michigan port city of Two Rivers at the southeast corner of the peninsula and work our way north along the coast. The West Twin River and the East Twin River converge here forming a harbor at the lakeshore.

The route has us traversing many miles of scenic and enjoyable waterfront county roads, those wonderful gray line roads on a map, away from the crowds and traffic. Begin the adventure by riding east on route 42 and when it turns north just keep heading east on 22nd Street. In just a few blocks you come to the well marked Sandy Bay Road / county road O. Turn left onto CR-O and follow it along the shoreline for a bit over six miles to county road V. Between these two points is the large Point Beach State Forest (which is more like a park than a forest). The Rawley Point Lighthouse is the main attraction here, unless you want to camp, picnic, or play on the beach. Turn right onto Park Road to see the lighthouse and keeper's house if this is your thing. A 113-foot high steel tower, the Rawley Point light is one of the tallest on the Lakes and with good reason. Prior to its construction there were 26 shipwrecks off this point of land. The light is part of an active Coast Guard base so it isn't open to the public but the facility can be easily viewed from the beach.

The second half of CR-O is especially nice, though a slow posted speed limit keeps the fun to a sedated level. CR-O ends at CR-V and the pavement only goes to the west. However, if you want free access to the beach there is a short drive to the east at this corner that goes to school property and open beach access.

We are on 'V' a very short distance until we arrive at state route 42, which fortunately is an enjoyable road to ride. It's fairly laid back with a lot of farmland rolling by as one rides north. The route has quite a few graceful curves and some gently rolling hills and occasional wonderful vistas of Lake Michigan in the distance as hilltop curves are rounded.

Kewaunee is the first town encountered northbound on route 42. It is a popular base for sport fishing excursions and also has a couple of attractions that might be of interest. On the waterfront *The Ludington*, an Army Corps of Engineers tug boat is berthed in the mouth of the Kewaunee River, which forms a harbor where sportfishing boats enter the big lake. There is a small park on the south side of the harbor where a person can walk out to the point and relax while viewing the lake and watching boat traffic and shore fishermen trying to catch dinner.

If touring old jails stirs your interest you may want to explore the Kewaunee Jail Museum, located at 613 Dodge Street, one block west of route 42 in town, on a high hill adjacent to the very cool old courthouse. The building dates from 1876 and back in the day it served as the sheriff's residence, office and jail. The original 1876 cellblocks with their tiny 5' x 6' cells are intimidating enough to have kept even the wildest hard drinking lumberjack on the straight and narrow.

The museum has a scale model of the *USS Pueblo*, a ship built in Kewaunee in 1944 and captured by North Korea in 1968 while it was in international waters. Allegedly, the Soviet Union wanted a new cryptographic machine that was on board to go with the decoding key they had recently obtained from a spy. One sailor was killed in the attack and North Korea held the crew for eleven months. They still hold the ship, which the Navy continues to consider as a commissioned American naval ship. Ironically, the *Pueblo* is being used as a museum ship by North Korea at the War Museum on the Potong River in Pyongyang.

Between Kewaunee and Algoma are many miles of the same sort of pleasurable riding as south of town. Traffic isn't a hassle and the ride is tranquil with the same occasional wonderful views of the big water. The Lake Michigan shoreline is a pleasant surprise in its light state of development. Neon quickly turns to woods and a wooded shoreline and farm fields almost to the water's edge are the rule, rather than condos and resorts.

Algoma is a pleasant town of about 3,500 souls. It dates back to 1851 and has been known by three names. The Pottawatomie called the site Ahnapee, meaning Land of the Great Gray Wolf, a legendary beast of Indian lore. The first settlers named it Wolf River, a loose translation of the Indian name. It was later called Ahnapee, and finally in 1879 the name was officially changed to Algoma—an Indian term meaning Park of Flowers. Perhaps early Algoma boosters thought that 'park of flowers' was a much more pleasing and agreeable nickname that could attract business and tourists, as opposed to being known as the site of a bloodthirsty oversized wolf. Algoma has an attractive waterfront that is an enjoyable pause on the trip.

In Algoma leave forty-two after many miles of pleasurable company. Immediately after crossing the Ahnapee River turn right onto Water Street, which becomes Lakeview Drive and finally county road S outside of town. It is well marked and easy to follow. We're on 'S' for 4 miles, then turning right onto CR-U. County road U is our host all the way north to the city of Sturgeon Bay. The first several miles are along the coast and then it moves inland as it works its way north. Both 'S' and 'U' provide miles of enjoyable two wheeling.

County road U rejoins with state route 42 again in Sturgeon Bay, and we use the highway 42 bridge to cross the Sturgeon Bay Ship Canal. It took ten years to dig the 1.3-mile canal connecting Sturgeon Bay with Lake Michigan. The shipping channel was originally dug by a railroad company, which later sold the canal to the U.S. government. It is currently operated by the Army Corps of Engineers. The canal effectively turned the northern portion of Door County into an island, connected by bridges to the mainland.

Our ride has us motoring along the north shore of the canal to the Lake Michigan shore. To accomplish this we need to turn right onto Utah Street less than a half-mile after crossing the bridge. (Watch for signs for the Coast Guard facility and CR-Tt). After just a few blocks turn south on Cove Road which then curves east as CR-Tt. This lightly traveled county road provides 2 or 3 areas to pull over to view the canal if you wish before it swings north at the mouth of the canal and the location of the Coast Guard station. The Sturgeon Canal lighthouse is at this point but it is not accessible. A small public parking area is available just outside the USCG station to view the light and canal from a short distance if wished.

County road Tt runs north from the canal along the lake as a designated Rustic Road and it earns that title with full honors. The road is narrow and twisty asphalt through a heavily forested area resulting in a very nice ride for its 3.5-mile distance. When Tt makes a ninety-degree swing west we are going to make a very short jog to the east instead, then following Lake Michigan Drive north along the shoreline to county road T. County road T is also a designated Rustic Road and it is just great. The narrow roadway twists and turns its way north along the shoreline through dense forestland. Just like CR-Tt, county road T eventually turns due west. At that point, however, we turn right and continue following the coastline on Cave Point Drive. We pass through Whitefish Dunes State Park but our destination is Cave Point County Park—a jewel of a park that must be seen to be appreciated.

The road to the county park turns into a narrow and tightly twisting drive and you suddenly find yourself at a parking area near the shore. A short walk leads to a series of small sea caves and rock formations that are gorgeous to behold. The waves of the lake crash amongst the tree covered rocks resulting in a visual and audio treat that makes this trip worth every mile ridden. I have been to this park a couple of times on a bike and have yet to see another person there while I was present. If the weather is cooperative sitting on the rocks overlooking the water for an extended period soothes your troubled spirits better than anything else I've ever found. Like many of the destinations I discuss in this book this is best done as a small group ride. The road into the park, and the limited parking area weren't meant for dozens of bikes, or for large RVs for that matter.

Follow the drive north out of the park and it eventually join with route 57 at the tiny town of Jacksonport. A sign in Cave Point Park clearly points the way to this town.

Ride 57 for a bit over eight miles to the north side of Baileys Harbor. This small town was the first village to form on the peninsula and that came out of necessity when Captain Justice Bailey sought refuge in the harbor during a fierce Lake Michigan storm in 1848. Signs for CR-Q and North Bay clearly point out our next turn. Take 'Q' as it goes east to the shoreline and then after several miles it swings back west again to re-join highway 57. For the period where it goes north along the shore it is a very nice and easily followed motorcycling path. The qualities that we are becoming accustomed to—curves, light traffic, heavily forested stretches—are all here, making for wonderful biking.

The Cana Island lighthouse is along this stretch. However, it is a fairly long and somewhat confusing ride out to the island, and once there you must park and walk across the island to the tower. It is a nice diversion but it requires parking your bike in an unprotected sand lot after following a confusing road system from 'Q' out to the island. Definitely doable, but you should really want to do it, as opposed to doing it just for the hell of it.

Once CR-Q joins route 57 it is a short ride north to the town of Sister Bay where we pick up SR 42 northbound. Follow 42 through Ellison Bay, Gills Rock, and finally Northport, which is literally at land's end.

Sister Bay and Ellison Bay are both high-end resort areas blessed with great natural beauty, waterfront locations, and well-established resorts and restaurants. Gills Rock and Northport are much smaller. From Gills Rock a person can take a cruise boat out to the islands north of the point, and the Washington Island ferry leaves from the dock, located at the end of route 42, in Northport.

The seven-mile wide strait between Northport and Washington Island is where the Door Peninsula derives its name. Long before the arrival of the first Europeans the local Native Americans learned the hard way of the danger of crossing this strait. Unpredictable winds, currents and waves made the passage treacherous and the Indians called the passageway the Door of Death. It earned this name following a battle between local Pottawatomie Indians who lived on the island and Winnebago Indians who had planned a surprise attack. Many warriors died when their canoes were swamped and the natives pledged that they must never attempt the passage again. In turn, early French explorers gave it the name *Porte des Morts*/the Door of Death. The name stuck and Door Peninsula was named.

Washington Island is a favorite getaway for those seeking some low-keyed R&R. The island was named in honor of George Washington by a Navy captain. In 1816 the captain of the U.S. schooner *Washington* paused here in a sheltered bay while waiting for the rest of his small flotilla of ships that were enroute to present day Green Bay to establish Fort Howard. While waiting he gave Washington's name to the nearby island.

We of course don't want to retrace our steps on the way south from the tip of the peninsula so we will take a different route as much as possible. Follow 42 back south to just west of Ellison Bay, to Old Stage Road. At this corner there are several tall antennas to mark the location for us. Old Stage Road is a pleasant ride through a region of newly regenerated woodlands and quite a few abandoned farms and orchards that are reverting back to natural cover. Old Stage Road makes a westerly turn eventually and crosses route 57 just east of the town of Ephraim. West of fifty-seven the road's name changes to Settlement Road, but it's the same alignment. Follow Settlement Road into town where it eventually joins with state route 42 on the waterfront. We'll follow 42 as it works its way southwest along the shore to Egg Harbor. This stretch is probably the least pleasant of the entire trip because of the likelihood of heavy recreational traffic during the peak vacation period. It isn't too bad, but I have had occasion to get caught behind large RVs or trucks pulling large boats, making passing difficult because of traffic density and curves. If you encounter this type of traffic just be patient, as you will soon leave it all behind.

In Egg Harbor watch for the sign for county road G (aka Horseshoe Bay Drive). CR-G angles off to the right front, following the water's edge while 42 skirts inland. We ride CR-G four miles, when it turns east, but CR-B continues straight south along the shoreline. It is easy to follow as we stay on the waterfront pavement regardless of name change. CR-B is our partner for many miles, in fact all the way south to Sturgeon Bay and the Michigan Street bridge across the shipping canal to route 42 on the south shore. County road B is a fun ride. Though it is near the water the views of Green Bay are not constant because of trees. Just north of the town of Sturgeon Bay notice the large stone quarry and high cliff wall on the east side of the road; quite impressive!

We are going to follow routes 42, then 57, southwest many miles toward the city of Green Bay. Eventually we cross into Brown County at a wide spot in the road called Dyckesville. A mile further is Bay Shore

County Park, and about two miles further along you come to county road T. Turn left onto 'T' and work your way south across many miles of verdant farmland to the village of Denmark. Route 29 bisects this region, with the land north of 29 being intensively farmed and quite flat, but south of 29 the scenery becomes more interesting with more wooded land and a nice rolling character. CR-T makes a jog just north of Denmark but the turns are marked and obvious. The road becomes Wall Street in town and then angles southeast as Wisconsin Avenue. Follow Wisconsin Avenue to its end on the southeast corner of town where it "T's" at County Road R / North Packer Drive and turn left.

Denmark is an interesting small town, which, true to its name flies the Danish flag. Obviously a pocket of ethnic history. Our next stop, four miles to the southeast on CR-R, is the Devils River and historic Rock Mill, located in the Devils River Campers Park. This is a very nice stop where a person can view the 1848 stone barn and original milling equipment. Nearby is the scenic rocky gorge where falling water once powered the water wheel to turn the mill's stone. It is a great place to camp should that be on your agenda.

After leaving Rock Mill continue south on CR-R just a mile or so to Cherney Maribel Caves County Park and some very scenic rock formations in the rugged valley carved by the West Twin River. On the near side of the river are bedrock cliffs of fifty feet or more in height and on the other is a flat lowland. The cliff line marks a geologic demarcation, separating the erosion resistant Niagara escarpment Dolomite from a region that was eroded and made flat through glacial action and subsequent erosion. Over the centuries water has carved several caves in the lower cliff faces for added interest. It is a short walk from the paved parking lot to the cliff face and a wood walkway has been built along the base of the cliffs to make access easy. It's a highly recommended stop. Check it out at https://www.maribelcaves.com/

Just south of Maribel park CR-R / Packer Drive intersects with state highway 147. Continue south on CR-R ten more miles to state route 310. A left turn onto 310 carries us the final seven miles back to Two Rivers.

5. Riding with Eagles and Hodags

NORTHEASTERN WISCONSIN is an enchanting area of forests and lakes and wildlife, where deer outnumber humans and the main attractions are creations of nature, not man. Because of the thousands of lakes and large wetlands, not to mention rivers, straight roads are truly a rarity in the region. And large blocks of state and national forest lands protect what is precious to us in the form of open spaces and forestlands. And fortunately for us the motorcycling roads in the region definitely meet the threshold of being some of the best in the Midwest.

This 245-mile two-wheeled outing takes in several of those popular roads. We begin in the town of Merrill, situated on the upper reaches of the Wisconsin River at the confluence of the Prairie River. It comes as no surprise given its location both on the rivers and in the forested north that it began as a lumber town. Today the city of about 10,000 located just north of the 45th parallel is the county seat of Lincoln County. A nice attraction in Merrill is the Historical Museum. It does a nice job documenting the logging history of the area and the older Native American history.

Going north from Merrill has us on state route 17. Some local riders might ask why not route 107 which winds north to Tomahawk following the turns of the Wisconsin River. Two reasons actually. Though 107 is a wonderful road that riders should certainly enjoy when in the area it does lead into the congestion of Tomahawk, which with several merging roads and summer tourist traffic can overwhelm fun motorcycling. Second, I want to take advantage of a ride through the Harrison Hills located to the east of highway US51, northeast of Merrill. Even though the route is not as well known as route 107 I think you'll enjoy it.

From town ride east on route 64 to just east of the US51 expressway and turn north onto route 17. This road brings smiles for twenty relaxing miles as we work our way northeast. As you approach the twenty mile mark watch for county road B on the left. Turn here and it carries us north in a very enjoyable winding manner through what's known as the Harrison Hills. This scenic region is home to many glacial hills or moraines, and hundreds of small lakes, created at the end of the last ice age as the mile deep glacier melted about 12,000 years ago. It truly is a unique and beautiful area and CR-B carves through the landscape in a most agreeable fashion.

CR-B eventually turns west and in the tiny town of Harrison joins with CR-D. For the sake of navigating there is a church at the northeast corner of the CR-B and CR-D intersection. We turn right / north onto CR-D. This road goes north for close to two miles and then curve right for three more miles until it meets state route 17 again. Turn left onto 17 and resume the journey. I'm certain you will agree that the ride through the Harrison Hills was more than well worth the navigational effort. State route 17 carries us the remaining nine miles to Rhinelander in a businesslike manner through typical northern Wisconsin countryside.

Rhinelander is a very typical northern town that began as a lumber camp and today the town of 8,000 serves the local economy and tourism. Like most existing towns in the north circumstances or wise planning allowed it to survive after the lumber boom ended; many towns didn't endure and today are just open spaces in the forest or old buildings along the road. The fact that Rhinelander was the county seat for Oneida County helped.

There are a few things of interest in this town that bills itself as the capital of Wisconsin's north. The Rhinelander Logging Museum Complex, located in Pioneer Park on Business U.S. 8 (Oneida Avenue in downtown), is an eye-opening stop to explore. It features an 1870s logging camp and museum, an old Soo Line Depot, a one-Room School House, a 1930s CCC Museum and the largest collection of authentic Hodag re-creations in the world. Admission is free with donations at the discretion of the visitor.

You can't go far in Rhinelander without seeing or hearing references to Hodags. This mythical creature has become an integral part of the culture and economy of the city. The story of how this phenomenon began is an interesting one that I think makes a good tale that should be told. It began in the lumberjack culture, where men whiled away their few hours of rest telling fantastic stories and tales. This story was created by local practical jokester and timber cruiser Eugene Shepard in the early 1890s. Shepard started the legend by telling a convincing story at a lumber camp where he was spending the night that he had encountered a vicious beast in the woods that he'd never seen before. He described it as having spikes along the length of its body and sharp points on its tail. Its fangs were like a tiger's and it was stronger than any bear in the woods. He called it a Hodag. Shepard led a group of lumbermen into the woods to capture the beast with dynamite—and returned with charred remains. A photograph of the reenacted kill was widely published.

Shepard was a prankster and well known for small jokes but the Hodag story was different, he kept it up for years. He claimed to have captured a live Hodag and kept it in his barn. Of course he then gave people the chance to view it, from a distance and for a charge, because after all it cost a lot to keep a Hodag alive in captivity. People came from near and far to see it.

When customers arrived Shepard would disappear from sight. The commotion and noise would become terrible with growling and snarling and sounds of violence and danger. After a few minutes Shepard would reappear looking much the worse for the obvious attack he'd just survived, and tell the paying viewers that the Hodag wasn't viewable because it was dangerously uncooperative. Soon he was working at county fairs and anywhere else where he could trick people into paying to see his mysterious beast. His sons worked behind the scenes, making the monster move. Shepard earned to up $500 in a weekend. He kept up the sham until an investigator from the Smithsonian Museum came to check out the incredible story. After the expert refused to accept weak claims and stories Shephard finally had to admit that the whole thing was just a story turned into a profitable scheme. Amazingly the underlying legend of a strange and dangerous creature of the north woods survived and is today a cultural keystone.

Rhinelander still has the Hodag as its mascot for the city and the high school and Hodag statues line downtown streets. From Rhinelander we ride north again on route 17. This road takes us mile after sinuous mile through forests and alongside tree-rimmed pristine lakes. Though this road crosses an area that is relatively flat it is nonetheless quite high in elevation, averaging near 1,600 feet. This region isn't without its own variety of development and commerce. Gifts left behind by the last ice age in the form of gravel are extracted in two large gravel pits along the road, and quarries and forestry products continue to be economically important to this part of the state. Farmers try to scratch out a living in scattered pockets along the way but poor soil conditions and short growing seasons pose serious challenges.

Eventually route 17 joins with state route 70, going east two miles to the City of Eagle River. Depending on your timing there are some fun events here to take advantage of. In June is the Up North Beer Fest, with dozens of breweries offering about 150 different craft beers for thirst quenching. The Paul Bunyan Fest in August features chain saw carving, arts and craft events and vendors, lots of food, music, and more. The Cranberry Festival in early October mixes food and music with gorgeous fall color riding.

Departing Eagle River we ride the wonderful northern Wisconsin route 70 through the Nicolet National Forest for twenty five miles to route 55. Once beyond the influence of Eagle River and nearby lakes and resorts the ride across the north of Wisconsin is through a near wilderness area. No serpentine curves but just mile after mile of scenic pleasurable riding. The character of the road improves after turning right onto route 55. We'll ride this premier motorcycle route for 90 marvelous miles, all the way south to route 47 at Keshena.

Along the way route 55 offers up some of the best riding in the state. The road carves through unbroken forests and curves around lakes and rivers, through charming small towns and past scenic parks and places to stop and try to soak it all in.

North of Crandon we join route 32 for a few miles and follow it to town. Crandon is located on the north shore of Lake Metonga and is the county seat for Forest County. It's perhaps bestr known by bikers and gearheads as the home of the Crandon International Off Road Raceway. This famous site has been in operation for four decades. At Crandon routes 8 and 32 head east, but we stay on state route 55 for beaucoup miles of entirely delightful riding between Crandon and Keshena. For the first several miles route 55 dodges between a number of lakes, then it picks up the Wolf River, which it shadows for many more miles with the usual meanderings of a streamside road, overall making for fabulous riding through a rolling land blanketed with mature forests. There are two historic markers of interest in this stretch. The first is at Mole Lake and it describes an 1806 battle between the Sioux and Chippewa over rights to historically important wild rice beds in the area. The Chippewa had harvested the wild rice each fall for many generations. A ferocious battle was fought when the Sioux came into the area from the west to take over this vital food source, resulting in at least 500 combatant deaths. The Indians from both tribes were buried in a mass grave near the marker. This spot of course has special significance to Native Americans, but it is also a reminder to the rest of us that people lived their lives here, and history was being made, long before the first white settler built a cabin in these woods. The Mole Lake Indian Reservation and nearby Rice Lake are modern reminders of this region's history.

Several miles south of Mole Lake, just south of the village of Pickerel, is another interesting historic marker. Located in a nice roadside park, this sign marks the location of the old Military Road carved through the harsh wilderness between Fort Howard (Green Bay) and Fort Wilkins, located at the tip of Michigan's Keweenaw Peninsula. Though authorized by President Lincoln in 1863, the road wasn't finished for several years. In the end it served as the means of travel for explorers and settlers more than it did for its originally intended military purposes. There are places in northern Wisconsin and the western Upper Peninsula of Michigan where the name Military Road is still attached to intermittent stretches of roadway.

South of the intersection with route 52 our road goes through a nice hilly region in an area called Ninemile Hills. The great riding continues all the way to route 64 and Langlade, alternating between flat lands near swamps and lakes, or rolling and rocky forested lands. At all times in this area the road is greatly influenced by the nearby Wolf River, matching it curve for curve.

Near Langlade there is another interesting roadside historical marker near the 55/64 intersection that tells the story of the Charles Michel de Langlade, who is sometimes referred to as the father of Wisconsin. The Village and County of Langlade were named for him. He was born at the trading post of Mackinac in 1729 and was among the first permanent settlers to locate on the present site of Green Bay about 1745. In 1759 Langlade fought under General Montcalm in the Battle of Quebec which ended the French Empire in North America. After active service with the British in the Revolutionary War de Langlade returned to Green Bay where he died in 1800.

The landscape opens up a bit near the village of Langlade but soon turns into forest again, and the road gets even better as we enter the Menominee Indian Reservation and route 55 accompanies the meanders of the river southward to Keshena. Just north of route 47, our next turn, a historical marker for Spirit Rock is a poignant telling of Native American spiritualism.

Following route 47 westward keeps us in the Reservation and in a forested landscape for many miles. At the reservation's western boundary the countryside suddenly becomes a 50 / 50 mix of forest and farmland as we ride the last few miles on 47 to route US45. Go north on 45 for nine miles to route 64. Follow 64 west into Antigo and beyond – all the way back to Merrill. Route 64 is a mixed landscape near the two ends – Antigo and Merrill – but between the two towns it traverses a mostly wooded region.

The Langlade County Historical Society operates a museum in Antigo at the old Carnegie library building at 404 Superior Street. Outside displays include a log cabin from 1878 and a beautifully restored steam locomotive and caboose. Admittance is free though donations are encouraged.

This ride takes in the best of northern Wisconsin's forest and lake region. You might not see a Hodag (if you do be sure to get a picture!) but you'll likely see eagles and other wildlife. The geologic history of this region is on the surface and easy to see and marvel at. Whether it's bedrock outcroppings or glacial moraines and lakes, the effects of the last ice age are still apparent in this lovely region today for all of us to marvel at. The roads designated on the ride are among the best. None of them are major commercial routes with heavy traffic. Of course logging trucks can be found on all northern Wisconsin roads so a rider must always be aware of them, and summer tourists are to be expected especially near lake resort area, but you won't find the congestion that mars busy connector and high volume routes. Kick back, relax, slow down a bit, and just soak in the beauty surrounding you and the smooth pavement rolling under your wheels.

6. The Great River Scenic Byway Ride

WHEN THE TOPIC comes to the best motorcycling routes in Wisconsin the route alongside the Mississippi River is always in the conversation. As it should be. There is a reason that Route 35 (for the most part, though a few other roads are used on this ride when they're better than W35) is called the Great River Road. It's great in many perspectives, ranging from pure scenic value to fun hills and curves, charming places to visit, and fascinating historical sites that might make a history nut out of folks who heretofore claimed to not care about times gone by. The 250-mile Wisconsin Great River Road is part of the ten-state Great River Road National Scenic Byway which follows the Mississippi River for 3,000 miles through ten states. It was established in 1938 by Franklin Roosevelt making it America's oldest scenic byway. The entire route is marked by a green & white pilot's wheel and National Scenic Byway signs. Obviously a premier scenic route such as this will be part of a book focusing on the best of the best. It's not only the miles of great asphalt that make this a wonderful ride, it's also the 33 towns along the route that are filled with fascinating things to see and do, especially if you have an interest in those lesser known aspects of local history.

This particular version of a Great River Road outing begins at Tennyson and Potosi on the south, at the intersection of route 133 and US61 & W35. The town of Prescott anchors the ride at the north end of the tour. Keep in mind that the underlying principle of this book is that we'll follow the water and enjoyable routes, not necessarily just official routes or designated byways. In this part of the state route 133 is preferable to 35; it's near the water, has less traffic and is just plain and simply more pleasurable to ride.

Potosi has some recommended stops, even before we start the ride. It is home of the Passage Thru Time Museum, an informative stop to contemplate the mining and agricultural history of the area, as well as Native American influences. Just beyond the Passage museum is the National Brewery Museum in the former Potosi Brewery building. Potosi also hosts a Catfish Festival on the second weekend of August. The event features lots of freshly grilled fish, music, and the usual enjoyable activities that make these small town festivals famous. Potosi also brings us into the traditional lead mining area, which sparked the original migration into Wisconsin nearly 200 years ago.

When ready, ride west on 133 and almost immediately the fun begins. The scenery is captivating with the rolling woods and fields on either side of the meandering highway as it winds its way to the town of Cassville.

For the most part route 133 is a couple miles inland, but when the road arrives at Cassville the Mighty Mississippi is at the town's doorstep in all its grandeur. The stretch of asphalt between Potosi and Cassville is typically exhilarating and scenic.

Cassville is surrounded by the scenic beauty that is the hallmark of the driftless area and the river, as well as being a particularly historic town. The southwest lead mining portion of Wisconsin saw the earliest development while Wisconsin was still part of the Michigan Territory. It quickly became clear that a port on the Mississippi River was needed to efficiently handle the ore being mined nearby. Cassville was founded in 1827 to fill that role. The town was named in honor of Lewis B. Cass, then governor of the Michigan Territory, which at the time extended west to the Mississippi River and then north to the Lake of the Woods on the Minnesota / Canadian border. The Wisconsin Territory was formed in 1836 after Michigan's status as a state became certain.

Early in its development speculators were confident that Cassville would soon become the capital of the newly formed Wisconsin Territory due to its central location in the Territory (as it looked then). After Madison became the capital hopes were dashed and Cassville never became the metropolis on the river that investors had hoped for. When the first territorial legislature met in Belmont in 1836, Cassville received just one vote less than Madison as the place where the new capital would be established. A site of interest in downtown Cassville that dates back to 1836 is the Denniston House, a large red brick hotel on the waterfront (commonly referred to as the Big Brick) that builders thought would one day soon house legislators and other officers of the territory in its new capital. The Denniston House was listed on the National Registry of Historic Places in 1975. Historic preservation groups are trying to raise money to fully restore the building to its former grandeur. Across the street from the Denniston House is a small but nicely done veterans memorial on the water's edge.

After checking out Cassville go north on route 133 to the north city limits where you'll see county road VV going off to the left front. This is our road, which quickly takes us to Nelson Dewey State Park, and Stonefield, a Wisconsin Historic Site. Nelson Dewey was a Connecticut native born in 1813 who migrated to the new town of Cassville as part of the wave of immigrants seeking to make their fortunes in this region. Dewey became active in local, and then state politics, and was elected as the first governor of Wisconsin in 1848. Dewey was always a major booster for the Cassville area and he bought a two-thousand-acre estate just north of town that he named Stonefield. His dream home extended from the edge of the Mississippi River up over the 500-foot bluffs. By 1868 he completed a handsome mansion that was called a "palace in the wilderness." On a snowy day in January 1873 fire swept through Dewey's dream home, and a financial panic that same year drove him into bankruptcy. He died a pauper in 1889 in the Denniston House, which ironically was part of the venture that first brought him to Cassville and in which he had earlier invested heavily. Dewey's own home stood in ruins until Walter Newberry of Chicago bought the land and restored the house. Using the foundation and standing walls of the house he had it reconstructed but in a significantly different style and size than the original. Today we can see Newberry's version of the Dewey mansion in Stonefield. The Nelson Dewey State Park and the Stonefield historic site sit on much of the land that was Dewey's estate. If you're interested in antique farm equipment and the way of life of late 1800s and early 1900s rural Wisconsin, Stonefield is an enjoyable stop. It houses the state agricultural museum with its amazing collection of farm machinery from a hundred years ago.

he first few miles of county road-VV are very enjoyable, though it straightens out when the road turns inland for a bit. Ride CR-VV north to the point where the road "Ts" at CR-A. Head west on A and follow this scenic road into the small town of Bagley. On the north edge of this village we pick up CR-X (Bagley Avenue in town) and follow it close to the riverfront as it winds its way north to the village of Wyalusing. The bluffs in this area are fabulous, especially just north of the burg of Wyalusing. Here, dramatic stone cliffs jut out at the water's edge, doing a serious impression of coastal Oregon.

This entire area is scenic and makes for great riding. County road-X winds around the picturesque perimeter of Wyalusing State Park and then straightens out and goes east. Taking time to explore the park will pay large rewards. Five hundred-foot cliffs, waterfalls, caves, and other geologic wonders await the visitor, as do magnificent vistas from the bluffs.

After a short but nice ride on CR-C we finally arrive at route 18, where a left turn carries us across the Wisconsin River, through the town of Bridgeport, and into Prairie du Chien, a city with lots of stories to tell, things to see, and history to share.

What might be considered the modern history of Prairie du Chien began on June 17, 1673. That's the day that Father Pere Marquette and Louis Jolliet floated down the Wisconsin River and entered the Mississippi River at this site. They were the first known non-native persons to see the upper Mississippi. The Fox Indian tribe lived on the prairie at the juncture of the two rivers and the chief of the tribe was named Alim, which translated to dog in English and chien in French.

Prairie du Chien soon grew into a key trading post where voyageurs and Native Americans met to trade for furs and manufactured goods.

The U.S. government built Fort Shelby to establish a presence and claim sovereignty of the area. The only War of 1812 battle in Wisconsin was fought at the fort in 1814. A force of British and Indians, under command of Major William McKay captured the fort, renaming it Fort McKay in what is officially referred to as the Battle of Prairie du Chien.

The British victory in June 1814 was short lived and the tide of the war turned following American victories in other major battles. The war soon ended and American sovereignty in the Great Lakes and Mississippi River valley would never again be seriously challenged by a foreign power. The Brits burned Fort Shelby prior to vacating it in 1815.

Fort Crawford, another wood compound, was built at essentially the same location as Fort Shelby in 1816 but floods in the 1820s destroyed the structure. A second Fort Crawford was constructed in 1829, but this time it was built of stone and situated on higher ground about a mile south. Troops stationed at Fort Crawford took part in the 1832 Black Hawk War and it was at this fort that Chief Black Hawk surrendered to Colonel Zachary Taylor to end the Black Hawk War.

Fort Crawford's story is preserved in a museum located at the corner of Beaumont and Rice Streets, just west of route 18. Most of the fascinating history that occurred in Prairie du Chien was on St. Feriole Island. Immediately adjacent to the river, this locale was the base of the fur trade for many decades. This is where the Battle of Prairie du Chien took place, and it was the location of the first Fort Crawford. Two attractions to see on the island today are Villa Louis, a mansion built in 1870 that became Wisconsin's first state historic site in 1952. Near Villa Louis is the Brisbois Store and Fur Museum. This stone building was built in 1851 by a fur trader and like Villa Louis is also on the National Register of Historic Places. The museum chronicles an important part of Wisconsin's early history. Of interest to military buffs is the annual re-enactment of the War of 1812 Battle of Prairie du Chien on St. Feriole Island.

When done exploring St. Feriole Island and Prairie du Chien continue north on magical 35. This road between Prairie du Chien and the LaCrosse area is nothing short of fabulous. You want great scenery? How about forested hills and rock cliffs on your right, while frequent glimpses of the mighty Mississippi River offer enchanting views to your left. Want variety in terrain and road characteristics? Then hills and curves served up on smooth pavement with light traffic and as many motorcycles as four-wheeled vehicles to share the road with should keep you in high spirits. This is a destination road that bikers travel from far and wide for the opportunity to ride, so if you live close enough to ride it frequently consider yourself truly blessed. A Corps of Engineers campground in Black Hawk Park near DeSoto offers a unique opportunity to camp on the river's edge if an overnight stop is in your travel plans. In this facility are also historical markers that tell the story of the bloody Battle of Bad Axe, the final battle of the Black Hawk War. Several historical markers and scenic overlooks are located along route 35 in this vicinity and I suggest a stop at each to learn about the area's history and to marvel at its scenic and geologic wonders. A few miles further north, at the Bad Axe River, is the Genoa National Fish Hatchery and Great River Road Interpretive Center. It's right on our road so a stop is easy and an interesting diversion.

Traffic picks up on the south side of LaCrosse when U.S. 61 joins route 35 and takes us into this spirited city of 52,000. The city sprang up from humble beginnings in 1841 when a fur trader went upriver to set up his own fur business away from the crowded fur markets of Prairie du Chien. The geographic site had been named back in 1765 when Zebulon Pike explored the area. He gave the name Prairie La Crosse after seeing Native Americans playing a game (lacrosse) with sticks shaped like a bishop's crozier or cross.

This is a fine place to take that Mississippi River cruise you've always wanted. Along the riverfront just north of the 14 / 61 bridge paddlewheel cruise boats berth at the docks just waiting for your call. La Crosse Queen Cruises offers a variety of cruise opportunities—from multi-day trips up and down the river to short cruises of an hour or two. They can be reached at 608.784.8523. The Riverside Museum on Veterans Memorial Drive contains artifacts and information about the history of this region, including its archaeology, steamboats, logging, and fur-trading, and has the largest collection of artifacts salvaged from the wreck of the *War Eagle* steamboat. It's open from Memorial Day through October, perfect for the curious motorcyclist.

The nature of the area changes for a bit beyond LaCrosse, with busier and straighter roads carrying us north again. By the time we arrive at Fountain City things are looking better again. Fountain City is one of the oldest places on the river. A small group led by a hardy entrepreneur by the name of Thomas Holmes settled here in 1839 to trade with the local Indians and to cut wood that steamboats burned as they began plying the river.

Every person or community capitalizes on unique attributes or occurrences that happen to them, and this village is no exception. In 1995, a 55-ton boulder fell off a cliff onto a house 400 feet below. Fortunately, nobody was injured but it did open the door of opportunity and the Rock In The House (as opposed of course to the House On The Rock) tourist attraction was born. The house is located on the north edge of Fountain City where a small sign points the way. A real estate agent bought the house, which is vacant except for the occasional tourist who paid a dollar to walk in the home to look at the huge boulder in the master bedroom.

Just a short ride east on Elmers Road is an interesting potential stop at Elmer's Auto and Toy Museum, located atop Eagle Bluff. This mom and pop operation has dozens of antique cars, motorcycles, bicycles, and more.

This area is one of the most striking along the entire length of the river. Two miles north of town is Merrick State Park, offering camping and recreation on the shores of the river. Just north of the park is the aforementioned Eagle Bluff, at 550 feet the highest point on the upper Mississippi. Fabulous views are afforded from atop this bedrock mount.

For the first roughly ten miles there is a broad plain between the road and the river, but the bluffs are tight against route 35 on the east side. Near the north end of this stretch we pass by the town of Buffalo, beyond that the strip of land on which we are riding between the hills and the river becomes narrow. Spectacular views of both are again the order of the day for mile after amazing mile.

There are of course many places along the river road to pull over at scenic overlooks, but if you want one that provides a marvelous view of a lock and dam system you can't do better than in Alma where Buena Vista Park provides a bird's eye view of the river and the lock system. Go east on CR-E a few blocks to Buena Vista Drive, then left to the top of the hill in the park. It's worth the short ride.

Eventually we arrive in the small town of Pepin, perhaps still best known by most people as the birthplace of author Laura Ingalls Wilder. The countryside north of Pepin was the location for her early life as told in the *Big Woods* stories. There is a small museum in town right along route 35 if you don't want to ride out of town several miles to see the log cabin replica. A small railroad museum is adjacent to the Wilder museum, and there is a small park in front, providing a handy place to take a break from the road. North of Pepin I encourage riders not to be in too much of a rush and take the time to stop at a couple of scenic overlooks and historical markers. The first overlook provides a marvelous view, as does the second, but that one is across from Lake City, MN, which spoils the view a bit. A historical marker 3 miles north of Pepin tells the story of Fort St. Antoine, built in 1686 by Nicholas Perrot to stake a claim for French sovereignty over this region. This was in response to British inroads along the Mississippi and upper Great Lakes areas. Other historical markers along route 35 north of Pepin tell the story of this region's long and fascinating history.

At the risk of sounding like I'm repeating myself I will just say that between Pepin and the end of our ride at Prescott is more of the wonderful same. Occasional signs point out attractions that might be of interest but the ride and the scenery speak for themselves and for many riders is all that's needed.

Prescott, where the blue waters of the St. Croix River meet the already brownish waters of the Mississippi River marks the end of our marvelous ride on the Great River Road. Upon arrival at Prescott you may wish to stop at the Great River Road Visitor and Learning Center, on Monroe Street on the south side of town, left turn off route 35. These museums do a great job telling the river's story.

Great Lakes Circle Tours

B y good fortune one of the most remarkable geographic features in North America, the Great Lakes, are in the Midwest. The far-reaching impact of these Sweetwater Seas in our lives is without measure. From the narrow perspective of this book we are blessed to have the scenic and riding opportunities they offer within a one-day drive of anywhere in the region.

Taking trips entirely around the Lakes has long been a desire of tourists and a book about the best motorcycling opportunities of the Midwest could hardly be considered complete unless these opportunities are discussed. I'm only including four of the five Great Lakes; Michigan, Superior, Huron and Erie. Lake Ontario certainly has its charms but it generally isn't considered as being in the Midwest.

Each of the Lakes are uniquely different and offer different rewards for making the effort to circumnavigate them.

Because I believe that the whole purpose of a Great Lakes circle tour is to see the lakes as much as possible, you will note that some of my routes differ from the official "circle" routes, which are based on state and provincial or federal highways. The Great Lakes Commission, in cooperation with the eight states that touch on the Great Lakes, plus Ontario, have created official routes around each of the five lakes. I suggest that, unless a person wants the simplicity of following signed routes on major highways, a traveler should disregard portions of the official routes and find something better. After all, shouldn't a rider stay as close to the water as possible and not ride several miles inland just to stay on a major state or federal highways? I believe so, and that's why I suggest waterfront roads rather than simply following the sanctioned routes. Following local roads always takes more skill and attention, but the rewards are well worth the extra effort.

But having said this I'm happy to point out that there are long stretches where the main state or provincial route is the only road available. For instance, US23 and M25 along the west shore of Lake Huron in Michigan, or route 17 along the north shore of Lake Superior. But as you will see there are lots of places where we will forsake official highways for local pavement next to the water.

Because we share three of these Lakes with our neighbor to the north (and to the east, if you live in Michigan), there are certain realities about entering and traveling in a foreign country that must be addressed. For a long time travel between Canada and the United States was easy and routine. The whole process seldom took more than a few minutes. While the border between the U.S. and Canada is still comparatively open and many thousands of people cross it each day for business, travel or recreation, things have changed. The requirement of travel documents, a passport or enhanced driver's license, being the most important. If your state offers an enhanced driver's license consider getting one prior to traveling to Canada. The enhanced license eliminates the need to carry a passport and this is especially convenient when traveling by motorcycle.

But don't let the border crossing process deter you from visiting Ontario. If ever two jurisdictions shared a special relationship it's the U.S and Canada. Our culture, history, economy, geography, and shared appreciation of the many natural splendors of this region unite us. And I find it very interesting to view the history of our two great nations from the 'other' perspective. Historical sites in Canada tell a different story than our historical traditions because for much of their existence they were associated with Great Britain while we of course fought a war to break from the Brits. There are sites in Ontario and Quebec where the story of invasion of that land by American forces or mercenaries is told in forts and battle sites. It's a fascinating bit of history. Additionally, many families in this region, my own included, have roots in Canada. One could correctly say we're more like cousins than just friendly neighbors.

On a more practical level, when riding near any of the Great Lakes be prepared for cool or foggy conditions. Fog, mist or cool temperatures can sometimes be encountered near the shorelines even if it's warm and sunny just a few miles inland. All that water creates its own microclimate and motorcyclists in particular must be prepared for the possible need of an extra layer.

Let's go do some great riding around the Great Lakes.

1. The Lake Erie Circle Tour

LAKE ERIE is a defining reality for those who live near its shores. Ohio proudly calls Lake Erie "Our Lake" and on the north shore Ontario feels equally honored. Michigan's portion of the lake is small but it is a favorite destination for sportsmen and women who take advantage of its fisheries and wildlife potential. And though not part of the geographic Midwest the states of New York and Pennsylvania are justifiably proud of their Lake Erie shoreline. The lake played a major role in the development of all of the jurisdictions that border the water and contributes immeasurably to our daily lives and economy to this day. Its presence creates a microclimate that allows vineyards and orchards to flourish along its shores. It is the source of the water that flows through uncountable faucets. Its productive waters offer endless opportunities for fishing and recreational boating and its miles of sandy beaches beckon to those seeking relaxation and maritime vistas.

To fully appreciate the fascinating history of the Lake Erie region and to explore the many attractions a trip completely around the fourth largest of the Great Lakes (though smallest by volume) is necessary. Depending on one's itinerary this tour could easily take two to four days.

Much of the tour is comprised of designated scenic drives. The Ohio portion is known as the Lake Erie Coastal Ohio Scenic Byway because of the historic and scenic value of the lakeshore route. On the Ontario side the Talbot Trail carries riders through a scenic landscape of historic lakefront villages and through a verdant land of orchards and vineyards. The segment through New York and Pennsylvania is part of the Great Lakes Seaway Trail. Numerous parks around the lake provide for waterfront views and activities.

A nice feature of circular tours is that a person can start wherever it's most convenient. For the purpose of this book I'm going to start in Toledo, located at the mouth of the Maumee River. The Maumee is steeped in history and the mouth of the river at present day Toledo is not only a major international port, this locale also played a pivotal role in the development of Ohio and the Northwest Territory. When in Toledo one should head southwest a few miles along the Maumee River to visit the Fort Meigs site and the Battle of Fallen Timbers park. These two places had a major impact on the history of the Great Lakes region as it affected the early U.S., native tribes, and Great Britain during the Northwest Indian Wars and later the War of 1812. The impact of these places and events in our history can hardly be overstated. The word Maumee is a version of the name of the Miami, the primary Native American tribe that lived in this area for centuries prior to European settlement.

Toledo is a large city of about 325,000 people. It was first settled in 1817, known then as Port Lawrence, and incorporated in 1833. The incorporators named it after Toledo, Spain – though nobody is quite sure why.

Take the time to explore this city and you'll be pleasantly surprised. There are many attractions, fine restaurants, museums, parks and things to do in this area. Toledo is crazy about its minor league baseball team – the Toledo Mud Hens - and their new stadium is a great place to watch a game. Touring the *SS William B. Boyer* Museum Ship near the river mouth is interesting, and as long as you're on the water take a cruise on the *Sandpiper* – a canal boat that carries passengers on an enjoyable cruise down the river to the lake.

Unfortunately heading north between Toledo and Monroe, Michigan leaves a person high and dry as there aren't any good coastal roads that connect the two cities. There are local roads of course, but no single highway that runs the whole distance on the waterfront. This means that a person must take inland roads such as I-75 or one of the nearby parallel roads. I recommend taking the Dixie Highway, which is Route 125 in Michigan and Detroit Avenue in Toledo. This road has lots of history, and of course prior to I-75 it was THE highway that got travelers from cities such as Toledo and Detroit to Florida. It takes you to Monroe and then turns east nearer the water as it proceeds north beyond Monroe. Just after crossing the River Raisin in Monroe the Dixie makes a one-mile jog to the east along the north shore of the river as State Route 50, and then turns northeast again along the coastline.

The City of Monroe has a long history – having its start in 1780. It also has a strong French flavor and until 1817 was called Frenchtown. It may be most famous for being the home of George Custer, renowned General of the Civil War and of course remembered mostly for the demise of him and his Seventh Cavalry by the Sioux at the battle of the Little Bighorn. There is a General Custer exhibit in the Monroe County Historical Museum which follows the famous General's life from birth in Ohio through his abbreviated military career. The museum is easily accessible on Dixie Highway / Monroe Street just south of the river. An impressive statue showing the general atop his horse is located on the bank of the River Raisin in town.

Monroe's interesting history is due to its location on the water highway used by the earliest explorers. Frenchtown was the site of one of the principal battles in the War of 1812. In what was called the River Raisin Massacre only thirty-three of nine hundred thirty-four soldiers escaped death or capture in January 1813. This was the largest battle ever fought on Michigan soil. The day after the battle a massacre of wounded and captured soldiers, mostly Kentucky volunteers, took place which enraged the Americans and energized them to fight all the harder. "Remember the River Raisin" became a rallying cry for American soldiers during the remainder of the War. A lonely stone obelisk in a vacant lot is all that marks the location today. The battle site is now a national park. Visit the River Raisin Battlefield Museum at 1403 Elm Street.

Saying *au revoir* to Frenchtown continue the tour north on the historic Dixie Highway. Because the Dixie is now replaced by I-75 it carries less traffic than it did in the past. Crossing over the Huron River and into Wayne County, Dixie Highway becomes River Road and then Jefferson Avenue. It follows closely to the Detroit River shoreline all the way to the Ambassador Bridge where we cross into Canada.

There are a number of small parks along this segment that allow access to the river itself, with its impressive vistas of strong currents, islands, and ocean-going ships heading up and down the waterway. This river now also supports a world-class fishery thanks to efforts of many in both the public and private sectors that cleaned up the river from its industrial sewer status of fifty years ago to the attractive waterway it is today. The economic boost that a healthy Detroit River and Lake Erie has brought to this area is immeasurable.

The last few miles of the ride up Jefferson Avenue are an eye-opener. This stretch of road is definitely not the usual byway sought out by motorcyclists, but it isn't very long and it's worth seeing. You'll pass by industrial complexes in places like Ecorse, River Rouge and Zug Island that served as the manufacturing backbone of our economy for many decades. Huge factories and steel mills – both active and abandoned – line the road and waterway in this stretch.

Just up the road from Ecorse and River Rouge is the Fort Wayne complex on the east side of the street. Fort Wayne has unfortunately fallen into disrepair, but it has a long and interesting history. The fort was built in 1854 on what is the narrowest stretch of river in that area because of serious border tensions with British Canada. Fort Wayne was to have the latest in artillery to defend shipping lanes and be capable of reaching the opposite shore.

The fort was fortunately never used in combat but it did serve as an induction center for every war from the Civil War to Viet Nam. Several original buildings at the fort still survive. I still have vivid memories of standing in one long line after another at Fort Wayne on a hot July day in my youth, completing my pre-induction physical.

At this point follow the signs to the Ambassador Bridge and head south to Windsor, Ontario. Yes, that's right, south. Detroit is the only border crossing point in the nation where you travel south to get to Canada. The Detroit River turns in an east / west alignment at this point, with

Windsor situated on the south shore. The Ambassador Bridge is unique in several ways. First, it is the busiest international crossing point in North America, and second, it is privately owned. One might assume that an international bridge would be a government-owned piece of infrastructure, but that's not the case. The Bridge was built with private funds in 1929 and is jointly operated by The Detroit International Bridge Company and The Canadian Transit Company. Over one-quarter of all Canadian / U.S. trade occurs over the Ambassador Bridge. It's such an important border crossing point that a second, government owned, bridge is being built.

Detroit and Windsor share a close relationship. They are sister cities in many ways with common links involving families, economics, sports, and recreation activities.

The Windsor area like Detroit is also steeped in history. As one might expect it has a more-decidedly British flavor, and is graced with beautiful gardens and parks along the riverfront. It has also become famous for its casinos. While in Windsor check out the plaque and small park dedicated to the 1838 Patriot War in which Michigan Militia of primarily Irish descent invaded Ontario, in conjunction with Canadian rebels, in an effort to wrest the southwest peninsula of Ontario from British control. It of course was a failed effort but is but another interesting chapter in the joint histories of the U.S. and Canada.

Crossing the Bridge puts riders on Ontario Route 3. Stay on route 3 until its junction with Ontario Route 20 / 18, then turn south along the Detroit River. While in Ontario we'll follow The Talbot Trail when it's near the water. This is a historically important land route completed in the 1820s along the north shore of Lake Erie. Its original purpose was to provide a land route for settlers and British military personnel between the Niagara region and Detroit in the strategically important Niagara Peninsula of then British Canada. The trail is named in honor of Colonel Thomas Talbot who oversaw laying out the more than three-hundred-mile route. The original trail adhered closely to today's designated memorial trail, comprised of Highway 3 and several numbered county roads.

The Trail begins in Windsor, continuing through Leamington, Wheatley, Blenheim and St. Thomas. It follows County Road 38 through Straffordville and Courtland then rejoins Highway 3 through Delhi, Simcoe, Jarvis and Cayuga. At Dunnville the trail splits from Route 3 again before rejoining Highway 3 near Wainfleet. This portion of the Trail ends at Fort Erie. This ride keeps us on the Talbot Trail to a significant degree but when the Trail goes inland too far we'll stick with lakeside roads.

And we leave the Trail almost immediately in Windsor so that we can follow the Detroit River south to the lake. There is much history along the shore of this major Great Lakes connecting water. Route 20 is initially

Ojibway Parkway, and later turn into Front Street for much of its length south to Amherstburg. Going south along the east shore is a bit like downriver Detroit – it's where a good deal of Ontario's chemical industry is located thanks to underground salt deposits.

Fort Malden National Historic Site in Amherstburg is a reconstructed fort originally built by the British prior to the War of 1812, but abandoned by them in 1813 and occupied by American forces for two years during that war. A restored 1819 brick barracks, earthworks from the 1840s, and various other buildings are preserved at the site. As with other Canadian forts it tells the British and Canadian side of the story.

Shortly after passing through Amherstburg O-20 swings eastward, and soon you'll encounter CR-50 heading south to the lake. Take CR-50 and follow it along the shoreline all the way to the town of Kingsville, where O-20 rejoins it. Continue east until you reach Leamington and Point Pelee Provincial Park. If you wish you can spend time in the park and walk to the southernmost point of land on the Canadian mainland. (Fish Point on Pelee Island in Lake Erie is the southernmost point of Canada) Pt. Pelee is renowned for bird watching during the spring and fall migrations.

A few miles west of Leamington the provincial road makes a ninety-degree turn north, but we stay on County Road 20 straight east to Leamington. When you see the Pelee Island ferry on your right you'll be at Erie Street – turn north and take this into Leamington and provincial route 3 – head east again on 3. Ontario Route 3 which is our host for about eighty miles to the small town of Wallacetown. In between Leamington and Wallacetown there are many attractions. You may be surprised at how lightly developed the north shore of Lake Erie is in this region – it certainly makes for pleasant and enjoyable riding with light traffic and good roads. This is a region of agricultural specialty crops, and fields of tomatoes and other vegetables are common. This is also Canada's tobacco growing region. Many fine vineyards have also developed in this southwest peninsula. Canada has many wonderful people, places and attractions, but is lacking in sunny southern resorts. This is Canada's south coast.

In Wallacetown turn south on county road 8 to route 16, which takes you to route 20, a one-mile jog south on CR22 just northeast of Port Stanley and then continue east on CR24. The route numbers change occasionally but if you just stay on the road that follows the coastline the most closely, you'll be all right. Route 24 follows along the coast to Route 42. This stretch of road from Wallacetown east to Port Rowan takes you past four Ontario Provincial Parks that are located on the lakeshore. Other attractions include the Port Burwell lighthouse and many small parks located in the villages that are located on the shore. Continue east on CR42 when Ontario 73 turns north.

East of Port Rowan turn left onto CR 16 for 2.5 miles and turn right on provincial route 24. Take Route 24 eleven miles and after it turns northerly Ontario Route 6 turns east taking you to Port Dover.

Follow Route 6 east out of Port Dover to Rural Route 3 (Dover-Dunville Road) and follow this road all the way through the town of Dunville. Stay on RR3, which is Taylor Side Road and then Main Road on the east side of Dunville. RR3 heads southeast where Ontario Route 3 turns northeast. We want Rural Route3, which continues along the shoreline (known as Lakeshore Road in the stretch east of Dunville) and after twenty-two miles RR3 delivers you back to Ontario Route 3 in Port Colborne (where the Welland Canal enters Lake Erie.) Once back on provincial route 3 follow it to Fort Erie to cross the Niagara River to Buffalo, NY.

Fort Erie, Ontario is a nice place to take a break and discover a little about Ontario history and learning more about our own history at the same time. The Old Fort Erie – another major War of 1812 site – is an interesting place to visit, especially for Americans. It provides a glimpse into the Canadian and British side of that war. Two American warships were captured at Fort Erie (The Ohio and Somers). Lake Erie of course played a significant part in the war with Commodore Oliver Perry's crucial victory against the British in a fierce naval battle on the lake in an attempt to free Detroit and Lake Erie from British control.

The nearby Ridgeway Battlefield Museum also describes a fascinating period of history from the Canadian perspective that most Americans aren't aware of. In 1866 a group of Irish-American Civil War veterans (The Fenian Brotherhood) invaded British North America (Canada) in an attempt to obtain freedom for Ireland. Obviously it was a doomed attempt, but it is an example of the continuing animosity between the British and Americans during that time period, and of course it shows that the British / Irish issue has been stewing for a long time. There were several other excursions into what was to become Canada during that period, all of which had the effect of speeding up the process of confederation of Canada as a nation to preserve its territorial integrity.

After crossing over the Peace Bridge into Buffalo follow I-190 / Route 5 south out of town. Of course if you wish this is the time to take I-190 north to Niagara Falls for a hectic but always impressive trip to this mighty cataract on the Niagara River, connecting lakes Erie and Ontario.

Continuing south on the tour, after just two mile I-190 goes east and Route 5 turns southwest along the shoreline all the way to Ohio. Take Route 5 for twelve miles and at the Wanaka Country Club you'll see Old Lakeshore Road quartering off to the right front. This road hugs the shoreline for fifteen miles while Route 5 goes inland in this stretch. Just after riding through Evangola State Park is Lotus Point Road – turn left and take it the short distance back to Route 5 and head west / right again.

Stay on Route 5 entering Pennsylvania and follow it through Erie where the road takes a one-half mile jog to the south and then continues west. Erie is an interesting city with a number of museums, lighthouses, parks, and monuments – including the Commodore Perry monument – that are of interest. It's a good place to do a little wandering on the shoreline and there are excellent waterfront parks available to accomplish this.

Continue west on Route 5 until just before the Ohio border where Route 5 joins US-20. Stay on 20 for just a few miles until Conneaut, Ohio where you'll get on Route 7 (Mill Street) which goes north to Ohio State Route 531. The stretch of coastline between Conneaut and Ashtabula is the least developed of all of Lake Erie shoreline in Ohio. The road follows a high bluff overlooking the lake and traverses through an area where there is still a lot of wooded land. The lake is almost always visible. SR531 takes you to Ashtabula with its bustling harbor and the Great Lakes Marine and U.S. Coast Guard Museum. It's located at 1071 Walnut Drive in Ashtabula. Continue on to Geneva State Park where route 531 meets state route 534 and turns south to U.S. 20 at the town of Geneva (birth place of Ransom E. Olds – inventor of the venerable Oldsmobile with its Rocket V8). Stay westbound on US20 roughly 14 miles and just east of Painesville where Ohio Route 2 angles off to the right.

If you have an interest in marine artifacts, and would like to climb a historic lighthouse to get a fantastic view of Lake Erie and the mouth of the Grand River, take the Painesville exit off US2. Head north on Richmond Street, which then becomes High Street and finally Water Street in Fairport as you follow the river out to the Fairport Harbor Marine Museum and Lighthouse. It's a fun and interesting stop and climbing old lighthouses is always a treat.

Take SR 2 west about eight miles and near Mentor you'll notice SR615 (Center Street) heading north toward the Lake. Take 615 a short distance and it'll deliver you to route 283 (known locally as Lakeshore Blvd.) which is our riding host for many miles. Mentor has one of the nicer local parks on the lake. On the east side of Cleveland, in Gordon City Park at the intersection of Martin Luther King Drive, at the Cleveland Lakefront Nature Preserve, Lakeshore Blvd. joins I-90 for a short distance through downtown. This immediate area has several fine attractions including lakeshore parks, the 1819 Dunham Tavern Museum, the *USS Cod* Submarine (which sank over a dozen enemy ships in WWII), the *Steamship William G. Mather*, the Rock & Roll Museum and more. You're also just a short ride from several worthwhile attractions in the north of Cleveland including the Auto-Aviation Museum, Jacobs Field and more. For these downtown and lakeshore attractions get off at the 9th Street exit. Most of these sites are between the highway and the lakeshore and are really easy to get to.

I-90 will leave and head south but you'll want to stay on what is now Ohio Route 2 / US6 / US20 heading west along the shoreline. This stretch of road is called the Cleveland Memorial Shoreway, then Clifton Blvd. and then Lake Road after crossing the Rocky River. Shortly after crossing the Rocky River just west of Lakewood routes 2 and 20 part company and our ride continues west along the shoreline on US6 all the way to Sandusky. Notice the Charles Berry Memorial Bridge when crossing the Black River in Lorain. It's the largest bascule or lift bridge in the U.S. Built in the late 1930s and opened for traffic in 1940, it was later renamed to honor Mr. Berry, a Lorain resident and Medal of Honor recipient killed at Iwo Jima. Be on guard when crossing the bridge as all four lanes are metal grid. In my mind Lorain is one of the nicer towns along the shore west of Cleveland. It has a very nice public park on the lake (Lakeview Park) in an area where public lake access is unfortunately scarce.

A destination I recommend for anyone with an interest in the history of the Great Lakes is the Inland Seas Maritime Museum located a few blocks north of US6 in Vermillion at the corner of Huron and Main Streets. Turn north at the corner of US6 and SR60 / Main Street in town. There's an unusual obelisk monument with a clock in it at this corner.

In Huron once again pick up Route 2 to cross Sandusky Bay to Marblehead Peninsula and the many attractions to be found there. The Lake Erie Islands and the Marblehead Peninsula are unique in Ohio and wonderful places to explore. Getting out to Marblehead Lighthouse (the oldest light on the lakes) requires heading east from SR2 on Bay Shore Road. Ferries out to the islands are available at three places on the peninsula between Marblehead and Port Clinton. These side trips are recommended – especially to Kelley's Island – the largest fresh water island in America - to view the fascinating glacial grooves carved into the island's limestone 30,000 years ago during the last Ice Age, and Indian pictographs on Inscription Rock. A ferry trip to South Bass Island, where attractions include the spectacular Perry Victory and International Peace Monument, Crystal Cave, Perry's Cave, state parks and much more, should also be high on anyone's to-do list.

When you've done and seen all that you can fit into your schedule take 163 back to Route 2 west of Port Clinton. Route 2 carries the rider all the way to the east side of Toledo and Woodville Road / SR51 / SR65, which we'll use to cross the Maumee River. This route takes us across the Anthony Wayne Suspension Bridge – a very impressive structure. It's much more interesting crossing the river on this bridge than taking the expressway! While still on the east side of the river you might want to head to the internationally famous original Tony Packo's Café for their sausage sandwich and chili specialties. Highly recommended by no less than Corporal Klinger himself! This iconic restaurant is located just off I-280 at exit 9, then right / east on Front Street. It's less than 2 miles north of the SR2 / I-280 interchange.

Thus completes this interesting and scenic tour around a great lake. I hope you enjoyed it and that you gleaned a bit of knowledge about the lake itself and the important historical aspect of the region.

I haven't gone into great detail about the motorcycling details of this ride because it is in the book for reasons other than serpentine roads and light traffic. It's about riding completely around a Great Lake, one of the most significant geographic and cultural features in North America. It's done for the broader experience of seeing and learning about the lake from atop a motorcycle, not just for fun motorcycling opportunities. To be sure, there are many miles of enjoyable riding. There are stretches in urban areas that are pleasurable motorcycling in the right mind-set but primarily fascinating opportunities to see, do, learn and appreciate.

2. The Lake Huron Circle Tour

THERE ARE two routes to choose from when considering a ride around Lake Huron. Each version offers a somewhat different experience and opportunities for the traveler. One option is to go all the way around both the main lake and Georgian Bay (the bay is so large it's sometimes referred to as the sixth Great Lake), while the second choice is to essentially split the lake in two by traversing ruggedly scenic Bruce Peninsula and taking a ferry across to Manitoulin Island. Because of my previously stated desires to stay off main roads, and be as close to the water as possible, I prefer the Bruce Peninsula/Manitoulin Island route. I also feel that this route offers more in the way of interesting scenery and experiences, so I'll focus primarily on the Bruce Peninsula option, with a bit about the entire Georgian Bay circle at the close of the chapter.

Lake Huron is the second largest of the inland seas with 23,000 square miles of freshwater. It has an astonishing 3,827 miles of shoreline, which includes shorelines of its 30,000 islands. Manitoulin Island, in northern Lake Huron, is the largest freshwater island in the world.

The lake was named hundreds of years ago by early French explorers in recognition of the Huron Indian tribe which lived along its shores. The surface of Lake Huron averages 577 feet above sea level (the same as Lake Michigan, which some scientists consider as actually being one huge lake because they're connected at the Straits of Mackinac.) It takes twenty two years for a gallon of water entering the north end of the lake to finally exit at the south end through the St. Clair River.

I'm going to use Port Huron, Michigan as the beginning point of this tour. One really should take the time to explore the places and commerce that makes Port Huron more akin to ocean seaports than cities in the center of the continent. This historically important port city is situated at the southern end of Lake Huron, at the beginning of the St. Clair River. It has long been a historically important location.

The city operates several museums and waterside parks to highlight its history, culture, nautical atmosphere, and scenic qualities. In town, the impressive Port Huron Museum is high on my list of places to visit while here. The museum, at 1115 Sixth Street, is housed in a stately limestone building of the Renaissance style, constructed in 1902 by Andrew Carnegie to serve as the city's library. It is typical of the beautiful architecture that exemplifies libraries built by this philanthropist a century ago. The Marine Gateway wing of the museum has the largest collection of model ships in Michigan.

Along the waterfront on the north edge of downtown the Thomas Edison Parkway offers paved walking paths along the St. Clair River. This park provides an easily accessible parking and walking opportunity to observe the waterfront and river as well as access to the Thomas Edison Museum. (Edison grew up in Port Huron. His family moved there when he was seven, and he left at age nineteen) A short distance south of the museum is the *Huron* Lightship Museum. Lightships operated for decades on the Great Lakes in places where it was impossible or impractical to install a permanent lighthouse. The *Huron* was the last lightship operated on the lakes by the Coast Guard; retired in 1970.

On the north edge of town, just a few blocks north of the Edison Parkway and Blue Water Bridge, is the Fort Gratiot Lighthouse and park. The first light at this site was built in 1825 at Fort Gratiot, a military fort established there in 1814 to guard this strategically important geographic position. This lighthouse was the first one built in Michigan and is the second oldest light on the Great Lakes. The structure is open to the public and can be climbed for an entry fee.

Standing on the shore and virtually feeling the massive power of the St. Clair River's current as it flows south can leave a person in awe as they try to comprehend the volume and colossal force of the swirling cold water. The powerful eddies and whirlpools created by the water as it rushes nearly a thousand miles down to the sea is at the same time impressive and frightening in its power. Great respect is gained for those who traveled this river in canoes for millennia before the first sailing and steam-powered ships arrived. Watching today's large freighters fight that current as they sail upbound to ports on the upper lakes is a fascinating sight.

A short ride over the recently upgraded Blue Water Bridge brings the traveler to Sarnia, Ontario. For several years Ontario used the tag line 'Friendly and Foreign' in its tourism promotional advertisements. I always thought that was a perfect description. Most of Canada truly is at the same time friendly and familiar while maintaining its unique cultural aspects and historic sites that are indeed decidedly foreign. But foreign or not, one quality that can always be counted on is the friendly and helpful attitude of Canadians toward their North American cousins.

Once in Canada you'll want to stop at the visitor center located at the east end of the bridge apron to exchange some currency and to gather travel information. Travel centers are a treasure trove of road maps and brochures and I always browse the shelves at these facilities to learn about new places to see. Ontario offers a veritable treasure trove of fascinating places to visit and a delightful landscape in which to roam.

A visitor to Canada should also keep in mind that they in fact are in a foreign country. So many things seem familiar that it's easy to act as if one were still in the states, but the many issues that could arise; legal, medical, currency values, roaming charges on a cell phone, language differences in certain locales of Ontario, firearms laws, and other issues require special attention and preparedness on a traveler's part. Speed limits are generally a little lower in Ontario, and speeds and distances are posted in the metric system.

The Blue Water Bridge puts drivers onto Ontario Route 402, a major expressway that connects Sarnia with all points east. This is the only stretch of superslab on the entire trip. Going east on 402 you can say adieu to the expressway at exit 34, which is Ontario Route 21. Stay on R21 along the east shore of Lake Huron all the way to Owens Sound at the southeast corner of the Bruce Peninsula.

This popular byway is the closest road to the water, but unfortunately it is inland just far enough so that a traveler on the road gets only occasional glimpses of the Lake. The various towns passed through along the way have parks or roads that takes you to the water's edge, however.

This part of Ontario is largely farm country, and you pass through miles of green fields, woods, and small towns. Many of the towns have local museums that tell the stories of this region. There are numerous campgrounds and parks that provide an excellent opportunity to camp, explore the local landscape, or simply take a break. Pinery Provincial Park in particular offers a break from the surrounding countryside. It is a unique 6,330-acre forested sand dune environment that is more typical of Lake Michigan's eastern shore than Lake Huron's normally rocky coastline. The park is home to a rare Oak Savannah ecosystem, the largest in Ontario.

North of Pinery Park, and about one hundred thirty kilometers into the trip, signs for Point Clark Lighthouse appear. This 110-foot high lighthouse, built in 1857, is a Canadian National Historic Site. The lighthouse and keeper's cabin are open to the public for tours and if you feel up to conquering the 114 steps, a climb to the top is an option. The view is tremendous. I certainly recommend taking the short trip west off R21 to visit this historic structure. It is open once again after being closed for several years for major structural repairs.

Kincardine, a town with a strong Scottish flavor, is a short ride north of Point Clark. I suggest visiting the lighthouse and museum on Harbour Street in the heart of town. The unique octagonal structure is 74 feet tall and is open for exploration. The Kincardine Yacht Club operates a museum as part of the structure. This lighthouse is one of a kind since it is actually located in town instead of being right on the lakeshore. If you enjoy Celtic music and pageantry try to arrange a Saturday evening visit to Kincardine to enjoy performances of the local Scottish Pipe Band. Every July the town hosts the Scottish Festival and Highland Games.

Continuing north, route 21 traverses the base of the Bruce Peninsula, taking us through a mix of farm and woodlands to the town of Owen

Sound. There are several waterfalls and other interesting attractions in and near this lively port city so watch for directional signs to them. As you're coming into town, turn left at Route 6 and drive the short distance to the parking lot for Jones Falls. It's an easy half-mile walk to these tumbling 40-foot cascades. By all means be sure to explore the Inglis Falls, on 2nd Avenue West, in a conservation area on the south edge of town. The Syndenham River creates a dramatic scene as it tumbles sixty feet over the Niagara Escarpment limestone into the rocky valley below. There is also a five mile long walking trail in this beautiful setting if time and energy allow. An old grist mill and the falls are mere yards from the parking lot.

The Niagara Escarpment is the same geologic formation over which the world famous Niagara Falls tumble further east. The Bruce Peninsula closely resembles the northern Midwest, with its rock formations, forests, hills, waterfalls, and lighthouses.

From Owen Sound we are going to hug the east coast of the peninsula on Grey County Scenic Route CR-1. Take 2nd Avenue West north from town. It eventually morphs into CR-1. There is also a 2nd Avenue East, but that street eventually delivers us a very long distance from where we want to go. 2nd Avenue West is west of the Syndenham River in Owen Sound.

North of Owen Sound the pure motorcycling aspect of this ride kick in. The roads and surrounding scenery improve significantly. The entire route is enjoyable, scenic and interesting, but the roads improve north of here.

About three miles north of town is a sign for Indian Falls. If you feel up to a fairly vigorous 15-minute walk through old forest and rocky terrain the end result pays off with interest. Indian Falls are a miniature Niagara Falls in that they are horseshoe shaped. They have a 45-foot drop, but beware that during the dry season the creek that creates the falls can nearly dry up and the falls will be just a trickle. But at other times the bridal veil type of falls are a striking sight.

Ten miles north of Owen Sound, and one-half mile north of a quarry, CR-1 veers to the right. This turn is easy to miss since it seems that our road keeps going straight ahead. Watch for this important turn. There is a small park at the corner, and small signs indicate a turn for CR-1.

Kick back and enjoy the waterside ride as we glide on mile after mile through a collage of scenic delights. CR-1 eventually swings west toward Wiarton as it shadows the lakeshore of Georgian Bay. An especially scenic stretch in this area has the high cliff of the Niagara Escarpment on your left, and a magnificent view of Lake Huron on the right. Just east of Wiarton, as the road climbs to the top of the escarpment, are the Bruce Caves, a geologically interesting and scenic place to explore and see some of the natural beauty up close. The caves were formed thousands of years ago by wave action when the Great Lakes were much higher than they are today. They're named after Robert Bruce, a hermit who lived there a century ago. The caves and local geology are definitely worth the time it takes to explore them.

Wiarton's most famous citizen just might be Wiarton Willie – the giant albino groundhog that predicts when spring will arrive north of the border. Motorcyclists customarily pay homage to the giant stone woodchuck in his home in Wiarton's Bluewater Park to help guarantee good riding weather.

At Wiarton take Route 6 north a couple miles to Bruce County 9, which carries us through a gorgeously wooded and rolling landscape north to the town of Lion's Head. Upon leaving Wiarton on route 6 you'll notice a sign for the Spirit Rock conservation area. This is a nice spot for a walk and scenic overlook views. Also the remains of a mansion that burned years ago.

After many miles on route 9 we'll arrive at Lion's Head. Its unusual name is derived from the shape of the limestone cliff along the waterfront. Early settlers thought a particular rock formation on the escarpment resembled the head of a lion, and the name stuck. Our route requires a turn just before entering the small town of Lion's Head, but I recommend taking the short side trip into town, if for no other reason than to take a gander at the Lion's Head lighthouse, situated on the water's edge at the base of the escarpment. The old light was torn down years ago but a group of local high school students built this replica structure, duplicating the original light.

We ultimately want to rejoin Route 6 just south of Lion's Head and continue north to Tobermory. Watch for signs along the way for the Bruce Trail and scenic overlooks. The east coast in this region offers spectacular views on top of the lakeshore sea cliffs that line the waterfront.

In the Bruce Peninsula National Park, at the northern tip of the peninsula, a hiking trail follows the edge of the lakeside cliffs. From these escarpments one can look out over Georgian Bay to the east of the peninsula. The cliffs at the water's edge are spectacular. Fathom Five National Marine Park off the northern tip of the peninsula is famous for its scuba diving opportunities, and glass-bottom boat tours, lighthouse tours, dinner cruises and more are available for those who want to spend some time and money on Bruce.

The road eventually temporarily ends in Tobermory, but the fun certainly doesn't stop. There are many things to see and do in this small waterfront tourist town. One option that should be high on a traveler's list is a cruise on Blue Heron Cruise Company tour boats. They offer tours that range from lighthouse and island viewing, to a glass bottom boat from which customers can view shipwrecks in the crystal clear off-shore waters. Flower pot Island and other picturesque delights can be viewed from shore near town.

A memorable part of this tour will be the ferry boat trip across the channel from Tobermory at the tip of Bruce Peninsula to South Baymouth on the southern coast of Manitoulin Island. While the Bruce Peninsula separates the main portion of Lake Huron on the west from Georgian Bay on the east, Manitoulin Island and other nearby islands create what is called the North Channel, that part of Lake Huron that lies between the islands and the Canadian and Michigan mainland to the north. This is a remarkably beautiful area with islands and blue water as far as the eye can see.

A ferry called ChiCheemaun (meaning The Big Canoe in Ojibwa) makes regular passages across the open water to and from Tobermory and South Baymouth. The ferry is operated by Ontario Ferries, and information can be obtained from ontarioferries.com or by calling 1-800-265-3163. Reservations are highly recommended. Motorcyclists often have the privilege of being the first vehicles loaded on the ferry, and the first vehicles unloaded. There is a special motorcycle parking area on the lower level of the ferry, with tie-down brackets in the floor and ropes provided to secure the bikes. Be sure to secure your bike as the water can get quite choppy and rough even in a moderate wind. This is a popular route for motorcyclists and one gets to meet an interesting collection of bikers from all around the U.S. and Canada. The ferry trip takes about two hours and operates from May 1st to October 16th.

Manitoulin Island is so large it has a mainland feel. There are things to do on the island, although making the roughly forty-mile trip across it on Route 6, which is the route used in this particular tour, is enjoyable by itself. If time and an adventurous spirt allow by all means take a loop ride on routes 542 and 540 across the bulk of the island to really appreciate what it's all about. The roads are enjoyable and traffic light. The roads have enough character to keep it interesting while passing through a landscape of stony overgrown fields and forests, with the occasional hard rock farm trying to make a go of it. As is the case on all good riding roads you have to choose whether to ride fast to enjoy the curves, or cruise more slowly and enjoy the scenery. Following route 540 all the way to the west end of the island allows exploration of the Mississagi Lighthouse on the rocky coast. Please note that the caretaker accepts only cash payment for restaurant and lodging services at the lighthouse.

Exit the island at the north end from a small town called Little Current on route 6. There is an interesting one-lane swing bridge here that connects Manitoulin to the next island. The bridge swings open to allow boat traffic through. It is quite rough so you want to have both hands on the bars. Route 6 makes it way north to the mainland, eventually terminating just north of Espanola at the Trans-Canada Highway (Canadian Route 17) on the Spanish River. There is an interesting story as to how it is believed this town got its name. Allegedly, an Ojibwe raiding party in about 1750 captured a woman south of the border who spoke Spanish. She ultimately married into the tribe and taught Spanish to her children. When French explorers showed up they were more than a little surprised to hear Spanish speaking people and the town and river got their Hispanic names.

Route 17 follows the northern shore of Lake Huron westward from this point all the way to Sault Ste. Marie (The Soo) Ontario. From Espanola to the Soo is approximately 245 km/160 miles.

While not a wilderness area this region is only lightly developed. Because it is a main trans-continental highway, there is a fair amount of traffic on the road, including trucks. Fortunately Route 17 has a good number of passing lanes constructed at strategic points to allow faster traffic to get by slow vehicles.

Due to the bilingual nature of Canada, you will have a chance to brush up on your high school or college French courses. All road signs are in both French and English, as are many brochures and other printed materials.

There are a number of interesting attractions along this stretch of road, especially in the several towns we'll ride through. On the east side of Blind River is the Northern Ontario Logging Memorial. You'll see what appears to be sails on masts blowing in the wind but in reality they're sculpted trees. This park has a logging camp, steam engines, blacksmith shop, and various artifacts, as well as statues that, along with the 'trees' make up the memorial to loggers. The town of Blind River, on the river of the same name, got its name because the mouth of the river, due to its layout, is virtually invisible to someone in a boat on the lake, thus the river was called the Blind River.

Further west is route 108 going north twenty miles to the town of Elliot Lake. Though this isn't on our tour if you have an interest in Uranium mining and nuclear physics this is a serendipitous find. When Uranium was discovered in this region after World War II a boom town resulted. From wilderness the town of Elliot Lake was built and by 1955 had 25,000 residents, virtually all connected with Uranium mining and processing. When the U.S. government stopped buying this nuclear fuel in the 1960s the town went bust. Today it has stabilized at around 12,000 people and has a more varied economy, including tourism and logging. The Nuclear & Mining Museum in Elliot Lake is unlike other museums around the Great Lakes and just might be an interesting side trip for the right person.

If you are into oddities and unusual roadside attractions then you should stop to take a picture of northern Canada's largest Adirondack chair just west of Thessalon. This popular style of wood seat is called the Muskoka Chair in Canada, due to the French influence. In any event, an 18-foot red one awaits visitors near the town of Thessalon on Route 17.

An interesting side trip, and one which continues the island hopping theme, is to follow the Canada National Park signs about sixty miles east of Sault Ste. Marie and take Road 548 onto St. Joseph Island. The road makes a scenic circular tour of the island, and takes you to Fort St. Joseph Historic Park. This fort was the most westerly of the various British frontier posts during the War of 1812.

The twin cities of Sault Ste. Marie anchor the International Bridge connecting Michigan and Ontario. A fascinating detail almost lost to history is the fact that these two cities, in different countries, were at one time one city straddling the river. Only after the Treaty of Ghent ended the War of 1812, and the border of Canada and the U.S. defined as the center of the St. Mary River, did they become separate cities.

The St. Mary River connecting Lake Superior and Lake Huron was named by French explorers in 1641. Because there is a fall of twenty feet in this short stretch of river, tremendous rapids were found by early explorers. Jesuit priests in 1641 gave the river the name of St. Mary in honor of an Indian mission by that name that they operated east of Georgian Bay. The Jesuits gave the name of Le Sault de Sainte Marie to this location meaning the falls (or rapids) of the St. Mary.

There are many things to see and do in the Canadian Soo. One interesting stop is at the Canadian Bush Plane Heritage Center, located at 50 Pim Street downtown on the river not far from the Bridge. Go to bushplane.com/ or call (877) 287-4752 for more information. They have many aircraft, flight simulators, and lots more artifacts and exhibits related to aviation history. If you have an extra day to spare, by all means check out the Agawa Canyon Wilderness Train. They offer wonderful day trips into the craggy wilderness north of the Soo. Highly recommended! Call them at 1-800-242-9287 for information or reservations. The Soo Museum on Queen Street has three floors of displays covering the history of the upper Great Lakes region and this part of Canada in particular. Finally, the Museum Ship *Norgoma*, a steamship that ran primarily between Owen Sound and the Soo, is berthed near the bush plane center and is another interesting sightseeing opportunity.

The International Bridge high above the St. Mary River carries travelers into Sault Ste. Marie Michigan, one of the oldest cities in America. The city was first established in 1668 when Father Marquette and others founded a mission here. French trappers, explorers, and missionaries had traveled through the area prior to this, but warring bands of Iroquois Indians from the east made any kind of settlement impossible. Even indigenous native tribes were forced out of what is now Michigan due to the Iroquois. In 1653 a series of major battles between Iroquois war parties and tribes from what is now Michigan and Wisconsin occurred. One of these battles is still remembered by the place name of Point Iroquois west of Sault Ste. Marie, Michigan. There is a lighthouse and an Indian mission cemetery at the spot today. By 1668 peace with the Iroquois was achieved and exploration of the Great Lakes region by French explorers began in earnest. Sault Ste Marie is either the second or third oldest city in the nation, depending on which reference resources are cited.

Like its twin city to the north, Sault Ste. Marie Michigan also has many attention-grabbing attractions. So give your bike a rest and let your feet do the walking for a bit. It is worth a few hours of your time to explore this unique city. Certainly watching the freighters going through the locks is a must for anyone visiting the Soo. Seeing these huge freighters just a few yards away is an amazing sight. The ultimate experience is to take a tour boat through the locks system. You can't get any closer to the workings of the locks than this. One of my most enduring and evocative memories of Upper Peninsula vacations both as a child and adult is the haunting sound of ship whistles and fog horns in the night while sleeping in a local motel or campground.

Because this region has such a long and varied history it should come as no surprise that there are several excellent museums that document and tell the story of the Soo area. The River of History Museum (531 Ashmun Street) is a great example. Its displays range from the immediate post-glacial period, through Native American eras, European explorers and settlers, and modern day. The Tower of History is another attraction worth some time. At 210 feet high it provides a great panorama of the entire area, as well as a museum of Native American and missionary artifacts. A tour of the museum ship Valley Camp, a 550-foot bulk freighter built in 1917 and retired in 1966, provides a unique opportunity to see the inner workings of a Great Lakes freighter. Its many artifacts and displays document Great Lakes maritime history and life on board freighters. Plan to spend a day at the Soo prior to departing on this tour. There is much to see and many fascinating blocks to walk. At the end of a fun day of sightseeing you will be hungry and thirsty, so plan on a stop at Antlers Tavern, close to the waterfront attractions. Their food and ambience are both memorable. But to be fair, there are many great places downtown at which to celebrate the end of a fun day with food and beverages.

Upon leaving the Soo to continue on the circle tour the official route has you take M-129 south from Sault Ste. Marie. For the most part this road follows the Prime Meridian, a straight surveying line the bisects Michigan from the Ohio border to the Canadian border. Naturally, that means that the road is straight. It's also quite flat, far from the water, not especially attractive, and not very entertaining for riders or drivers. Interesting sites along the eastern portion of the St. Mary River are missed by taking M-129. A better route is to take Portage Street, the main east/west street in Sault Ste. Marie, all the way east until you see signs for the Sugar Island Ferry, with Sugar Island just offshore. The road then turns south, becoming Riverview Road. It follows the shoreline for several miles, allowing great views of the river, islands, and freighter traffic. Unfortunately, even this county road runs inland for a bit, but it is much more enjoyable and scenic than the state highway.

Stay on Riverside Dr. for about thirteen miles to the four-corner town of Barbeau, which brings you to 15 Mile Road. If you wish at this intersection you can go east for three miles to the Village of Neebish, and then south along the shoreline to the Village of Munuscong on what appropriately enough is called Scenic Drive. Neebish Island is just across the channel. There is no outlet so you have to retrace your steps back to Barbeau but this scenic detour is well worth it.

Back in Barbeau continue south on Riverside Drive. After a couple of easy to follow jogs it finally ends at 22 Mile Road. At this point go west one mile, and then continue south again on Pennington Road for two miles where you hit Gogomain Road. Take Gogomain Road east about eleven miles and you're once again on the shores of the St. Mary River. The pavement curves south and becomes Raber Road. Gogomain/Raber is a good road to ride. There is little traffic and good scenery. Raber Road goes through the small village of Raber on the water, and then finally south to state highway M-48. Be careful in Raber as there is a deceptively tight curve coming out of town on which you can easily end up on the wrong side of the double yellow line.

We have no option but to take M-48 south for four miles to North Caribou Road. Turn east on North Caribou Rd and take it to the road's end in DeTour Village. This small waterfront town offers a ferry to nearby Drummond Island. There are interesting things to see on Drummond Island but some of the good sights really aren't accessible by touring or sport bikes. Serious adventure bikers or Jeep aficionados, with the right equipment, will have a ball on rural rocky roads in the eastern portion of the island.

Following the waterfront in DeTour brings you to State Route 134. While I try to stay off main roads M-134 is fine because it's a great riding road in its own right, and besides, there is no alternative. M-134 hugs the northern Lake Huron shore with the Les Cheneaux Islands (locally referred to as 'the snows') and endless blue water dotted with white sail boats on the left, and thick cedar forests on the right. The town of Cedarville is an especially nice stop along this expanse of blue water and is worthy of some time spent on the waterfront. Fans of antique boats will want to stop at the Les Cheneaux Maritime Museum, and also schedule the ride to catch the Antique Wooden Boat Show held on the Cedarville beachfront each year during the second week of August.

M-134 carries smiling riders west to Mackinaw Trail, which takes you south along the shoreline and through St. Ignace to the Mackinac Bridge. There really isn't much to see if one takes the I75 expressway from M-134 south to St. Ignace so I highly recommend taking the old road instead. Many people unfortunately never see downtown St. Ignace, located on the waterfront, because they blitz through this area on the expressway. Each year in late June St. Ignace hosts one of the largest classic and antique car shows in the Midwest. An antique tractor show is also on the yearly schedule with a parade of old tractors chugging across the Mighty Mac, making quite a sight!

St. Ignace shares honors with the Soo as one of the oldest cities in America. It too was founded by the same explorers and missionaries, though like the Soo, the landscape certainly wasn't vacant when the French arrived. Native Americans lived in the Straits region for millennia. They enjoyed an agrarian lifestyle and the local forests and waters provided whatever was needed in the way of meat and fish. French Jesuit missionaries named the location after St. Ignatius Loyola. While we don't often speak of French monarch Louis XIV and Michigan in the same breath, the king in fact administered this part of the world through representatives at Fort de Buade, located here. The Fort de Buade museum occupies the spot on BR75 in downtown St. Ignace where the original fort stood 300 years ago (334 N. State St.). Stop in to learn a bit about this regions fascinating Native American and European history.

Crossing the five-mile wide Straits of Mackinac on the Mackinac Bridge is a thrill in itself. Suspended high above the water with Lake Michigan on your right and Lake Huron to the east, the view is a montage of islands, lighthouses, working tugs, sailboats, Mackinac Island ferries with their proud rooster tail plumes of water, and freighters loaded with goods and raw materials coming and going on this water highway. Take your time and enjoy the few minutes you have to soak in this unique ride and splendid scene. Be aware that maintenance is never-ending on the bridge and that the outside paved lane is frequently closed due to maintenance trucks and workers. This means that a rider often has to cross the suspended portion of the bridge on the iron grid which comprises the interior two lanes of the four-lane bridge. The Mackinac Bridge Authority has employees who are licensed to drive bikes and cars across and transport the owners in a vehicle if a person is fearful of driving themselves. It's a free service. For a fee the Authority will trailer motorcycles across also.

Throughout the Lower Peninsula of Michigan it is easy to hug the shoreline of Lake Huron by following U.S.-23 from Mackinaw City all the way south to the town of Standish at the northwest corner of Saginaw Bay. This puts the traveler as close to the water as is possible without getting wet, and is an enjoyable and scenic ride. The list of attractions along this so-called sunrise shore of Michigan is too long to list. Lighthouses, museums, parks, beaches, scenic pullovers, monuments, huge limestone quarries, wildlife refuges, campgrounds, and many other points of interest and attractions await the curious rider. Don't be in too much of a hurry and be mentally prepared to stop frequently to smell the roses. As an interesting side note – Presque Isle and Alpena Counties, in the Rogers City and Alpena areas, are home to some of the largest limestone quarries in the world. For over a century this area has supplied quality limestone and calcite products for North America's steel, building, and concrete industries.

A few 'don't miss' attractions on this portion of the tour include a stop at the 40 Mile Point Lighthouse and museum, located seven miles north of Rogers City. The red brick house and white tower are a favorite subject for artists. On the beach nearby is the wood skeleton of the *Joseph S. Fay*, a ship that sank in 1905 during a fierce storm. Fifteen miles south of Rogers City are the Presque Isle lighthouses; one from 1840 and the 'new' one built in 1870. The 1870 light can be climbed and at 70-feet it is the highest on the Great Lakes that can be climbed to the light deck. These two structures are several miles east of US23. At the north end of Grand Lake (and it really is) take county road 638 east across the north tip of Grand Lake to the Lake Huron shoreline. It's definitely worth the short scenic drive. If a stop at these two lighthouses is made, Grand Lake Road can be taken when commencing the tour, following the east shore of Grand Lake south back to US23.

The Sturgeon Point Lighthouse and museum just north of Harrisville and the Tawas Point light at Tawas City are also worthy of a stop.

South of Harrisville and just north of Oscoda are signs for the Wurtsmith Air Museum. Wurtsmith was one of several sprawling Air Force bases located around the country during the height of the Cold War. The base was closed two decades ago but a group of volunteers is working hard to preserve its history and of military and civilian aviation and planes in general. There are many fascinating planes and other displays that make a stop well worth your time.

Tawas State Park at the twin cities of Tawas City and East Tawas is a great stop if the lighthouse and a walk on miles of sandy beach are on the agenda. It's one of the most popular parks in Michigan so if camping is on the list of things to do there be sure to make reservations. South of

Tawas City takes the traveler through an area where much gypsum mining took place for many decades. All that's left now is the name Alabaster and the long rail dock sticking out into Lake Huron that can be seen from the right vantage points.

In the town of Standish turn onto M-13 and take this south along Saginaw Bay to the small town of Kawkawlin and ultimately the large port town of Bay City. Traffic lets you know that you're not in the calm and quiet north anymore, but once through Bay City all is well again. Stay on M-13 as it becomes Huron Road just south of Kawkawlin and take it the four miles into downtown Bay City where M13 intersects with M25. Route M25 is our guide for the remainder of this tour.

In Bay City you have the opportunity to take a three-hour sailing trip on Saginaw Bay on one of two schooners (the *Appledore IV* and the *Appledore V*) operated by BaySail, located near Wenonah Park on the Saginaw River. Call 989.895.5193 or go to baysailbaycity.org for more information. Reservations are strongly recommended. The only surface warship that has been converted to a museum ship is berthed on the Saginaw River in Bay City. The *USS Edson 946* is part of the Saginaw Valley Naval Ship Museum. It's located a few blocks north of M-25. Hours are limited at the museum so call them at 989.684.3946 or go to their web site for specific tour times. The museum and ship are always open on summer weekends.

Following M-25 out of Bay City and heading east takes riders back up and around what Michigander's call "the Thumb" on the east side of Saginaw Bay and finally south again along the Lake Huron shore back to our starting point of Port Huron. "The Thumb" is a particularly unique Michigan colloquialism, used in normal daily conversation. The Lower Peninsula of Michigan looks remarkably like a person's hand, and the portion east of Saginaw Bay is the thumb. Remain on M-25 the entire way past Bay City except for any side trips you may wish to make following signs to lighthouses, parks, and other attractions.

Fortunately US23 and M-25 haven't been replaced by expressways and one can leisurely travel for an entire day with views of Lake Huron being a common treat. The east coast of Michigan is in general less developed and less hectic than the west side of the state.

On the Thumb portion of the route there is the opportunity to have a freshly caught fish sandwich at Bay Port, lay on the beach at Caseville or Port Austin, rent a kayak for a water excursion along the coast to see unique rock formations near Port Austin at the tip of the Thumb, see the old grindstones at Grindstone City, view lighthouses, take a charter boat fishing for Great Lakes salmon or Lake Trout, or just ride along and enjoy the scenery.

The aforementioned rock formations at Port Austin can be best seen from the water. The Port Austin Kayak Company rents kayaks and guides group tours along the shoreline to view Turnip Rock and other formations. The rock formations are on private property so there is no overland access. There is also a park and long pier at Port Austin that juts quite far out into the water, making for an enjoyable way to see the town and adjacent waters. Many different watercraft ply these waters during the warm months. The Port Austin Reef Light, located 2.5-miles offshore north of Port Austin, has helped keep boaters safe since 1878. This part of Michigan is an oft-overlooked portion of the state and it has much to offer the inquisitive traveler beyond just the ride and the scenery.

Continuing east on M-25 there are a couple of suggested stops – the Huron City Museum and the Port aux Barques Lighthouse. The Huron City Museum is actually a small village with several structures dating back to the late 1800s, including a small log cabin in which a large family lived! The lighthouse gets its title from the point of land named by early French explorers because they thought that the stone formations along the shore resembled boats at anchor when viewed from a distance. Lake Huron in this vicinity is a treacherous place, with at least 105 known shipwrecks in the immediate offshore area. Watch for signs for the Lighthouse County Park about six miles north of Port Hope, as you begin the southward portion of the trip along the lakeshore. The light is open every day during the summer.

We continue the tour following M-25 south through a landscape of fields, woods, and small towns, with the lake always not far to the left. The towns passed through offer one of a kind opportunities in the form of homemade food at local restaurants and plenty of small motels, Bed and Breakfast lodgings, or campgrounds. Most towns and villages have local museums that tell the history of the region, including massive forest fires that swept across the Thumb in 1871 and again in 1881, destroying entire towns and killing an unknown number of people.

Ultimately we arrive back in Port Huron and the conclusion of this marvelous several day motor voyage around a great lake.

I noted at the beginning of this chapter that a person can choose to go completely around the lake and Georgian Bay, rather than cutting across the lake via the Bruce Peninsula and Manitoulin Island. If you choose Option B and wish to long way simply stay on Ontario Route 21 and don't take the turn onto Bruce Peninsula at Owen Sound. Route 21 turns into Ontario Route 26 and continue east to Barrie. Ontario Route 400 is an expressway that takes you north from Barrie to Parry Sound, where the expressway ends and you continue north on Ontario Route 69 to Sudbury.

Sudbury is a mid-sized industrial and mining town, a bit larger than the Canadian Soo, and while there you'll want to explore the local nickel mining industry and visit the large Science North Museum. Going west out of Sudbury on Trans-Canada Highway 17 takes you back to Sault Ste. Marie. Unfortunately the route around Georgian Bay is for the most part inland far enough so that side trips are necessary to see the lake.

So there you have it, a fabulous trip of almost exactly 1,000 miles (add about 150 miles if going around Georgian Bay). A person truly can experience some of the most fascinating scenic and geologic wonders of the northern Midwest along these roads as they traverse regions of forests, waterfalls, and stone. But the traveler also experiences the reality of centuries-old history, places, and purpose-built structures that remind them that though they are many hundreds of miles from the ocean, there is no doubt that they're in the heart of a nautical wonderland with a long and intriguing political and maritime history.

3. The Lake Michigan Circle Tour

IF THE IDEA of taking a drive around the largest lake in the country was brought up in conversation a person could be forgiven if their first thoughts were Lake Tahoe, Great Salt Lake, Lake Okeechobee or another large lake in the U.S. They perhaps wouldn't think of one of the Great Lakes. They're so large that we often don't think of them in the same way we think of 'normal' lakes, and some folks might think that all five of the Great Lakes are politically divided between the U.S. and Canada. But Lake Michigan is the exception. It is the only one situated completely within the U.S. This means that it is the largest lake in the country. It's also distinctive because of the vast difference between the lightly developed northern lake and the heavily industrialized and populated southern portion. Almost all of the 12-milllion people who live in the lake's watershed live in the south half. Interestingly, Lake Michigan itself also differs from south to north. There are two distinct basins in the lake, called the North and South Chippewa Basins, separated by an underwater plateau that runs east and west across the lake roughly between Milwaukee and Muskegon. These basins affect the lake in several ways, including depth, water temperature, and biology. Lake Michigan is the third largest of the Great Lakes at 22,394 square miles. It takes almost exactly one hundred years for a gallon of water entering the lake at the south end to finally make its way through the Straits of Mackinac to begin another twenty-two-year retention period in Lake Huron. This long holding period is but one reason why it is so critical to protect these freshwater seas from pollution.

The greater Chicago urban area makes a trip around Lake Michigan a difficult and even hazardous undertaking. One must either skirt around Chicago and never see the lake or go through many miles of heavy urban congestion in order to stay somewhat near the water.

But there is another option: take a ferry across the lake. This adds a special flavor to the trip, as well as allowing one to avoid the Chicago and Gary Indiana megalopolis. There are two quite different ferry options to choose between depending on route and destination choices, and personal preferences. Cutting across the vastness of Lake Michigan on either ferry is an enjoyable and eye-opening experience in itself. The boat ride truly does add another element to a motorcycle trip. Keep in mind that it is necessary to securely tie motorcycles down on both ferries, and that it's advisable to bring your own tie-down straps as the ferries have only a limited supply.

The *SS Badger* is a 410-foot coal burning steamship and is the only one like it in America. This tried and true ship has been ferrying people and vehicles since 1953. It was originally built to transport rail cars and train passengers across the stormy waters of Lake Michigan on a year-round basis. The rail portion of their business ended in the 1980s and since 1992 the ship has been rededicated as a ferry for motor vehicles and passengers. It sails between Ludington, MI, and Manitowoc, WI. The *Badger* is a large but at 15-knots still a relative fast ferry and has a cruise ship feel, including staterooms and on-ship amenities. It takes about four hours to complete the 60-mile trip. Call 800.841.4243 or surf over to ss-badger.com for schedules and reservations. To get to their docks, in Ludington take US10 to James Street on the east side of downtown. James Street takes you south to the port. In Manitowoc follow W42 south to 10th Street, a one-way street going south. Take 10th Street south to Madison Street then east a short distance to the docks.

The second ferry is the *Lake Express*, which sails between Muskegon and Milwaukee. This service started operations in 2004 and takes a different approach to crossing the lake. Four Detroit Diesel engines, each cranking out 3,000 horsepower, move this 192-foot vessel across the lake in two-and-a-half hours. It's designed to skim across the surface rather than plow through the water. Because of its smaller size the *Lake Express* offers fewer amenities and creature comforts. Riding on the upper deck and feeling the wind and spray of the water as the boat slices through the waves is quite an adventure in itself. A noteworthy point about this ferry is its special relationship with motorcyclists. During several weeks in the spring and fall there is no charge for motorcycles, only the passenger fee (and the surcharge fees for fuel, docking and security). Call 866-914-1010 or go to lake-express.com for reservations or sailing times.

The *Lake Express* dock is located on the south shore of Muskegon Lake, at 1918 Lakeshore Drive, at the Great Lakes Marina. In Milwaukee it's at the Port of Milwaukee, 2330 South Lincoln Memorial Drive. Get off at exit 3 of the I-794 expressway, or follow Lincoln Memorial Drive south along the shoreline.

This tour is based on starting the ride in Muskegon, and assumes a Muskegon-Milwaukee crossing. This doesn't reflect a recommendation of one ferry over the other, but simply because it provides the greatest amount of road information. If one takes *SS Badger* ferry then road data south of Ludington and south of Manitowoc is of course irrelevant.

As with the other Great Lakes circle tours, I also avoid the official route as much as possible to get off major highways and expressways, and onto lakeshore roads. The ride is almost 900-miles on land if the Milwaukee / Muskegon ferry is utilized. Add nearly 300 more miles if the entire loop is done via lakeside roads. The complete circle tour via pavement is about 1,150 miles.

Begin this counter-clockwise ride in Muskegon, a fairly large old industrial town which in recent years has taken great pains to change its image as obsolete chemical and manufacturing plants have closed, or been replaced with new and cleaner and more attractive operations. Start on the southwest shore of Muskegon Lake near the shipping channel into Lake Michigan. Pere Marquette Park, at the point where the channel empties into the big lake is a nice place to view boating traffic and get the first good look of this freshwater sea.

If you have interest in World War II fighting ships then a stop at the Great Lakes Naval Memorial & Museum in the shipping channel is a must. It is the home to *USS Silversides*, a WWII Pacific Theater submarine. A tour onboard the submarine is a fascinating and humbling experience. On Lakeshore Drive just east of the submarine is the *SS Milwaukee Clipper*. It's the oldest passenger ship on the Great Lakes and a Historical National Landmark. Tours explore all parts of the ship.

Follow Lakeshore Avenue to the east end of Muskegon Lake, and turn north onto Business-31 to see another rare vintage naval vessel. LST (Landing Ship Tank) 393 is both a museum ship and a veterans' museum. LSTs played a major role in moving assault vehicles and troops across the oceans and in amphibious combat during World War Two. They were referred to as Large Slow Targets by the crewmen who manned them. After the war a few survived the scrap mill to serve in Vietnam before they were officially retired. Few remain today. LST393 carried tanks and troops into battle on Omaha Beach on D-Day. Almost straight across Business US31 from LST393 is the Fire Barn Museum with antique firefighting equipment including a 1923 LaFrance Pumper.

Continue north on Business 31 a short distance to M-120, Whitehall Road, and cross the river channel. You soon see Ruddiman Road. Turn left onto Ruddiman, which soon turns into Memorial Drive. This lakeshore route goes west along the north shore of Muskegon Lake. Memorial Drive terminates within the boundaries of Muskegon State Park and at this point turn north on Scenic Drive, which runs along the Lake Michigan coast for roughly the next eight miles. This is a very nice stretch of road along which one gets their first impressions of the sand dune geology of the east shore of Lake Michigan, and of the unique agricultural niche that the maritime climate creates.

The Lake Michigan coast is lined with what are technically called drowned river mouths. These are lakes that formed when a river has been 'impounded' by the rebounding of the earth's crust following retreat of the last glacier that covered this area with a few thousand feet of ice, and sand dunes at the shoreline, creating a lake with a narrow opening or channel at the point where it empties into Lake Michigan. Most of these drowned river mouth lakes don't have bridges across them at their channels resulting in the need to skirt around them by going inland. This is not only the case with Muskegon Lake, but with White Lake, located eight miles north, and several others up the line.

Scenic Drive becomes Shore Drive as it skirts White Lake on the south shore. Before turning right at this point, however, I suggest you continue north a short distance to the mouth of the White River and the White River Lighthouse and Museum. This short section of road ends at a parking lot for the lighthouse. When done with this visit ride east along the south shore of White Lake to Business Route 31.

Cross the White River on BR-31 into Montague. Notice the impressive sail boat weather vane sculpture in the small downtown park. It's the largest weathervane in the world. Make a west turn again right after the bridge on Old Channel Trail which follows the north shore of White Lake and delivers you back to the Lake Michigan shore. The shoreline road makes an east, and then a west, jog as it continues north into Oceana County, becoming 48nd Avenue. At this point you're about a mile inland, but one-and-a-half miles into Oceana County a left turn puts you back on Scenic Drive and more coastline travel. No turns are involved, but Scenic Drive becomes 16th Avenue on its way north. At Buchanan Road our road takes a half-mile jog east then continues north until it Ts at Silver Lake Road, also called Lighthouse Road heading west to the Lake Michigan shore. I recommend taking this short ride out to Lake Michigan to see Little Sable Point Lighthouse. This light reaches over one-hundred feet high and makes a pretty picture as it stands alone surrounded by sand dunes on one side and the blue water of Lake Michigan on the other. As is often the case it's easier to ride these roads than it is to describe them in print. The primary pavement route is usually obvious and these are the gray roads depicted on maps that motorcyclists so envy.

Riding east on Silver Lake Road delivers you to Silver Lake State Park and the famous Silver Lake sand dunes. This park has a wonderful beach of unlimited sand, and several dune buggy concessionaires are more than happy take you for memorable rides on the dunes in their specially modified buggies. The Silver Lake area is a popular summer vacation destination. You'll either love it or want to leave it as quickly as possible. It is a beehive of activity. A word of caution; windblown sand frequently covers the roads in this vicinity making them potentially hazardous for riding.

Drive around Silver Lake to its east shore then head north again, first on Shore Drive for a short distance then onto Ridge Road. Ridge Road closely follows the Lake Michigan shore heading north. The circumnavigation process has to be repeated again several miles up the road to get around Pentwater Lake. This time BR-31 is the road we take back west once beyond Pentwater Lake. As BR-31 makes its way back east toward the expressway you'll see Lakeshore Road heading north on a narrow strip of land squeezed between Bass Lake on the east and Lake Michigan on the west. Take Lakeshore Road north about eight miles to Iris Road which we must take east to get around Pere Marquette Lake – yet one more drowned river mouth – this time for the Pere Marquette River.

Before turning east on Iris Road to Old 31 I recommend you head north on Lakeshore Drive to view two worthwhile sites. First, you'll ride by a memorial to Father Jacques Marquette, 17th century French missionary who (some claim) died near this location in 1675. Further north on this dead end spur is White Pine Village, an entire reconstructed community of old buildings that recreate Ludington's past. It's a 'living' interpretive village museum that has thousands of fascinating displays and artifacts.

About halfway between Bass Lake and Pere Marquette Lake you'll pass the giant Consumers Energy Company pumped storage facility perched on the hillside to the east. This is an electrical power generating plant using water from Lake Michigan pumped uphill to the lake-sized pond during low energy demand periods, and then released through tubes that feed waterpower to generators to create energy during high-energy demand periods.

Upon reaching Old US31 take it north two miles to the intersection with US10. I recommend taking US10 west at this point to Lake Michigan, and then turning north on M116. State route 116 is a dead end road that goes out to Ludington State Park. The Park itself isn't the destination here as much as the ride out there along the lakeshore. It's a great place to stop and enjoy the shoreline and scenery.

If you just want to continue north and not take the M116 side trip, then just ignore the previous paragraph. But I encourage folks to go into downtown Ludington and the lakeshore area. There is much to see and do in this old and enjoyable lumber town turned resort and vacation town.

When ready to resume the tour go east on US-10 two miles to Stiles Road. A left turn resumes the north bound ride. After one small easterly jog at Townline Road, the south Manistee County line, Stiles Road turns into Maple Road in Manistee County and it takes you north all the way to the city of Manistee and US-31.

Manistee is one of many towns around Lake Michigan that have an interesting history. Like most towns in this area it started out as a lumbering port city, from which White Pine lumber left Michigan bound for Chicago and other burgeoning Midwest markets. Underground brine deposits also caught the attention of chemical companies well over a century ago. The Manistee County Historical Museum tells the stories of the people and events of this region. It's located in an old store in downtown Manistee. Just north of town on US31, on the northwest corner of Manistee Lake (yes, another drowned river mouth) you'll find the *SS City of Milwaukee*, a museum ship, and the Coast Guard Cutter *Acacia*. The *City of Milwaukee* is particularly impressive. This ship was able to carry an entire freight train across Lake Michigan, and its icebreaker hull meant it could cross the lake in the worst winter conditions.

Just north of the museum ship Old M-110 veers to the left from US31, going straight north along the shoreline. I suggest taking this old road along this scenic stretch and it eventually swings easterly to get around Portage Lake. This allows you to avoid the congestion near the casino just north of Manistee on US-31. Our old road connects with M22, a pleasingly scenic and fun riding road that is our riding companion for many miles, taking us to the tip of the Leelanau Peninsula and to Traverse City where we finally leave it behind.

M22 between Portage Lake and Traverse City is a wonderful mix of hills, curves, farms and forests, and perhaps most of all, great scenery. It's a destination road for Midwestern motorcyclists. There are many things to stop and see along the way. North of Frankfort is Point Betsie Lighthouse, a short ride west of M22. Further north, just south of Empire, take Wilco Road to the Empire Bluffs Trail. This 1.5-mile round trip walk delivers you to high dunes that overlook Lake Michigan and offer a stunning vista of forested hills and endless blue water, with the Sleeping Bear Sand Dunes to the north. I visited this site again in 2018 and happened to be standing near a family quite clearly from the Asian subcontinent – either Indian or Pakistani based on accent and appearance. The family was in awe at the vast expanse of freshwater and the father reverently said "And they call this a lake!" May we all have the same reverence and respect for this marvelous treasure.

Stop at the Sleeping Bear Dunes National Lakeshore headquarters at the intersection of M22 and M-72 to learn more about this marvelous park. Just north of Empire we temporarily leave M22 for an even more enjoyable ride. Turn left onto M-109 and follow it north into the heart of National Lakeshore. After just over a mile you'll arrive at Pierce Stocking Drive, a fun one-way circular scenic byway through the park and to the top of the dunes. There is an entry fee for this drive. Do the dune climb if you dare, but let good judgment guide you; remember, you have to climb all the way back up the dune once you reach the water. The Sleeping Bear Dunes Park is truly a magnificent place. Natural beauty of a most unique type abounds here like nowhere else.

Continue north on M-109 and it eventually circles back to rejoin M22 after passing through additional points of interest. As you cruise M22 north in the Leelanau Peninsula you'll encounter wonderful small towns like Leland and Northport. I encourage you to park your bike and explore these towns, especially Leland, on foot. You'll pass lighthouses and wineries, grand overlooks and historic sites, and all the time riding with an appreciative smile.

In Northport M22 circles back south, but we want to continue north out to Lighthouse Point and historic Grand Traverse Lighthouse. To get there go north from Northport on M-201 which soon morphs into county route 629, which delivers you to land's end. Lighthouse Point is a beautiful locale and exploring the 1850 lighthouse and keeper's cabin is icing on the cake.

After Northport, M22 takes one south along the east side of the Leelanau Peninsula, and along the west coast of Grand Traverse Bay. A half-mile north of M72, just prior to entering Traverse City, is a business called Traverse Tall Ship Company on the water's edge. They have a large sailing vessel, the tall ship *Manitou*, on which one can sail Grand Traverse Bay. At 114 feet in length, *Manitou* is one of the largest sailing vessels on the Great Lakes. Sailing on this ship is an enjoyable diversion from everyday life, I've done both one day and four day trips. Sit back and watch the crew work the sails, or help with the cranking and lifting if you wish, either is okay, and enjoy the scenery and the sound the wind. They offer afternoon and evening dinner sails, as well as the 4-day excursions. Call (231) 941-2000 for more information.

Even the best roads come to an end, including M22. When it does we'll be in the heart of Traverse City eastbound on M72 / US31, which runs east and west along the south shore of Grand Traverse Bay. There are plenty of places to park along here, and a large waterfront park offers great access to the water. Downtown Traverse City, another major Midwestern destination, is just one block to the south of the waterfront. I recommend parking your bike and exploring the restaurants and shops of the town that Michiganders refer to simply as TC.

Follow US31 through town and take it up the east side of Grand Traverse Bay. Just northeast of Traverse City near the town of Acme is the Music House. If you're into music, especially automated musical instruments, consider stopping here. Plan on over an hour for the guided tour and demonstrations. The museum has one of the world's largest collections of rare and historic automated instruments.

Like M22, US31 transports riders through scenic countryside and along the lakeshore for many miles. The road isn't technical in any sense but it's an enjoyable ride through picturesque orchard country with the occasional coastal town. It's also a region blessed by the microclimate created by the presence of Lake Michigan's on-shore winds and warmth, and as a result is a major producer of apples, cherries, and grapes for wine. There are many roadside stands where fresh fruit and refreshments are available. The upcoming stretch of coastline; Elk Rapids, Charlevoix, Petoskey, and Harbor Springs, is a fairly upscale area with old vacation destinations and resort towns that have served many generations of families. It's a land of well-kept houses, small towns with flower-lined streets, and lots of history. You might call it Michigan's Gold Coast. It is iconic author Ernest Hemingway's youthful stomping grounds, vacationing with his family on Walloon Lake near Petoskey and getting married for the first time in nearby Horton Bay. There's a small Hemingway museum display at the Little Traverse History Museum Center, located in an old railroad depot in Petoskey on the waterfront. If you are a serious Hemingway fan, or you simply love home cooked food and wonderful home baked pies, stop at Jesperson's Restaurant at 312 Howard Street in downtown. Hemingway and the owner of Jesperson's were close friends and he frequently ate there while living in Petoskey for six months recuperating from World War One wounds. A plaque on the building commemorates his relationship with owner Yorgen Jesperson.

While in Petoskey I also suggest stopping at Sunset Park, just north of downtown. Park either at the bottom of the stone cliff along the lakeshore, or atop the bluff for an elevated view of Little Traverse Bay. And keep in mind, it's called Sunset Park for a reason. In the evening it offers a spectacular sunset view. Continue northbound on US31 to the east side of Petoskey where a left turn onto M119 takes us to the next excellent part of this journey.

M119 is an average motorcycle road for the first few miles. First you have to get through the upscale town of Harbor Springs, another unique northern Michigan municipality where you may want to park and walk around. Once beyond Harbor Springs M119 gets progressively better, until it turns into the "Tunnel of Trees", as it is called. M119 is one of few state highways where special rules apply. There is no shoulder and the trees are literally on the edge of the pavement. There is also a severe shortage of straight sections. Many of the curves are tight, so even though it is tempting to go fast try to show some semblance of restraint and keep your speeds reasonable for the road you're on. M119 runs along the crest of a high bluff overlooking Lake Michigan. Unfortunately the land all along it is private, with many drives heading down the bluff to palatial second homes. M119 is a blast to ride, which of course means that bikers have a lot of company. On any warm day the road sees numerous motorcyclists, bicyclists, sport car enthusiasts, walkers, and of course minivans full of kids. Enjoy the ride but know that it is Michigan's version of The Dragon, unfortunately located in a popular tourist area. The Tunnel of Trees is a motorcycle destination road for the Midwest.

The state highway ends in Cross Village, another suggested stopping place. The attraction here is iconic Legs Inn Restaurant. Legs Inn is one of those places that a person has to see for themselves. I guarantee that whether you go in the restaurant to check out the unusual ambience or the great food you won't be disappointed. The parking area along the street is often packed on summer weekends so plan on a wait if eating lunch or dinner is your goal. Fortunately, a stroll on their property behind the restaurant building provides a place to relax and enjoy the magnificent view while waiting for a seat.

Though M119 ends in Cross Village our lakeshore route continues north several more miles. Continue following Lakeview Drive north following the pavement tight along the coast until it finally gives up and curves inland heading east. Stay on the easterly pavement and it becomes County Road 81 that after going east for several miles turns and goes straight north to the shoreline and Wilderness Park Drive. Turn right on Wilderness Park Drive and follow it into Mackinaw City and the Mackinac Bridge. Just west of Mackinaw City on our road one sees signs for McGulpin Point lighthouse, which is another of the 124 lighthouses that Michigan calls its own. This is more than any other state.

Common questions that tourists ask in the Mackinac Straits area include: Why is the word Mackinac spelled two ways, and what or who the heck is a Mackinac anyway?

As is common in Michigan the word has its origins in Native American language. Mackinac is a French derivation of michilimackinac which itself is a shortened version of the Ojibwa word "missilimaahkinaank" which means "at the territory of the mishinimaki," which was an Indian tribe that lived in the straits area long ago. The traditional spelling was Mackinac, but the British anglicized it to Mackinaw when they occupied the area following their victory in the French and Indian War and the 1763 treaty that ended the war.

Mackinaw City is another ideal place to park yet again and walk. You won't be the only biker there. It's a favorite gathering place for motorcyclists, and you'll see quite a selection of machines parked in the lot that runs the length of downtown. Relax, eat some fudge, and watch the other people who are trying to figure out which T-shirt or tourist knick-knacks to spend their money on. Fort Michilimackinac and the old Mackinac Point Light are favorite sites to explore. Old Mackinac Point Light in particular is a great spot to sit in the shade near this marvelous old structure, watch the boating activity on the Straits and be amazed at the size and beauty of The

Bridge. If possible, take a day trip over to Mackinac Island to truly explore and appreciate the long and unique history of the Straits area. Ferries to the island operate from both Mackinaw City and St. Ignace.

After downing your last bite of fudge it's time to head across the Mackinac Bridge. If you've never been across it before you're in for a real treat. I've ridden across dozens of times and it is still a thrill each time. The view from the top of this five-mile long suspension bridge is incredible. Water horizons stretch forever to the east and west, freighters are making their way through the center channel of the straits, and smaller boats leave their white wakes in the dark blue water nearly two hundred feet below. Riding on the inside lane of the suspension portion of the bridge, where an iron grid rather than concrete forms the roadway, is an extra source of excitement as one can look down through the grid while riding across and see the water below. If this isn't your idea of fun, the outside lanes in each direction are paved and solid. Be aware, however, that since maintenance and painting are a never-ending activity on the bridge, quite frequently the outer concrete travel lane is blocked by maintenance vehicles. Probably one half of the times I have crossed the bridge I have had to use the interior iron grid lane. The Mackinac Bridge Authority will transport nervous riders or drivers across at no cost.

The city of St. Ignace anchors the north end of the Mackinac Bridge and is the primary gateway from the Lower Peninsula to the Upper. There are some well-established colloquialisms encountered when making the passage across this bridge. The Upper Peninsula (UP) is the home of the Yoopers and the Lower Peninsula is home to the Trolls (beneath the bridge). Michiganders have had fun for many years with the cultural differences between the two peninsulas that make up the state. So if you hear a local refer to you or your riding group as flatlanders, trolls or fudgies, don't take offense.

Established in 1671, St. Ignace is either the third or fourth oldest city in the country. Not all references are in agreement. Regardless, it is an area with a tremendous amount of history going back well over 300 years. To appreciate this unique past a bit more, plan to spend some time there.

Begin this exploration by turning east onto business route 75 / State Street to go into the downtown portion of the town. Many people miss the main part of town because they immediately head west onto route US2 at the interchange just north of the bridge.

St. Ignace is situated along the waterfront and provides the setting for an enjoyable stroll. Walk along the water's edge on the boardwalk or follow the sidewalk on the west side of the street to take advantage of shops and restaurants. One recommended stop is the Fort de Buade

Museum, located at 334 N. State Street, in town. This museum tells the story of the area from the perspective of the early French explorers and the Native Americans they found living in the Straits area. The museum is at the location of a fort manned by the French from 1683 – 1701.

When ready to resume the journey west ride back across I-75 and set your sights on Escanaba, about 150 miles over the western horizon. Just west of the expressway is a road that leads south to the Father Marquette Memorial. South of this small memorial the road continues to the lakeshore and one of the most popular parking areas for an impressive view of The Bridge.

When ready, turn west onto US2 and let the fun begin. US2 is an interstate highway with a long history. With the exception of upstate New York, it travels across the northern tier of states from the Maine border with New Brunswick to Seattle, Washington. This highway not only gives travelers who prefer two lanes over expressways an up-close view of the northern USA, it is also an enjoyable riding road across the breadth of the country. During the Named Highway period, roughly from 1915 to 1925, this road was part of the Theodore Roosevelt International Highway. It was international because part of the route went through Ontario and Quebec. Interestingly, there is a gap in U.S.-2 today between New York and Michigan just as there was in the TR Highway a century ago.

US2 from St. Ignace west to Naubinway is fun and impressive. In many areas the pavement is just yards away from the shoreline with continuous imposing vistas of Lake Michigan. Scenic pullouts are commonplace and I certainly urge a driver or rider to take advantage of them. A few miles west of St. Ignace the road runs literally on the shoreline. While this presents fabulous views of the lake (and crashing waves on windy days) it creates some unique potential problems. Many cars park along the beach to swim or sun bathe, causing congestion and pedestrian issues. Also, if it's windy sand blowing across the road can create potentially dangerous conditions for motorcyclists.

The state and federal highway departments have upgraded the highway to make it safer without turning it into a soulless superslab. Passing lanes and center turn lanes have been strategically placed along its entire UP length creating a safe and efficient means of moving traffic. Because it is a primary northern USA transcontinental highway there is a fair amount of truck traffic, including large logging trucks as well as more typical commercial vehicles. In the dozens of times I've ridden across US2, however, I can say that truck traffic has seldom been a problem. They travel at the speed limit or above and frequent passing lanes allow the ability to get around trucks or RVs when desired. The portion of US2 west of St. Ignace is a gem and it's best experienced on two wheels.

Proceeding west, there are two attractions near Naubinway. Six miles east of town check out the Garlyn Zoo. It's a marvelous stop with many native and exotic animals. In Naubinway take time to visit the Top of the Lake Snowmobile Museum. This unique attraction tells the story of snowmobiling and has numerous antique and vintage snowmobiles. The museum is open year-round and is located right on US2. They have been so successful that the museum was recently expanded to include a library and media room, as well as space to display 33 rare snow machines given to the museum by the Bombardier Museum in Quebec.

After Naubinway the highway turns inland and doesn't touch the shore again until Manistique. About 12 miles after crossing the Schoolcraft County line the small village of Gulliver awaits. There is a large Sunoco station located at the main intersection with a flashing caution light to catch your attention. If a person is on a bike that can handle some hard-packed gravel and enjoys exploring and climbing lighthouses a southerly turn at that intersection delivers them ultimately to the Seul Choix Point Lighthouse.

This light, pronounced sis-shwa by the natives, is 80-feet tall and visitors can climb to the top via 96 steps. The navigational aid was con-structed in 1895 and is still in operation. It is unusual for visitors to be able to climb a still-functional light. The view from the top is of course spectacular. The lighthouse keeper's living quarters has been restored to the early 1900s period and also serves as a museum. An adjacent boat house museum has artifacts and displays that tell the story of the shipping and fishing history connected with this strategic locale.

The first half of the roughly seven mile trip to the lighthouse is on County Road 432, which is paved. The second half is on CR 431, which is hard packed stone – smooth and trouble free when dry but not quite as user friendly when wet. This is limestone country, and two large limestone quarries, and a shipping port are on CR 432 east of the lighthouse.

Beyond M77 our road angles southwest back toward Lake Michigan and the town of Manistique, an important commercial and tourism center at the mouth of the Manistique River. On the east side of town the high-way runs along the lake's edge and a parking area provides a good spot to check out the shoreline – which is much rockier here than further east.

A boardwalk provides a convenient and scenic walk along the Lake Michigan shoreline. When entering the town a brick tower to the right catches your attention. This structure is the old water tower. It was built in 1922 and its 200-foot height makes it the tallest structure around. It is octagon shaped in the Roman architectural style. It is now part of the Schoolcraft County Historic Park. For music lovers, Manistique offers visitors the annual Folk Festival on the second Saturday of July each year. The cultural event includes music, crafts, food, and much more.

Six miles west of Manistique is M149, a short highway going north to Palms Book State Park and the Big Spring, the largest spring in Michigan at 200 feet wide and 40 feet deep. Visitors can go out on the small pond created by the spring on a glass bottomed raft to observe crystal clear water streaming out of fissures in the underlying limestone at the rate of 10,000 gallons per minute.

About 10 miles farther west and about 120 miles west of St. Ignace is state highway 183, going south into what's called the Garden Peninsula. This large peninsula juts south into Lake Michigan to nearly meet Wisconsin's Door Peninsula. The two peninsulas form Green Bay to the west. The Garden is off the beaten path, but is a recommended destination. The primary attraction is the restored ghost town of Fayette and Fayette State Park. From 1867 to 1891 Fayette was a company town and was one of the state's largest iron-smelting operations. Large limestone bluffs line the lake in this vicinity, and the limestone was used in the iron ore process. The town site, furnaces, and charcoal kilns have all been restored by the state. The scenic beauty is also outstanding and excellent camping opportunities are available in the park. On limestone cliffs near Fayette, known as Burnt Bluffs, the Indian cliff paintings found there are estimated to be 1,500 years old.

Resuming our westward trip along US2, about three miles past the tiny town of Ensign, CR513 heads south on the Stonington Peninsula to Stonington Point and its lighthouse. This is a pleasant side trip to take, especially if you're into lighthouses. Be aware that the last couple miles can be a bit rough following heavy rain. The majority of the road south to the point is lightly traveled pavement.

Stonington Peninsula separates Big and Little Bays de Noc. These bays are named after the Nokay (Noquet in French) Indian tribe that lived in the area many years ago. The bays are famous for fishing, especially walleye.

On the west side of Little Bay De Noc, US2 swings south along the shore through Escanaba. Escanaba had once been a major iron ore port, where ore from the nearby mines was shipped to various mills around the Great Lakes. It is now a major port for recreational boating and fishing. It's a fun place to take a break for some exploring. The town hosts a large antique car show called Krusin'Klassics each year just after Memorial Day. This worthwhile event includes cruises, car shows, tractor pulls, food, dancing, and in general a good time for young and old. Escanaba is also the home of the large UP Steam and Gas Engine Show, held each summer in late August.

Beautiful Ludington Park is on the waterfront. Within the boundary of the park is the Sand Point Lighthouse, open Memorial Day to Labor Day for tours. It was constructed in 1867 when shipping of iron ore, copper, and lumber made this city a busy port. Behind the lighthouse if the Delta County Historical Museum. In the downtown section is one of the most famous buildings in the region, the House of Ludington Hotel. This iconic structure, built in 1864, was the home of lumberman Nelson Ludington.

We leave US2 in Escanaba as it continues its westward journey to the State of Washington, and we head south on M35 to Menominee. M35 is about as close to the water's edge all the way between Escanaba and Menominee as you can get without benefit of an off-road vehicle. This stretch of highway is flat coastal plain and runs through a mix of low-lying cedar forest and occasional farms and resort areas. It's a relaxing unchallenging section of roadway that makes for a fun ride all the way to Menominee, at the mouth of the Menominee River, which forms the Michigan / Wisconsin border.

There was a Native American tribe in Lake Michigan's Green Bay area called the Menomini by neighboring tribes. The name is apparently a derivation of the Algonquin word for wild rice, which was a staple of the diet for Indians in that region. Prior to settlement there was a large marsh where wild rice was abundant at the mouth of the Menominee River.

US41 joins M35 just north of Menominee and it carries traffic across the boundary river into Marinette, Wisconsin. Lakeside travel gets a little trickier in Wisconsin because there isn't one road such as US2 or M35 that provides a water side route. A person must either take one of the major roads and stay away from the water, or when possible take the various county roads that do get a person off the major highways but unfortunately it means extreme focus on navigation if county roads are to be used extensively because they're intermittent. So we'll hit a happy middle ground and use more state and federal roads than usual but still use waterside county roads when it's safe and practical. In Marinette stay on US41 as it heads southwest to the town of Peshtigo.

While almost everyone has heard of the famous Chicago fire of October 8, 1871 fewer people have heard of the much more disastrous fires that struck Wisconsin and Michigan on the same day. Peshtigo was caught in the middle of the worst recorded forest fire in North American history. The fire burned a huge tract of Wisconsin and the Upper Peninsula of Michigan, killing between 1,200 and 2,400 people in its path. Due to the near wilderness nature of the area at that time, and the lack of communication systems and roads, the true number of victims was never determined, but entire communities were wiped out as well as many isolated cabins and farmsteads. While the Chicago fire became part of our country's history and lore, this much worse fire has largely faded from our collective memory. The Peshtigo Fire Museum located at 400 Oconto

Avenue in Peshtigo is an interesting and recommended stop. For more information go to peshtigofiremuseum.org/ or call them at (715) 582-3244.

From Peshtigo to Green Bay the county road system unfortunately becomes difficult to follow, to the extent that trying to maintain a waterfront route requires so much confusing detail so as to make it impractical. In this stretch the option is US41. The riding is easy and relaxing if not exhilarating. Oconto is the next town encountered. Located on the Oconto River, the town's history goes back to French missionary days but the commercial heyday for this locale was based on lumbering and commercial fishing. The town today caters to recreational boaters rather than the cargo carriers of a century ago, and weekend fishing boats fill the docks rather than commercial tugs. You might want to follow Business Route 41 into town to check out two interesting sites – the Beyer Home and Carriage Museum (with antique cars) and the Copper Culture Museum. The Copper Culture site contains artifacts documenting the ancient history and peoples of the region and is an ideal spot to stop for a nice walk and outdoor lunch on the river trail. And entry is free though of course donations are gladly accepted to cover costs.

It's no coincidence that almost every town of any size around Lake Michigan is located at the mouth of a river. Water transportation was critical in the early days of settlement and those same rivers floated logs down to sawmills located at river mouths where cut lumber could be loaded onto vessels. These same towns also supported a commercial fishing economy until the 1950s when invasive species such as the Sea Lamprey decimated native fish populations.

US41 joins forces with US141 for about seventeen miles to the northern suburbs of the City of Green Bay, at which point we get on the I-43 expressway to get across town and over the Fox River. There are of course several places to visit and things to do in this large city so do a little homework prior to arrival. Lambeau Field and associated Hall of Fame and Museum are obviously a favorite stop for football fans, but the nearby National Railroad Museum is also an interesting attraction for lovers of antique railroading paraphernalia.

On the east side of town head north along the east shore of Lake Michigan's Green Bay on the Door Peninsula by exiting I-43 onto Wisconsin Route 57. Route 57, aka Sturgeon Bay Road for part of its length, carries us for many miles as it winds its way up the peninsula to the Sturgeon Bay Ship Canal. State route 42 joins 57 for the second half of the distance to the canal.

We're not crossing the canal on this particular ride, rather we'll work our way east to the Lake Michigan coast and continue south. The east end of Sturgeon Bay was excavated to make a connection with Lake Michigan proper during the 1880s. There were several large quarries in this locale and prior to the Lake Michigan canal connection ships heavily loaded with limestone had to sail north in Green Bay and enter Lake Michigan at a treacherous zone of the lake off the tip of Door Peninsula that earned the title Death's Door because of the many shipwrecks that occurred there. The canal east of Sturgeon Bay not only eliminated that hazardous passage it also cut many miles off the trip.

Just before Route 57 / 42 reaches the canal and the bascule bridge (the eastern-most of the three bridges over the canal) we want to turn south onto CR-U from Tacoma Beach Avenue and take it south along the coast for many miles. Just north of the town of Algoma CR-U becomes CR-S that we take into town. County road U is a wonderful ride south along or near the shoreline. For several miles the pavement shadows the meanderings of the wooded shoreline, making for an enjoyable ride on a road that most of the traffic is ignoring. In Algoma CR-S joins Wisconsin 42 which takes us all the way to Manitowoc.

As is evident while traversing the Door Peninsula, this is orchard and vineyard country. There are several ag-tourism places to stop for some wine tasting and educational tours. The von Stiehl winery in Algoma is one such example. Algoma, at the mouth of the Ahnapee River, is a typical coastal town in this region with historic sites or structures to see along the waterfront and a pleasant downtown to walk around in.

Route 42 is our partner south of Algoma, and the first few miles are tight on the water's edge. The next city we encounter is Kewaunee, labeled as *The Spirit of the Lakeshore*. Locals pride themselves on their maritime culture and it shows. The local lighthouse is a historic structure that draws a lot of attention, as is the Corps of Engineers tug boat *The Ludington*. The Kewaunee Jail Museum on Dodge Street, next to the old courthouse, is another interesting Kewaunee diversion.

Nearly twenty-five miles south on W42 brings us to the city of Two Rivers. (Six miles north of Two Rivers you might wish to follow CR-V over to the coast and ride CR-O south through Point Beach State Forest for a more scenic view and chance to see the Rawley Point Lighthouse. The light is part of a Coast Guard base so it isn't open to the public, but the facility can be viewed from the beach. CR-O delivers you to Two Rivers and W42 again).

The origin of the name of Two Rivers is easy; the West Twin River and the East Twin River converge here, with the harbor being the river mouth. I encourage spending some time in this small but interesting town. There are some unique museums, Including commercial fishing, farm equipment and rarest of all, a woodtype and printing museum.

It's a short ride along the waterfront to Manitowoc. Route 42 heads inland at this point so we need an alternative coastal route. In downtown Manitowoc turn south from W42 onto 10th Street and follow it south as it becomes CR-LS. (If you're taking the *SS Badger* back across the lake the port is on 10th Street south of Wisconsin 42) An attraction that history and navy enthusiasts might enjoy is the Wisconsin Maritime Museum. Located near the waterfront at 75 Maritime Drive, this hands-on museum is also the proud owner of the *USS Cobia*, a World War II submarine. Call them at (920) 684-0218 for information. On January 8, 2019 the power of Lake Michigan was witnessed when a massive wave knocked the south pier light into the lake. The twenty-foot structure had survived numerous storms for many decades but one thing lakes states residents can tell you, never underestimate the power of Great Lakes storms.

It's a bit early for motorcycle tourists, but local bikers might be interested in attending the Charity Motorcycle Show and Dance at the Manitowoc Expo Grounds. Sponsored by the Ant Hill Mob Motorcycle Club and Hoban's Cycle, the event is held in late April.

As you travel further southward the CR-LS pavement becomes Lakeshore Road, and then 15th Street in the city of Sheboygan, known as *The Spirit of the Lake*. This large city of fifty thousand is a bustling place with lots going on. It's at the mouth of the Sheboygan River and of course the waterfront has attractions and beaches to explore. An unusual local attraction is the Lao, Hmong and American Veterans Memorial at Deland Park. It's in recognition of military members who served in Laos from 1961 to 1975. The memorial is made up of 24 panels that collectively tell the story of that little known conflict taking place in Laos during the Vietnam War.

The lack of an easily followed local road along the lakeshore south of Sheboygan impacts on the next phase of this tour. In Sheboygan the best option unfortunately is to follow W23 west a mile to I-43. We'll ride this highway south; next stop Port Washington. The town of Port Washington is home to the Port Washington Lighthouse and Museum. They sit high atop St. Mary's Hill at 311 Johnson Street. This 1860 structure is one of the few lighthouses where the public is allowed to climb the steps to the top.

If you don't visit Port Washington just stay on 43. If you do visit the town and the lighthouse museum turn south on Wisconsin Street and follow it as it turns into County Road C and then Lakeshore Road and once again it is called CR-C (just follow the pavement). County Road C does eventually turn westward and allows entry back onto I-43.

As the Milwaukee metropolitan area approaches I suggest exiting 43 at W100 / Brown Deer Road / W32 and following the shoreline. This road is one mile south of the Milwaukee County line. Riding through the community of Fox Point on W32 gives a glimpse of how 'the other half' lives. For several miles the boulevard cuts through the scenic, wonderfully maintained tree-filled community. Visitors pass by mansions and estates set deep in wooded lots with Lake Michigan occasionally visible behind the palatial homes. This gorgeous area has more trees than people and traffic is surprisingly light on the wide avenue.

Route 32 goes through the suburbs of Whitefish Bay and Shorewood as we ride through the northern Milwaukee suburbs. You'll finally see Lincoln Memorial Drive veer off of W32 to the east where it follows the lakeshore. Take LMD south as it winds past Lake Park and then the large and attractive Veterans Park, where the Drive seamlessly merges with I-794, an in-town access expressway. This highway carries traffic over the Milwaukee River with the Port of Milwaukee, home of the *Lake Express* ferry to Muskegon, visible to the east. Look for signs to the port at the south side of the river.

If you don't mind expressways and want to avoid riding through the many towns along the shoreline, then get on the I-43 expressway just west of Manitowoc and take it south to Milwaukee for the last leg of this trip. There are of course a ton of things to see and do in Milwaukee. The Harley-Davidson Museum immediately comes to mind, but there are many other attractions; too many to list here. Do a little Internet research and come prepared to spend a day exploring this historic city.

This Muskegon – Milwaukee trip is about 900 miles in length (not counting the ferry ride) and I recommend at least three days to complete it, four days are better. As usual, there is just too much to see and do along the way to hurry. Taking a ferry adds several hours to the trip when one considers the loading process, the trip itself, and the offloading.

There are those folks who consider a trip around Lake Michigan as not officially complete for bragging rights purposes unless one rides the entire circle – no shortcuts across the water to avoid the metro Chicago area. I have motorcycled completely around Lake Michigan, including the southern portion of the lake through downtown Chicago on several occasions, and have ridden that fearsome strip of I94 from I80 near Gary north to Milwaukee quite a number of times. Every time I'm in Chicago I see bikers battling the trucks, short tempered taxi drivers, and multi-tasking distracted commuters and am amazed at the ability and courage of these metro bikers. And of course local riders fight on this vehicular battleground every day so we know it can be done.

Continuing our counter-clockwise direction of travel follow Wisconsin route 32 south from Milwaukee to the Illinois line. This is not a non-stop blitz, however. There are plenty of things to do and places to see along this route. Just north of Racine a turn to the east on 3 Mile Road out to Wind Point and the Wind Point Lighthouse is recommended.

In Kenosha, follow the signs and make the short detour east to the lakeshore, especially to Simmons Island Park and the nearby museums and statuary, including a Civil War Museum and the Kenosha Public Muesum. The entire lakeshore area has been nicely restored and is a marvelous place to stop for a break and some exploration on foot. The Southport Light Station Museum is a recommended stop with views available from the top of the light. The restored electric streetcar system is worth a stop all by itself.

At the Illinois state line route 32 turns into route 137 / Sheridan Road; no turns necessary. Though the landscape is quite urban along this main road there are several miles of natural areas just to the east, along the lakeshore. The North Dunes Nature Preserve, Illinois Beach State Park, and the Illinois Beach Nature Preserve offer roads where the traffic can be left behind for at least a short excursion in the woods. (The Zion Nuclear Power Plant is hidden away in the middle of this urban savannah).

Highway 137 carries us just south of Waukegan where it turns west. I recommend following 137 west to I-94 and get on the expressway at this point unless the desire is to take local roads through Chicago. The I-94 expressway will of course carry a rider south and then east through the greater Chicago and Gary area.

If a person wants to follow the lakeshore route perhaps the best option is to exit 94 onto US14 just north of Chicago and take 14 east to US41. Forty One goes east at that point to lake shore parks and attractions. If you're not in a hurry this is an interesting and not unpleasant ride. This road can be followed all the way south to the Indiana Tollway / I-90 in far northwest Indiana. Ninety eventually intersects with I-94. Regardless of the point at which a person got onto I-94, get off at exit 26B and ride Indiana state route 49 north a couple miles to US12 and the Indiana Dunes National Park, just recently promoted from a National Lakeshore. The Park offers ample opportunities to walk through the unique sand dunes or to just take a break and relax on the beach on Lake Michigan's southern shore.

US12 is a path of history in its own right. The highway was originally part of the famous Sauk Trail used by Native Americans to travel between the vicinity of the Detroit River to southern Lake Michigan and ultimately the Mississippi River. This trail was used for centuries by native tribes for a wide variety of purpose before the Europeans arrived. It ultimately took on important strategic and military value during the period of the French and Indian War and later the War of 1812. The British called the trail The Military Road, which they improved slightly after capturing the Great Lakes region from the French and used it to connect their forts at present-day Detroit and Chicago. In the 1830s, after completion of the Erie Canal in New York connecting the Atlantic seaboard directly with the Great Lakes, the road became an important settlement route for immigrants migrating west. Stage coaches started running between Detroit and Chicago in the 1830s on this very road, and as they say, the rest is history.

A person has only to gaze upon the moving hills of sand or walk the miles of sandy beach in the Indiana Dunes Park to be amazed by the unique geology. The state and national parks that protect what remains of the once much larger area of dunes are also testament to the fact that a small group of people, fighting for a cause, can overcome overwhelming odds. The parks came close to not happening and this entire region was nearly bulldozed flat and converted to industrial development but for the tireless efforts of a small number of people that knew that this natural wonder needed to be preserved for future generations. A string of state and local parks awaits the traveler all along the east coast of Lake Michigan.

Michigan City is on the east edge of the Lakeshore. One attraction here that I suggest taking a few minutes to visit is the Old Michigan City Lighthouse and Museum; it's just a few blocks north of US12 in the downtown area. Turn left onto Pine Street, which curves and becomes Franklin Street, which will cross Trail Creek. The light is on the left after crossing the Franklin Street bridge. The museum and lighthouse are open every day but Mondays during the warm months.

Shortly after leaving Michigan City on 12 we'll cross the state line into Michigan and arrive at the village of Michiana. A stone's throw north of Michiana is the small town of New Buffalo. Though the American Bison, or buffalo, did wander nearby prior to arrival of the settlers, the origin of this town's name is less exciting. It seems that in 1834 a sailboat captain from Buffalo, New York ran aground near here. He was so struck by the beauty of the area that he filed a claim for a tract of land at the mouth of the Galien River and named his future development New Buffalo, after his home town. This area was a popular resort and vacation mecca from the late 1890s until the Depression. A string of hotels and resorts lined the shore, attracting vacationers from Chicago. The country's first highway travel information center was built nearby.

The New Buffalo Railroad Museum is located at 530 South Whittaker Street and is a fun, and free, place to check out railroading artifacts. They're open noon – 5:00 daily during the summer season. I've noticed that most riders are gearheads and that most gearheads love the mechanical aspects of railroading equipment.

Just beyond New Buffalo leave US12 and go north on the Red Arrow Highway. This highway is named in honor of the Army's Red Arrow Division. The unit was originally part of the Army National Guard and made up of members from Wisconsin and Michigan. The Division became well known and respected for its major combat roles in both World War one and two.

Just south of the town of Bridgman is Warren Dunes State Park. This 2,000-acre park has a tremendous beach and is noted for its impressive sand dunes. This park is a favorite destination for many people in this part of the country, so if you wish to camp make a reservation well in advance utilizing Michigan's state park reservation system.

At Bridgman, Red Arrow Highway crosses Interstate 94 and moves about a mile inland on the east side of the xway, remaining there for seven miles. A short ride further north takes you to Grand Mere State Park at Stevensville. If you're looking for a bit more of a relaxed and close to nature experience than what is found at bustling Warren Dunes State Park Grand Mere will be more to your liking.

On the north side of Stevensville, Red Arrow Highway crosses back to the west side of I94 and becomes BR94 leading you through downtown St. Joseph as Main Street, just a couple blocks from the coast. I suggest spending some time in St. Joseph. It is an upscale coastal town with lots to offer. Silver Beach Park and the awe-inspiring shoreline help give the title Riviera of the Midwest to this locale. I suggest walking along the shore south of the river mouth to view the many boats berthed there, and while you're at it, stop in at the carousel museum at Silver Beach Park. An old time carousel, with an adjacent museum, make for an interesting stop. The North Pier Lighthouse is also a should-see stop.

In St. Joseph we say adieu to Red Arrow Highway and BR94 as they veer off to the northeast heading inland, while the pavement we're on continues north uninterrupted as M63, which we'll follow for roughly nine miles. At that point M63 ends and the Blue Star Highway begins. The designation of being a Blue Star Highway had its origins in 1944 when a New Jersey Garden Club wanted to honor the military. The idea of calling a highway a Blue Star Highway took off and now includes many roads in the nation. The National Garden Clubs, Inc. is the sponsoring organization, along with state and federal transportation agencies. During World War II, families who had members serving in the war flew a service flag that had a blue star in the center.

Though it's on the same alignment and no turns are necessary, the Blue Star has a distinctly different look. It is narrower and in general is more interesting than M63. Just north of the point where Blue Star Highway begins is a small roadside park on the Lake Michigan shore.

It's a nice spot for a walk down the dune to the beach and for views of the lake.

Continue following Blue Star Highway north into the resort town of South Haven. There are many tourist-related activities in South Haven, from great beaches and parks to small shops and restaurants. It is a town in which it's easy to park your bike on the main drag and walk to various attractions and restaurants. The waterfront is a must.

If you have any interest in maritime matters visit the Michigan Maritime Museum located downtown on the Black River. A lighthouse keepers house, commercial fish tug, a U.S Lifesaving Service building, and boat shed are also part of the museum. An electric river launch called the *Lindy Lou* is available for rides on the river. The museum's mission is research, preservation of the maritime culture of the region, and education. It is truly a fascinating place to spend a couple hours. Call 800-747-3810 or go to michiganmaritimemuseum.org for more information.

The Blue Star Highway goes north through South Haven and continues for almost exactly nine miles, to the tiny village of Glenn, at which point it veers northeast and then continues north inland of the I-196 expressway. In this stretch the road is also called A2, an Allegan County primary route.

When the Blue Star Highway veers right at Glenn you will see 70th Avenue / aka Lakeshore Drive heading straight north. Turn left off Blue Star and continue north on 70th Avenue / Lakeshore Drive. Follow this road, much nicer and closer to the water, north where a right turn at 130th Avenue takes you the one mile back to Blue Star Highway, which by then has curved back to the coast in the town of Douglas.

Turn north onto Blue Star Highway following it across the Kalamazoo Lake causeway into the neighboring community of Saugatuck. This is a popular resort area with great beaches and access to the lake. The downtown section is a frequent motorcycle destination. Park the bike and walk along the river to gawk at the large boats or to enjoy lunch at any one of the many restaurants that line the street. There are a couple interesting nautical options also. Take a ride on the Star of Saugatuck paddlewheel boat. The boat operates on the Kalamazoo River and offers spectacular sunset cruises on Lake Michigan in the evening. It is located at 716 Water Street, 269-857-4261.

Since there is no good lakeshore road alternative between Saugatuck and Holland, continue north on the Blue Star Highway all the way to Holland. Just south of Holland the road becomes 58th Street. You will cross both the I-196 and US-31 expressways. When you cross the US31 expressway 58th Street / Blue Star Highway becomes Washington Street, it then angles as Michigan Street, then turns straight north again as River Avenue in Holland and crosses the Macatawa River.

Holland, as the name suggests, is a pocket of Dutch culture in Michigan. The town celebrates its heritage in several ways, but most notably at Windmill Island Gardens and each May during the annual tulip festival. Windmill Island is just a few blocks off our route and is highly recommended. The village, beautiful gardens, and Dutch windmill are impressive indeed. The authentic windmill was shipped over from the country of Holland and reassembled in the park. Called DeZwaan, the windmill is an imposing structure. It is 125-feet high and over 250 years old. Built in Holland in 1761, it was disassembled and moved to America in 1964. A year later it was dedicated in this park. The windmill is open for tours that include climbing several levels inside the structure. It is a fascinating and rare opportunity to see these giant towers, and their impressive internal mechanism, up close and personal. Getting to the island park is easy. Once in town turn right onto 9th Street, taking it to Lincoln St. Turn left onto Lincoln and it goes directly into the park.

When ready to continue the ride cross the river on River Avenue and turn left on the second street(Douglas Street) after crossing the river and follow it west along the north shore of Lake Macatawa where it becomes Ottawa Beach Road. Near the west end Ottawa Beach Road becomes narrower and is essentially the access road for Holland State Park. Just before that point is Lake Street going straight west where Ottawa Beach curves southwest. Follow Lake Street west, make a very short north jog on 168th Avenue, and Lakeshore Road angles off from 168th heading north and northwest. This is ultimately our route.

However, you might want to follow Ottawa Beach Road to the end and visit Holland State Park. It has a great beach and the Big Red Lighthouse is at the river mouth. Holland State Park is one of the most popular beach destinations in Michigan and the large parking lot is often filled on summer weekends.

To resume the trip go north on Lakeshore Road all the way into Grand Haven. Once in town it becomes Sheldon Street and eventually curves east on Grant Street to join business route 31, onto which we turn left. Lakeshore Road south of Grand Haven is an enjoyable roughly twenty-mile stretch of road.

Grand Haven is where the Grand River, Michigan's longest river and largest watershed, empties into Lake Michigan. There are two nice state parks near here. Grand Haven State Park located on Lake Michigan south of the river mouth, and P.J. Hoffmaster State Park located north of town on the big lake. Hoffmaster Park in particular is a nice place to enjoy the beach and to explore the natural beauty of the freshwater dunes environment. There are several walking trails through the 1,130 acres of forested sand dunes and an impressive visitor center with displays that tell the story of these unique dunes. Grand Haven State Park is smaller and consists primarily of lakeshore beach opportunities. Both are popular, and if you wish to camp at either be sure to make reservations well ahead.

Downtown Grand Haven is host to what for decades was the world's largest musical fountain. This fanciful display synchronizes music, light displays and water fountains in a memorable spectacle that can be enjoyed at dusk each evening from Memorial Day through Labor Day. The Fourth of July show and fireworks is especially impressive. It's located downtown on the river at Harbor and Washington Avenues, west of US31.

Grand Haven is an officially-designated Coast Guard City USA. It has a close relationship with the Coast Guard, which makes sense because it is a nautical community with lots of boating and water activity. Every summer Grand Haven hosts a huge Coast Guard Festival, which is so popular that about 300,000 people show up. It is also the time when the Coast Guard honors those members who have died in service to the country. The Tri-Cities Historical Museum on Washington Street is a fun place to learn about the history of this area. There is also a wonderful waterfront path that offers splendid views of the water and boating activity.

North of Grand Haven there is no lakeshore route so we're going to do the next best thing. Ride BR31 across the Grand River and in a few blocks 3rd Street appears on the left. Turn onto 3rd and it soon curves north and become 174th. Motor north on 174th the few miles to Pontaluna Road. Turn west to Lake Harbor Road. This is your opportunity to visit Hoffmaster State Park and the Gillette Sand Dunes Visitor Center. It's worth the diversion. To go to the park just follow the signs on Pontaluna Road. The east shore of Lake Michigan has more freshwater sand dunes than anywhere else in the world. They are an amazing scenic and geologic wonder and a fascinating ecosystem. The Gillette Visitor Center has excellent displays that explain the formation, evolution, and ecology of the sand dune environment and nearby trails help to enhance the experience.

To head to Muskegon go north on Lake Harbor Road. It isn't a lakeshore road but it gets the job done. Along the way is impressive Mt. Garfield and the home of the Muskegon Motorcycle Club. Continue north and eventually Lake Harbor Drive morphs into Seminole, which in turn jogs on Norton to Lincoln Street. Sounds more difficult than it really is. Ride Lincoln north to its end at Lakeshore Drive along the south shore of Muskegon Lake. Just to the left are Pere Marquette Park on the Lake

Michigan shore, and the channel connecting Muskegon Lake with the big lake. This is where the Lake Express Ferry docks.

So there you have it. A traveler around Lake Michigan can do the entire route by land through Chicago, or they can choose to cut across on one of the two ferries. At the trip's end a rider will appreciate even more just how amazing and diverse America's largest lake is.

Point Betsie Lighthouse, Frankfort, Michigan

4. The Lake Superior Circle Tour

ALL OF THE Great Lakes circle tours are unique enjoyable trips in their own right, but the trip around Lake Superior just might be the crown jewel. The tour is one of the great road trips of North America. No matter where a person is on the tour; Michigan, Minnesota, Wisconsin or Ontario, they are never far from magnificent vistas, waterfalls, historic lighthouses, picturesque small towns with great stories to tell, majestic overlooks, and always that view of the lake itself with its freshwater horizon stretching forever into the distance. Adjectives fall short when it comes to describing this area. Superlatives like tremendous and spectacular are overused today and thus watered down. The Lake Superior region is one place where they really are applicable.

Knowing that one is riding through a land populated with wolves, moose, bears, and woodland caribou adds to the flavor of the trip. This is still mostly wild lands not fully subdued by man's hand. The roads are wonderful with enough motorcycling character to satisfy the most demanding two-wheeling aficionado.

For those unfamiliar with the Lake Superior region there are realities to keep in mind. First, the weather in that area can change rapidly, and even in the summer the temperature frequently drops into the forties.

Cold and dense roadside fog can develop near the water and the nights can get quite cool. This isn't meant to discourage anyone but be prepared with cold and wet weather clothing in case it's needed. Riding near Lake Superior is like riding in the Rockies. Be prepared for extremes. Chances are it won't happen, but I've been caught in some sudden cold spells where it went from eighty degrees to fifty in short notice along the lake and a good rain suit was mandatory for comfort. Be prepared for pleasantly cool nights if camping. Secondly, make sure your machine is in good working order and keep the gas tank topped off. It's of course not unbroken wilderness but there are places where one does not want to run out of gas or have a mechanical problem due to lack of maintenance. Motorcycle dealers and repair shops are few and far between.

Finally, watch out for wildlife. It's a thrill to see them in the woods or swamps near the road but you certainly wouldn't want to hit a thousand-pound moose that chose that moment to cross the road to eat the greener grass on the other side.

As with any circular trip there is no one start and end point, just what happens to be most convenient for each rider. For me that was always Sault Ste. Marie, Michigan, and I've done this ride in both the clockwise and counterclockwise directions from the Soo. Let's arbitrarily begin at

Michigan's side of the twin cities and go north by crossing the International Bridge into Sault Ste. Marie, Ontario. Before leaving the Soo area I suggest checking out some of the popular sightseeing attractions. On the Michigan side that would certainly include viewing ships making their way through the locks. The Soo Locks is the largest and busiest lock system in the world. The first lock was built in 1855 to facilitate shipping from Lake Superior to the lower lakes. A 20-foot drop in the St. Mary River results in dramatic rapids that blocked shipping. Prior to the first lock vessels were pulled out of the water and carried and dragged overland to a point where they could be floated again below the rapids. The twin cities' name, Sault Sainte Marie, literally means "falls or rapids of the Saint Mary" – the name given this river in the 1600s by French missionaries. For thousands of years before the French arrived on the scene the river had a different name of course. The Ojibwe called it Baawitigong, meaning "place of the rapids." Native tribes not only lived in the region but the falls were an especially important food gathering spot during the whitefish spawning season.

There is much more to do so check the local visitor centers for more ideas. I hope to provide a sampling of attractions in my various trip descriptions, but this book could never be an exhaustive list of all the attractions in any region or ride. Don't be in too much of a hurry, be willing to stop to investigate the options and take the time to participate. What a shame it would be to simply ride through beautiful places with those proverbial blinders on.

Because you will be in Canada for about 350 miles a stop at the Visitor Center just beyond the bridge to pick up brochures and maps and exchange some currency is recommended. Some common items such as gasoline do cost a bit more in Canada but the exchange rate for the U.S. dollar is often at least slightly in the favor of visitors from south of the border. Besides, given the wonderful trip ahead of you and the friendly Canadians you're about to meet, it isn't unreasonable to pay for the experience. The Ontario government does an excellent job of providing informational brochures about the Lake Superior region.

The Ontario portion of the loop is easy; just get on and stay on the Trans-Canada Highway / Route 17 from the Canadian Soo all the way to Thunder Bay. In Sault Ste. Marie, Ontario you will be on 17B when you get off the bridge. This road changes names as it goes through town, but it's always 17B. (Bay Street, Queen Street, Church Street, Pim Street, and finally, Great Northern Highway) Once you reach the northern city limits on Route 17 / Great Northern Highway, you don't have to think about directions for the next three hundred miles.

Sault Ste. Marie Ontario is a fairly large city (at least for this part of the country) and has congestion typical of any other hub city. Heading north along the east shore of the lake the surroundings and the road gradually improve for the better. After about a half-hour you'll start enjoying what the trip is all about – great scenery and riding. Between the Soo and the town of Wawa there are so many things to see that one just has to be willing to stop occasionally and smell the flowers – or watch the moose. You'll see signs for attractions such as waterfalls, scenic overlooks, light-houses, historical markers and so on. The stretch from Batchawana Bay Provincial Park north to the town of Wawa is just one scenic delight after another. This is true for the entire trip. Lake Superior can be said to be lacking in only two things – warm water and sandy beaches. It definitely isn't lacking in motorcycling credentials. The road north to Wawa is noth-ing short of fabulous for two-wheelers.

South of Wawa in Lake Superior Provincial Park an enjoyable trip through the park should include walking to the Agawa Rock Indian Pic-tographs. These ancient drawings on the shore of the lake are reached by a trail that is fascinating in its own right. One walks in a deep cleft between two rock walls, which are actually massive boulders and uplifted rock that has split forming a narrow roofless 'tunnel' to walk through. If you're riding an adventure bike the short but rewarding side trip to view the Magpie Falls just south of Wawa is an option. I do not recommend making this trip on a large touring bike, especially with a passenger, due to the rough gravel and stone road.

For many years I made annual motorcycle camping and hiking trips to Lake Superior Provincial Park. I spent several days each summer wan-dering the wilderness and rejuvenating my soul. This small corner of Ontario is a marvelous place to visit and explore. This area was also the last link in the trans-Canada highway. The rugged hills south of Wawa are comprised of some of the hardest rock on earth. Cutting and dynamiting through was so difficult that this final link of the cross-continent highway wasn't completed until 1960!

Just north of the park is the town of Wawa (Ojibwe for Land of the Wild Geese). It is a good place to stop and refuel both yourself and your bike. You know you're there when you see the famous Wawa Goose perched high on a hill south of town.

Route 17 curves inland for a stretch northwest of Wawa around Pu-kaskwa National Park, a large wilderness park on the lake. The next town you'll come to is White River. If you're into canoeing, fishing, wilderness hiking or hunting then this is your place. It is far from Lake Superior, but surrounded by hundreds of lakes and streams, and miles of forest. White River has gained some fame in a most unusual manner. In 1914 a veterinarian in the Canadian Army on his way to Europe and World War I bought a bear cub he named Winnie at White River as a mascot for his unit. The bear was left in the care of the London Zoo in England where a certain Mr. Milne and his son Christopher Robin noticed it and fell in love with it because of its playful ways and personality. That bear of course became the basis for the lovable bear known by children everywhere as Winnie-The-Pooh. A park in White River honors this endearing bear.

Upon leaving White River Route 17 begins its westward march. Lake Superior curves north to meet the road near the village of Marathon. Shortly west of there is Terrace Bay and just west of Terrace Bay is Aguasabon Falls and Gorge. They're just off the highway and are a must see. Like so many fabulous scenic delights around the lake crowds are nonexistent and access is often free. When these falls first come into view they elicit an insuppressible gasp of awe.

The town of Nipigon is nestled at the northernmost point of Lake Superior, just before the shoreline starts angling southwest. Southwest of Nipigon the next interesting suggested stop is Ouimet Canyon Provincial Park. Ouimet Canyon road is a two-lane pavement that carries the few visitors that make their way to this out-of-the-way park through the woods about ten miles to the small parking lot. A trail through the woods provides access to the canyon viewing overlook. Though it is a provincial park there are no buildings or services, just a sign kiosk and voluntary pay tube buried in the ground. This marvel of nature was formed by rock faulting and is quite a spectacular sight with 300-feet high vertical canyon walls defining a deep gorge that seems out of place. Just before reaching the park there are signs for Eagle Canyon Adventures, a private business that offers zip line rides across one end of the canyon.

Continue following Route 17 west and signs for the Sleeping Giant Provincial Park appear. This side trip, down Sibley Peninsula which juts far into Lake Superior, is a scenic delight. The enjoyable round-trip ride on route 587 to get to the park is frosting on the cake.

The City of Thunder Bay is the next big thing. It is the largest city in the region and is a major transport center for both highway and maritime trade. Make time for a visit to historic Old Fort William – billed as the world's largest recreated fur trading post – for a look at late 18th and early 19th century Upper Canada. Thunder Bay is a fairly recent creation. In 1970 the residents of two towns, Fort William and Port Arthur, voted to become the new city of Thunder Bay.

The city seems sprawling and busy after a couple hundred miles of bucolic calm and beauty. Route 17 joins Canada Route 11 near Thunder Bay and these two roads are combined through the busy city. In the southwest portion of Thunder Bay Routes 17 and 11 intersect with Route 61, and 17 and 11 continue through western Ontario and all points west while route 61, our road, follows the shoreline toward Minnesota. By good planning or just good karma the road remains numbered as Route 61 after entering Minnesota so you'll stay on Route 61 from Thunder Bay to Duluth.

The "arrowhead" country of Minnesota is as spectacular as the Ontario portion of the trip, perhaps even more so. Lakeside cliffs, waterfalls, forests, hills, light traffic and a wonderful riding road make this a stretch you'll want to come back to time and again. The fun begins immediately after entering Minnesota.

Very quickly there are signs for the High Falls of the Pigeon River. These 120-foot cascades, the state's highest, are definitely a must see. Grand Portage National Monument is also nearby. This national facility has many interesting displays and buildings that recreate the important role that this locale played in trade, transportation, and the early settlement period of this region.

Not far down the road in Magney State Park are the Devil's Kettle Waterfalls on the Brule River. Next comes the city of Grand Marais and a bit further the small town of Lutsen, located in the Sawtooth Mountains. Lutsen Mountain Ski Area offers the longest and tallest ski runs in the Midwest and the gondola on Moose Mountain or the chairlift on nearby Eagle Mountain offer rides to the top in the summer for spectacular views of the surrounding area.

Further southwest the 1,400-foot-long Silver Creek Tunnel is an unexpected surprise. This tunnel opened in 1994 and eliminated a dangerous narrow strip of pavement that had perilously clung to a roadside cliff. This section of the road has countless spectacular views of the lake as the pavement hugs the shoreline. Nearby Splitrock Lighthouse and Gooseberry Falls are also not to be missed. As I noted earlier, the attractions on this route are just too numerous to write about them all. Be willing to take the time to explore sites as you pass them on the road and I guarantee you won't be disappointed. The only way a traveler might be dissatisfied is if he or she just keeps riding (which is tempting because it's so great!) and doesn't stop to enjoy the natural beauty and sights.

Duluth, a port city at the far western end of Lake Superior and thus essentially in the middle of the continent, is the next large town on the tour. One of the quickest ways to learn about this area and its history and culture is a stop at The Depot. Technically it's the St. Louis County Heritage and Arts Center Historic Union Depot. You can understand why it's known locally simply as The Depot. This fascinating museum houses everything from old railroad cars and locomotives to historical and cultural artifacts and displays that span two centuries. This busy railroad depot opened in 1892 and once served seven different rail lines and 5,000 people per day walked through its doors. It has been beautifully restored and is a highly recommended stop on your journey through the Superior region.

If a rider happens to be in Duluth, which after all isn't on everyone's destination list on a regular basis, he or she might want to stop at Aerostich/RiderWearhouse. What Bass Pro Shops or Cabela's is to outdoors folks, Aerostich is to bikers. If it involves a motorcycle or rider, they've got it.

In the city Route 61 merges into I-35 for a short distance until its juncture with US2 where the tour turns east toward Superior, Wisconsin. On your way to Superior you will be on US2 / I-53 for much of the way.

In order to stay near the lakeshore and take a much more scenic route, at the southeast portion of Superior head east on Wisconsin Route 13 and abandon US-2, which runs inland many miles. Route 13, a designated scenic road called The Lake Superior Byway, carries riders out to the tip of the Bayfield Peninsula and to the Apostle Islands National Lakeshore, a lovely archipelago of twenty-two islands, rock formations and historic lighthouses. Boat tours through the islands are popular, as are hiking trails on the islands themselves. The village of Bayfield is a highly suggested stop. Spend a bit of time exploring the waterfront and nearby nautical museum, as well as the historic and hilly downtown portion of town. Bayfield hosts two large events each year that might fit into your schedule. First is a boating regatta over the July 4th week, and on the first weekend of October the Apple Festival brings tens of thousands of visitors into town.

Beyond Bayfield Route 13 curves south along the shore of Chequamegon Bay and rejoins US2 just west of Ashland, WI. Chequamegon (pronounced she-WAH-ma-gon) is an Ojibwe term meaning roughly 'place of the sand bar'. The southern end of the bay is quite shallow and each spring for centuries Native Americans harvested spawning fish in these sandy shallows.

Just west of the W13 and US2 intersection is the Northern Great Lakes Visitor Center – another recommended stop. This federal facility has impressive informative displays that portray the natural and cultural history of the northern Great Lakes region.

Get back on US2 and take it east through Ashland. US2 will be our host for the next forty miles across northern Wisconsin to the Michigan border town of Ironwood. There are things to see along the way so watch for signs. Just before crossing the state line the Interstate Falls, dramatic waterfalls on the Montreal River, are a very nice diversion. Turn left onto Center Drive to the parking area. From Ironwood ride six miles east on US2 to Bessemer. In town turn left / north onto Moore Street. After a few blocks the name changes to Black River Drive / CR513, a National Scenic Byway.

Ride this excellent road up to the Black River Harbor on Lake Superior, even though it requires doubling back on the same road to get back on US2 (you won't mind riding this road twice). The Black River Drive is a scenic fifteen-mile stretch of winding road along the Black River, replete with waterfalls, hills, curves, forests and wildlife. Eagle sightings are common in this area and five waterfalls are easily accessible from the road. You also pass the Copper Peak Ski Flying Hill – the world's tallest ski jump. The view from atop the 18-story observation deck is unlike any other in the Midwest. Even when just viewed from a distance this structure gives an entirely new perspective on ski jumping, and respect for the men and women who fly off the lift with nothing but a lot of cold air beneath them!

After completing the Black River Drive diversion take it south to US2 and head east again a few miles to Wakefield where US2 intersects with M28. Turn north on M28 for about a mile and you'll intersect with CR519 – the road we want. Take 519 north to the South Boundary Road of the Porcupine Mountains Wilderness State Park. Follow this great stretch of backwoods road east as it meanders through the southerly portion of this large wilderness park, ultimately turning north and ending at M107 on the shore of Lake Superior. Turn west on M107 and climb it to the overlook at the Lake of the Clouds, an absolute must-see on this trip. This is the kind of place where a person ought to sit on the rock cliff and just let the beauty of the place soak in, and the only reason to use the ever-present cell phone should be to take pictures. There are many hiking trails in the park, some short and some long wilderness trails. Bears are common in this area so if you camp or hike listen to the advice of the park rangers and take appropriate precautions regarding food storage.

When you've finally soaked in enough of the beauty of the Porkies head east on M107 to Silver City where the road joins M64. This road takes you to the town of Ontonagon. Take M38 (The Ontonagon-Greenland Road) out of Ontonagon all the way past the small town of Greenland, where you turn east onto M26 which you take up to the Keweenaw Peninsula.

In Greenland, on M38 you'll see the Adventure Mine – an early copper mine that operated from 1850–1920. Daily-guided tours into the mine are offered. It's an informative and interesting diversion.

Continue on M26 across the Upper Peninsula's rugged beauty all the way to Houghton, cross the Portage Canal Bridge, and turn right again on M26 in the town of Hancock. The Keweenaw Peninsula deserves a day or two all to itself. There are several great routes on the peninsula. In this tour I'll define the various circle tours that the Keweenaw offers. You can either just take US41 up to Copper Harbor and head back south – missing much of what the Keweenaw has to offer – or you can take the several small tours that I spell out here in order to see the peninsula the way it should be seen and experienced.

If you're in a hurry and must do the peninsula in one round trip then take US41 to the end at Copper Harbor and head south on Brockway Mountain Drive out of town. The Keweenaw County portion of U.S. 41 is fabulous. Brockway Mountain Drive is a should-do though in recent years the asphalt has become quite rough. The Drive ends at M26 at its south end and 26 then joins U.S.41 to the south, making the loop easy to do.

However, I highly recommend that you don't just do the US41 / Brockway Mt. Drive loop. You'll miss out on so much! Instead, when you enter the peninsula at Hancock, stay on M26 as it goes easterly, then north, to the town of Lake Linden. In the small town of Lake Linden you'll see Bootjack Road going east off M26. Take this road a short distance and Traprock Valley Road goes to the north. Take Traprock Valley Road a little less than two miles to Gay Road then turn right and ride all the way to the water where it turns to the north and hugs the coast of Keweenaw Bay. The nearly abandoned village of Gay has definitely seen busier days. A century ago it was a major copper processing facility. The huge chimney, part of the old stamping mill, still stands. The Gay Bar is a popular place to stop for a break or to take a picture by the sign. The village was named after Joseph E. Gay, a founder of the Mohawk Mining Company, which operated the copper processing facility that once stood next to the huge chimney.

Continuing north, kick back and cruise scenic and fun Gay Road north along the water's edge almost twenty miles to the small crossroads town of Lac La Belle. Traffic in this part of the peninsula is light and the rewards for going the extra mile are high. Turning left on Lac La Belle Road eventually takes us to U.S.-41 near the town of Delaware, and the Delaware Copper mine site. This underground mine was in operation from 1847–1887 and guided or self-guided tours of the mine are available. The mine is an interesting place to visit. In addition to the well-lit mine tunnels they also have a display of antique machinery and engines. The mine is located on US41 and is open 7 days per week from June–October.

When you're done touring the mine, head north on 41 to Copper Harbor. Whether you're on a bagger or crotch rocket you will find yourself leaning forward and playing road racer on this renowned motorcycling road. Along the way is the Keweenaw Mountain Lodge. Spending a night at this famous resort is an experience you'll never forget. The Lodge is an intriguing building, built during the worst of the Depression when the local mines had shut down and unemployment in the region was severe. The building of the Lodge was one of many surviving federal WPA projects that put unemployed men and women to work. Today in addition to the Lodge there is a beautiful golf course for those skilled enough to play on the rough and hilly terrain.

Copper Harbor is Michigan's northernmost city and is the northern terminus of U.S. route 41. A boat tour of the islands in the bay and to the Copper Harbor lighthouse is a great way to really appreciate this unique area and see the 1800s lighthouse up close. Fort Wilkins State Park is literally at the end of the road just east of Copper Harbor and is an interesting stop. The fort was built in 1844 and manned by army troops to keep the peace. You can imagine that the soldiers stationed there must have felt that they were truly at the end of the world, especially in the long cold winters. The need for the fort quickly faded and it was abandoned in 1870. As a state park the fort has been reconstructed and has interesting displays of military and frontier life during the 1800s in the Lake Superior wilderness. Depression-era programs to get people working were largely responsible for the restoration of this fort. The park is a convenient and enjoyable place to camp if the day is near its end.

When ready to depart from Copper Harbor there are two loops that can be taken out of town – requiring doubling back – but what a reward there is for this effort. Head out of town on south M26 (though you will actually be heading west, not south) for about eight miles to the southerly junction with Brockway Mountain Drive. Head back to Copper Harbor on BMD to enjoy some spectacular vistas on this nine mile long narrow sightseeing byway. It is the highest above sea level drive between the Rockies and the Alleghenies. The brutal northern winters haven't been kind to this narrow strip of asphalt so keep your speeds down and your focus up. Marvelous scenic views abound and the extra time and miles are well worth the effort.

Retrace your route on M26 and continue following the shoreline south along the peninsula's west shore through the coastal towns of Eagle Harbor and Eagle River. Unless you're on a strict diet you might want to stop at the Jampot, a small roadside bakery operated by monks just south of Eagle Harbor. They make arguably the best breads, pastries, and preserves as one can find anywhere. This entire area is a nice place to just sit and watch the waves crash onto the rocks.

Eagle Harbor is a small harbor town today but was a boom town a century or more ago because of several active nearby copper mines. The Eagle Harbor Lighthouse is at the rocky entrance to the harbor and is a working lighthouse. It still guides boats of all size across the northern side of the Keweenaw Peninsula. The original lighthouse was built in 1851 but was replaced in 1871. The lighthouse is furnished with period furnishings and open to the public from mid-June to early October. Three Museums are open at the same time. There is a small admission charge to the Light Station complex. If the buildings are closed visitors are welcome to walk around the grounds.

Though ancient bedrock and stone hills make up much of the Keweenaw there is a stretch of M-26 between Eagle Harbor and Eagle River that is called Sand Dunes Drive due to the sudden appearance of sand dunes in this small part of the Keweenaw shore. At Eagle River the coast turns mostly rocky again and this is a popular place to hunt for agates and colorful stones, even bits of copper. There are many wonderful things to see in Copper Harbor, Eagle River and Eagle Harbor so don't be in too much of a hurry.

Continue on 26 and soon it meets up with US41, onto which we turn south. Even more attractions await us at places such as the Quincy with its famous mine and associated museum. Stick with 26 south until it joins with 41 again and turn southbound onto US41.

There is so much history on the peninsula that the Keweenaw National Historic Park was established in 1992. This unique park encompasses communities and attractions in a manner that allows their stories to be told and protected while allowing them to remain in their 'natural' condition as functioning commercial and governmental entities. The city of Hancock and the Quincy mine are examples of this historic preservation. Hancock is the gateway to the Keweenaw Peninsula, situated on the north shore of the Portage Canal, and named after John Hancock, signer of the Declaration of Independence. The town was founded by the Quincy Mining Company in 1859 during the heyday of the Keweenaw's copper mining boom and for decades the Quincy Mine was the economic backbone of the area. Nicknamed Old Reliable, the mine produced copper continuously for 83 years. Tours are offered at the old mine shaft and associated buildings.

When you see the signs for Calumet and M-203 it's time to turn so we can explore the historic town of Calumet and then the far southwest corner of the peninsula. In Calumet a recommend stop is at the old Fire Station, also called the Red Jacket Fire Station. This fascinating building, built in 1899, is typical of much of the wonderful architecture in this region. The towns and citizens had some wealth a century ago and they used it to build impressive and long-lasting buildings. The structure is on the National Register of Historic Places and is part of the Keweenaw National Historic Park. Today it houses the Upper Peninsula Firefighters Memorial Museum. It's on 6th Street just one block south of M-203.

Continue west on 203 to take in the southwest corner of the Keweenaw. There are two highlights in this corner of the peninsula; McClain State Park and the Portage Canal. McClain Park has a marvelous beach and is famous for sunsets. It faces west across the vastness of Lake Superior and sunsets are legendary. If you're into camping you can't do much better than this location.

Just south of the park 203 turns east along the canal. At the west end of the waterway you get a good view at the Keweenaw Waterway Upper Entrance Lighthouse. From this point east to Hancock 203 hugs the north shore of the canal and offers a bounty of grand views and vistas.

When ready to leave the Keweenaw ride US41 across the lift bridge again and then south along the shore of Keweenaw Bay to the towns of Baraga and L'Anse. At Baraga you might want to stop at the Bishop Baraga monument. Baraga was a priest who worked with local Indians in the 1830s. He earned the name Snowshoe Priest because of the amount of time spent traveling through the wilderness catering to the needs of the indigenous population.

About 3 miles southeast of L'Anse on US41 Old 41 veers off. Old 41 is a more interesting and enjoyable riding road, so I recommend taking this loop. It rejoins the new highway just north of the town of Alberta, and then Old 41 veers off again a mile later just south of town, this time for quite a bit longer stretch.

It is no accident that Old 41 goes through the Village of Alberta. This village has an interesting history. It was a company town built out of the wilderness by Henry Ford and Ford Motor Company in 1935. Ford at one time had huge holdings in the Upper Peninsula, in the range of 500,000 acres. Ford wanted a dependable supply of the right kind of timber for his automobiles, which in the 1920s and 1930s had a significant amount of wood in them. Ford built several large sawmills in the UP, and in fact in the town of Kingsford at one time 8,000 people worked in his various plants and mills.

Ford wanted his workers to live near the land and to work on the land. As a former farm boy Henry Ford never lost his love of the land and his belief that working the land was one of man's highest callings. Alberta was built out of the forests with comfortable homes for the workers and a state-of-the-art sawmill. In the 1950s, when wood was no longer utilized in cars or trucks, Ford Motor Company donated the town and 2,000 acres of surrounding land to Michigan Technological University for use as a forestry research and education center. There is a museum in Alberta that tells the fascinating story of Alberta and Henry Ford.

After splitting off of the new highway just south of Alberta, Old 41 eventually rejoins the new highway in the burg of Tioga. This is moose country so if you're alert you may see one of these large animals in a nearby swamp with its head submerged eating aquatic vegetation; better there than on the road in front of you!

Head east on US41 all the way through and just past Marquette. But don't be in too much of a hurry because a person can easily occupy an entire day just in the Marquette area. Ishpeming is home to the United States National Ski Hall of Fame and nearby you'll pass by Da Yoopers Tourist Trap and Museum. In Negaunee, stop to see the Iron Mining Museum and learn about Michigan's nationally important iron mining history.

In Marquette you can tour the beautiful and historic county courthouse, made famous in the movie and book *Anatomy of a Murder*. The Marquette Maritime Museum and Lighthouse, on the waterfront on Lakeshore Boulevard, is another stop you should make while in this enjoyable city. Before departing Marquette I also suggest a ride north on route 550. Take it all the way north to the end of the road at Big Bay if you have the time, but if not, at least ride out to Presque Isle Park, and Sugarloaf Mountain. The view from the top is wonderful, well worth the walk. But for the lack of tides and saltwater Marquette could easily be mistaken for a coastal town on Maine's rocky coast.

Where M-28 and US41 split east of Marquette stay on M-28 as it hugs the shoreline east all the way to Munising. There are many things to see and do in this area so it is difficult to list them all. Watch the road signs for waterfalls, scenic overlooks, lighthouses, and other attractions. Near Au Train there are some delightful places to pull off the road to view the lake, just a few feet away. Take a picture in front of the sign for the village of Christmas; it'll come in handy when you send out Christmas cards in a few months.

In Munising, boat trips to the Pictured Rocks formations on Lake Superior make an enjoyable diversion. The only way to truly see the impressive sandstone cliffs, stained in many different hues from the various minerals that have leached through the rock over the millennia, is from the water. There are a dozen easily accessible waterfalls within ten miles of Munising, and the list of things to do and see is impressive indeed. There is a reason lots of folks come to Munising for their entire vacation – one can easily fill a week here and not run out of things to do.

When ready to move on, follow the signs east from Munising on route H-58 to H-13 (Miners Castle Road) and turn left. An enjoyable ride through dense forests north to the road's end at the Lake Superior headlands delivers grinning riders to the sea cliffs that are the basis for the Pictured Rocks National Lakeshore.

A pleasant 20-minute walk to Miners Falls is a recommended option while traversing Miners Castle Road enroute to the lakeshore. The Miners River plunges forty feet into a rocky gorge and the sight and sound of the cascade are well worth the easy hike on a hard-packed trail from the parking lot. Once at the Lake Superior shore things get even better with a stunning bird's eye view from atop the cliffs, and the iconic and much photographed rock formation called Miners Castle.

Motor south back to H-58 and shadow this recently paved road east through the beautiful Pictured Rocks Lakeshore as it twists, dips, and weaves its way to the village of Grand Marais at the east end of the park. Route H-58 has become a motorcycling and sports car destination and it definitely won't disappoint.

There are several scenic attractions along the way, especially the majestic, and totally unexpected, Grand Sable Sand Dunes tucked between Lake Superior and Grand Sable Lake. Miles of impressive sea cliffs suddenly give way to some of the largest freshwater sand dunes in the world. The Lakeshore's visitor center and impressive Sable Falls are also just west of Grand Marais near the dunes and are both recommended stops.

Unless you are equipped to ride on gravel and sand you have to take M-77 to Seney and M28 where we once again head east, this time to the junction of M123. (If you are on an adventure bike you can continue east of Grand Marais on H58 and take a series of gravel and paved roads to Newberry. Deer Lake Road / 407 eventually takes you to Newberry.) For touring bikes, ride 77 south to 28 and go east. A left turn onto route 123 soon delivers a rider to Newberry (designated by the state legislature as the Moose Capital of Michigan) and beyond. M-123 is a delightful road to ride. The main attraction between Newberry and the town of Paradise on the Lake Superior shore are the Tahquamenon Falls. Like so many places in this region the Tahquamenon River gained its name from Native Americans. It means 'dark waters', a name derived from the river's dark copper colored waters, which is caused by high levels of tannic acid as a result of flowing through the coniferous forests of the area.

The Upper Falls of the Tahquamenon is an impressive sight that you don't want to miss as the 200-foot wide river plunges fifty feet over a cliff. This rock formation is part of the same Niagara Escarpment that a rider sees in Ontario's Bruce Peninsula and that the Niagara Falls tumble over. The well-marked entrance to the state park where the falls are located is on M123.

This is also Ernest Hemingway country. The setting for some of Papa's 'Nick Adams Stories' is the wild country near Newberry and Seney, where the Big Two-Hearted and Fox rivers flow today much as they did nearly one-hundred years ago when Hemingway camped along them and fished for trout.

When someone tells you that a person can go to both Hell and Paradise in Michigan they're being truthful. Hell is in southeast Michigan and Paradise is on the Superior coast near Whitefish Point where M-123 hits

Whitefish Bay. From Paradise we ultimately need to follow M123 south, but first another side trip is in order, this time north to Whitefish Point.

Going north out of Paradise on Whitefish Point Road takes you to the Point, with its shipwreck museum (including the two-hundred-pound brass bell from the *Edmund Fitzgerald*), the Audubon Bird Observatory, and lighthouse. It is well worth making the approximately twenty-mile round trip to the Point and back. In the spring and fall this is a favorite spot for birders as the Point is a funnel for a wide variety of birds migrating across Lake Superior. Near the midway point between Paradise and the Point is the ghost town of Shelldrake and the river of the same name. For many years it was the location of a Native American village and in the late 1800s a lumbering town sprung up there. With tales of ghosts of shipwrecked sailors being encountered by visitors it has a reputation as a true ghost town.

Eventually departing southward from Paradise, M123 carries us along the west shore of Whitefish Bay. A few miles south of Paradise, at the mouth of the Tahquamenon River, a large boating access site provides a spot to check out the shoreline. Almost ten miles south of Paradise is a paved road going east – take it. This shoreline road hugs the southern coastline and it's a more scenic and interesting option than going inland to M28 as the designated Official Circle Tour route recommends. The road, called the Curley Lewis Highway which later becomes Lakeshore Road, (also designated as the Whitefish Bay Scenic Byway) goes past Iroquois Point lighthouse, an old Indian Mission, and the Bay Mills Indian Reservation with its large gambling casino.

Iroquois Point was the site of a major battle between Native American tribes in 1662. The invading Iroquois were defeated in a surprise attack by outnumbered local Chippewa Indians. The two surviving Iroquois warriors were sent back east to warn other Iroquois bands to stay out of the upper lakes area. This battle was instrumental in opening up the upper Great Lakes region for further exploration by eliminating the Iroquois threat which up to that time had significantly hindered movement by Europeans and Natives alike.

Lakeshore Drive ultimately delivers you to Brimley, on the southeast corner of Lake Superior. While passing through this area check out the Wheels Through History Museum. This Bay Mills and Brimley area museum on Whitefish Bay is in a pre-1905 passenger railroad car and caboose. Exhibits include artifacts and photographs of area railroads, early telephones, logging, fishing and the old Bay Mills town site.

Lakeshore Drive turns into 6 Mile Road east of Brimley. These last few uneventful miles deliver us to Old Mackinaw Trail where a left turn brings us back into Sault Ste. Marie, marking the end of an incredible trip around a truly superior lake. Depending on how many of the side trips one takes, the total tour is in the range of 1,500 miles in length. Scheduling a five, or preferably a six-day trip around Lake Superior makes for an enjoyable tour with time to do some additional things such as boat rides, waterfall excursions, exploring historic lighthouses and museums, short hikes, and much more.

Some Suggested Tips for Safe Riding

L iving an active life comes with risks. It's reality. Driving, skiing, bicycling, hiking, motorcycling, even walking the dog; they are all more dangerous than sitting on the couch watching television or playing computer games.

As motorcyclists this increase in potential danger is something we knowingly accept. Motorcyclists after all are participants in life, not spectators. Any intelligent person will of course take steps to reduce possible dangers, regardless of the activity they are involved in. As motorcyclists we should do the same by making safe riding habits an ingrained part of how we think and ride.

After 45 years and a few hundred thousand miles on two wheels I feel I've learned a thing or two. I try to learn something every time I'm on the bike by observing and thinking. Conversations with fellow riders often revolve around incidents that can be used as learnable moments.

The safety suggestions that I offer below aren't official rules copied from motorcycling safety manuals, they're things I've learned by experience from a lifetime on the seat of a bike. Readers also no doubt have their own lists of safe practices developed from personal experiences. The most important factor is that safety is a never-ending process. It's something riders must think about and put into practice on a daily basis because each ride creates a whole new set of circumstances and possibilities.

So I offer the following in no particular order.

Always assume you are not being seen by others on the road. In your mind pretend that you are invisible to drivers and assume that they will act as if you weren't there, and be ready for such actions on their part. They may well in fact not see you, and for sure you are not the number one priority on their mind. They are all deep in thought and probably doing several things besides driving their vehicle. If riders want to survive an encounter with these and all other vehicles it's up to us to take the necessary precautions and defensive actions. Being in the right means nothing when it's a contest between a motorcycle and a four-wheeled vehicle.

Always leave a margin for error in curves, on wet pavement, or other potentially dangerous conditions and situations. I find that if I ride a bit below my limits, rather than at or above them, I actually have more fun and at much less risk to myself and others. Fun curves are the fudge and cherry on the motorcycling sundae but unfortunately they have potential dark sides in the form of unexpected gravel or sand, vehicles on the wrong side of the yellow line, animals, slow cars, and so on. Be prepared and always use caution in a curve of unknown radius. Throughout my riding career I have played a mind game to help ensure my safety in curves. I imagine that the yellow center line and the white edge line are like the third rail in an electric subway system. Touch the third rail and you die. I thus ride with a concentrated mental effort to ensure that I don't cross the center line or the white pavement edge line because if a rider does either in a curve the consequences could be severe. Oncoming cars and roadside trees are unforgiving.

If you find that competition takes over when riding with a group and you end up taking chances or ride over your head to stay with your friends, then ride alone or with a different group. If you are uncomfortable with any aspect of a group ride then don't participate. This is one area in which an individual rider always has the final say and responsibility; ride how, where, when, and under the circumstances you want – not what a group dictates. Riding with a group carries great responsibility and each rider is expected to have certain skills and know the rules. If you lack the experience or desire then don't do it. Find your own small group to begin with and learn before doing rides with a group that includes strangers you've never ridden with.

As for group riding in general: it is critical that every group have a leader and that before every ride that leader makes clear how the ride will be managed; passing vehicles, yellow & red lights, spacing, stops, what to do if separated, mechanical problems, the ride sweep, hand signals, anticipated speeds, routes and turns, and any other variables that could arise. This is particularly critical if there is even one new rider or new group member. I have ridden in countless group rides for every reason, group and cause imaginable over more than four decades. But I ride solo a lot because I believe group rides to be inherently more dangerous than solo riding. (plus of course more limiting as to options) Most of the close calls I've had while riding have been when with a group of mixed riders who had not ridden together before. The worst was on an Autism Research Fundraiser ride near Chicago. I was in the middle of the column and as we approached a yellow light that was about to turn red I began braking at exactly the time when the man behind me aggressively accelerated. He intended to stay with the group even if it meant running a red light. (there was no police escort and it was expected that we abide by all traffic regulations) As this rider swerved at the very last moment and clipped my rear fender we almost both went down. If we had it would have been in the center of a busy four-lane intersection where cars were already crossing from the other direction. If there had been a clear directive by the group leader on that ride that stoplights must be clearly adhered to then perhaps this person might not have felt the need to run a red light in order to keep up with the front half of the group. When in a group we are responsible not only for our own safety but the safety of every other rider.

When the stoplight turns green for you, always look each way before proceeding. Vehicles unfortunately often continue through red lights during that one or two second period after it turns green for you and red for them.

When slowing for a stop light or stop sign make it a habit to flash your brake light as you're decelerating and even when stopped, until the car behind you is also at a dead stop. Do whatever it takes to get the attention of the driver behind you. When stopping, potential danger is usually behind you. For that reason I use my brake light in the same manner as a turn signal; to inform those near me of my intentions. I flash it two or three times to let drivers behind me know that I'm about to slow down or stop.

Speaking of stopping at lights, always test the stability of your boot on the pavement for a millisecond before leaning the bike over and putting weight on your anchoring leg. If a rider doesn't automatically perform this test each time they stop sooner or later the boot will slip out from under them because they set it down on oil or water, and the bike and rider will unceremoniously fall over.

When stopped at a stop light or stop sign, leave your bike in gear and leave six to eight feet of space between you and the vehicle in front of you; enough room to maneuver. Always have an escape route planned in the event it's needed. Watch your rear view mirror to spot any vehicle approaching rapidly from behind that appears unable to stop in time. Pay as much attention to what's happening behind as to what is going on in front of you because in this situation danger is more likely approaching from the rear, not from the front or sides. Vigilance must continue even when at a standstill. And it isn't just at stop signs or red lights where you need to watch your behind. On open country roads the danger is potentially even greater. If you have to stop or slow down to turn on a stretch of open road drivers behind you aren't expecting it and represent a real threat. Monitor your mirrors and be ready to take appropriate action if a vehicle approaches at a speed that indicates the driver isn't seeing what's occurring up ahead and won't be able to stop in time. Of course this is also a situation in which you want to be flashing your brake lights to help get the attention of someone closing from the rear.

Official accident reports will often list speed or some other driving condition as the cause of an accident. But very often the real reason the accident occurred lurks behind the superficial cause that's listed. I have noticed that three emotional states are in reality the cause of many injuries and fatalities. These mental states are impatience, anger and distraction. If we become either impatient or angry while motorcycling we're much more likely to do something stupid. In this case stupid can kill. These two mental states override cognitive processes. Under normal conditions we wouldn't think of suddenly swerving from one lane to another to pass a vehicle or taking other unwise and dangerous actions, but when we're angry or impatient we do it without thinking. The ultimate condition that did us in might be speed, passing in a no passing zone, an unwise quick movement causing loss of control, failure to see a dangerous condition, inability to stop in time, or other surficial reasons, but often the underlying factor behind finding ourselves in these suddenly dangerous circumstances is that we became impatient or angry due to circumstances beyond our control. It is essential that motorcyclists maintain their cool. Distractions of course are rooted in different causes but can have the same deadly consequence. And their causes are many and varied. The temptation of built-in electronic distractions are especially alarming. I know of two local accidents in recent months caused by misuse of new technology; one rider adjusting his music volume and another interacting with a GPS unit – while riding at speed. With electronic options on today's touring machines resulting in a display module resembling a jet's cockpit it's easy for a rider to focus on buttons and touch pads rather than on the task at hand – keeping eyes and mental attention on the road and surrounding traffic.

Riding through an intersection where oncoming traffic is present always poses potential danger. Is that car coming at you going to decide to turn left in front of you without warning? There is no magical solution to this problem except extreme awareness and vigilance on our part. Have a couple fingers on the brake pedal and formulate a plan in your mind as to what you will do to avoid a collision if a car driver does turn across your path. Slow down to allow time to react and evade the danger should it arise at the last second. Don't ever just assume that it won't happen. I always try to make eye contact for a moment, glimpse at their wheels or steering wheel use to detect direction of travel changes, and watch a car driver's head to see where they're looking and if they are actually looking and focusing or simply taking a quick glance.

One of the most maddening habits that many car drivers have is approaching a stop sign or stop light at a high rate of speed and hitting the brakes hard at the last moment to stop. They may have intended to stop all along but from a motorcyclist's perspective it sure looks like they're going to run the stop sign. At every intersection where I have the right of way or green light – whether it's a country road with very light traffic or a typical urban intersection – I watch vehicles that are approaching from the side very carefully to ensure that they're showing indications that they are in fact going to stop. When I see a car approaching a stop sign at a rate of speed that seems too fast I assume they're not going to stop and I will slow down considerably while ascertaining their intent.

When operating a motorcycle with a single headlight I ride with my headlight's high beam on during the daytime when on open roads. It's much more important to me that I'm as visible as possible to others, than whether one or two percent of car drivers are annoyed due to my "brights". The reality is that I almost never get signaled to lower my lights. In urban traffic or if I'm right behind someone at a stoplight or heavy highway traffic I lower the beam out of courtesy. Of course if your bike is equipped with dual lights or accessory lighting fixtures then operating with your high beam on isn't necessary, and in fact can be distracting and annoying to oncoming traffic. I'm referring only to single headlight configurations. For decades I have noticed the conspicuous difference between riders who were using the low beam or high beam, and the difference in visibility is very substantial.

If you ride from dusk to dawn remember that the odds against you are significantly increased. Not only are you even less visible to others, but you are also more likely to encounter impaired drivers, debris on the road that can't be seen, and wildlife. The populations of large wildlife, ranging from coyotes to bears, have increased all across North America. From dusk to dawn is when you're most likely to encounter one of these animals. Deer of course represent the greatest danger to motorcyclists. Scan the area of the shoulder and ditch for deer and at night search for the reflection from deer's eyes in the area adjacent to the pavement. And keep in mind that they almost always travel in small groups or family units.

Speed Kills. Ironically, it's the enticing and enjoyable back road speeding that's most likely to be fatal, not speed on boring uninspiring superslabs. Expressways are designed for high speeds and few surprises (such as a car suddenly deciding to turn left in front of you) but you never know what is just around the next curve on a fun two-laner in the boonies.

Never follow behind a loaded pickup truck, or any kind of open or uncovered loaded trailer. It doesn't matter if it's a boat trailer or flatbed trailers. I've seen everything from ice chests to two-by-fours fly off of trailers and mattresses and back yard grills fall out of pickup trucks as they're being driving down the road. You don't want to be the vehicle right behind the truck or trailer when this occurs!

Along the lines of positioning, avoid riding beside semi-trucks and do not linger in the blind spot of any vehicle, especially large ones, for any longer than it take to pass the vehicle. When passing a vehicle accomplish it as quickly as possible.

We've long been reminded to keep adequate space between us and the vehicle in front of us to allow a safe stopping distance. For motor-cyclists there is another equally important reason for maintaining a safe distance and it has nothing to do with stopping distance. Bikers also must leave enough room between themselves and the car ahead of them so that they can spot debris or a large pothole in the road in time to take evasive action. While a car driver will nonchalantly pass over a muffler or piece of wood or a large hole, straddling it with their wheels, a biker has problems if he or she suddenly sees such an object in their path. Keep a healthy distance between you and the vehicle ahead of you not only for safe stopping ability, but also to be able to see road conditions ahead of you relative to your speed.

Pay attention to brake light action ahead of you on open roads. If a driver touches his or her brakes there is a reason, even if it isn't immedi-ately apparent. Maybe it's a large pothole, perhaps it's a radar car, debris on the road, or deer just out of your sight in the ditch. If you see brake lights up ahead that have no obvious reason, slow down and anticipate the possible need to stop or take evasive action.

Most of us would agree that motorcyclists have qualities and traits that lead us into this activity in the first place. One of these is a feeling of independence and separation from the crowd, and another is a sense of confidence in our ability to handle situations that arise. As a result too many of us eschew advice or training, with an attitude of 'I don't need no stinking training, I learned how to ride motorcycles the old fashioned way – I just got on and rode'. The reality is that while this approach may have worked 50 years ago when traffic was lighter and rural areas less developed, and there were far fewer distracted car drivers on the road than today, it is a recipe for disaster given current realities. Everything has changed; roads, traffic, power and speed capabilities of the machines, congestion, distractions, far more unskilled car drivers out there, cell phones and texting, you name it. Bottom line – take a training class, and if you are already an experienced rider continue your training with constant skills practice or formal classes. Piloting a motorcycle is much like flying an airplane – both types of pilots need constant training and practice.

Wear proper gear. I know I'm going to alienate myself with some readers by saying this, but when given the choice as to wearing a helmet or not I suggest wearing one. It just might save your life or prevent head injury in even a minor accident. I too believe in choice. I wouldn't force anyone to wear a helmet. I choose to wear a helmet and seat belts because I think it's the smart thing to do. I value my life and health more than whatever enhanced feeling of freedom I might experience with the wind blowing in my (thinning) hair. Years of trail and street riding, and an active imagination with which I can vividly imagine what will happen if my head strikes a tree, the pavement, or a car bumper at even low speed, causes me to wear a helmet even when it isn't required.

I shudder when I see riders in T-shirts, shorts, and beach thongs passing me on the highway. A rider doesn't have to dress like Darth Vader, but for your own sake please do wear protective gear – at a minimum a jacket, gloves, proper footwear, and long pants. Professional racers would never consider racing without proper gear. And they're riding on a controlled course where there are no cars, deer, debris in the road, or impaired drivers likely to do something stupid in front of them. If it's good enough for them it ought to also make sense for those of us who are less skilled and who must ride in conditions that are far less safe and predictable. Motorcycle apparel has made tremendous gains in recent decades, both in form and function. It's actually more comfortable, and thus the ride more enjoyable, (in my opinion) to wear proper motorcycling apparel that's designed to deflect the sun's burning rays and enhance the cooling effect of air movement than to ride with bare skin exposed to the sun and the various flying insects and debris that are encountered on the road.

Despite the aura of the hard-drinking biker as an American icon, the reality is alcohol and bikes are not a good mix. Alcohol can negatively influence the fighter pilot-like reflexes needed to safely and skillfully operate a motorcycle. Each rider must of course decide for him or herself whether he or she can safely enjoy a drink while in the course of a ride, but intelligent thought needs to go into if and how many. I love a cold beer at the end of a ride, but almost always stick with Coke or coffee or simply the water bottle that I always try to carry while riding.

I've seen and heard a lot of motorcycle enthusiasts, including instructors, make the comment that there are two kinds of motorcyclists; "those who have crashed and those who haven't crashed yet," implying of course that sooner or later everyone will crash. I think this attitude is unfortunate and plays directly into the hands of those who believe motorcycling is a dangerous antisocial activity that should be tightly regulated. I know a number of veteran motorcyclists who have never had an accident or gone down. These skilled riders operate in a manner that minimizes the possibility of an accident while still very much enjoying the thrills of motorcycling. It might sound macho to make statements about the inevitability of crashing but it harms our sport and sends the wrong message. Instead, let's talk about how safe riding habits, training, experience, and skill at piloting a motorcycle greatly reduce the possibility of an accident.

Whenever someone tells me that they are thinking of getting a motorcycle I always give the same advice – if you can't focus one hundred per cent of the time at one hundred per cent intensity on what you're doing, then reconsider. Motorcycling isn't the activity for daydreamers and others who can't concentrate totally on the task at hand. The penalty for letting one's mind wander while riding is severe.

Always expect the unexpected – it will happen.
Overconfidence is deadly.

Last but not least – Have Fun. We're participating in one of the most enjoyable and exciting activities in the world. I couldn't imagine life without it.

Be safe and ride smart today so you can ride again tomorrow.

Index

ILLIINOIS
Alton, 25–26, 33
Alto Pass, 17

Badger Mine and Museum, 30
Bald Knob Cross, 17
Bartonville, 25
Beardstown, 25
Brookport, 22
Browntown, 29

Cahokia Mounds State Historical Site,
   34
Cairo, 21, 32, 34–35
Castle Rock State Park, 27
Caterpillar Visitor Center, 25
Chester, 18, 34–35

Driftless area, 19
Driftless ride, 19
driftless zone, 13, 30
Dubuque, 32
Dutch Immigrant Windmill, 33

East Dubuque, 32
Elizabeth, 19
Elizabethtown, 23

Fort Kaskaskia State Historic Park, 35
Fort Massac, 22
Freeport, 29–31

Galena, 19–20, 29–32
Golconda, 23
Grafton, 26
Grand Detour, 27
Great River Road National Scenic Byway,
   32
Great River Scenic Byway, 26, 32

Hanover, 20
Hardin, 23, 26
Horseshoe Mound, 19, 31

llinois River, 25–26, 33
Illinois Rural Heritage Museum, 16
Indian Mounds Historical Site, 33

John Deere Historic Site, 27
John Deere Pavilion, 33
Jonesboro, 17–18

Kampsville, 26, 33
Kincaid Mounds, 22

Lewis and Clark State Historic Site, 33
Lewiston, 25
Lincoln Museum, 25
Little Egypt, 16

McFarland's Tavern, 23
Metropolis, 21–22
Mississippian Culture, 34
Mississippi Palisades State Park, 20, 32
Mississippi River, 16, 18–21, 25–26,
   32–33, 35
Moline, 33
Mound City, 21
Mound City National Cemetery, 21
Mt. Carroll, 31
Mt. Horeb, 31
Murphysboro, 16–17

National Great Rivers Museum, 26
New Liberty, 22–23
Northwest Territory Historic Center, 27

Ohio River, 14, 21, 23, 35
Ohio River Scenic Byway, 14, 21
Old Shawneetown, 21, 23

Pecatonica River, 29
Pere Marquette State Park, 26
Perry County, 16
Pinckneyville, 16, 18
Portage, Wisconsin, 31
Pyramid State Recreation Area, 16

Rockford, 27–28
Rock River, 27
Ronald Reagan's boyhood home, 27
Route 3, 18, 34
Route 4, 19
Route 73, 29
Route 78, 31
Route 84, 20, 32–33
Route 96, 26, 33
Route 127, 17
Route 146, 23
Route 100, 25, 26, 33
Route 150, 18

Scales Mound, 19
Segar Park, 18, 34
Shawnee National Forest, 17
Shullsburg, 29–30
Stagecoach Trail, 19
Stockton, 31
Superman, 21–22

Thunder Bay Falls, 31
Trail of Tears State Forest, 17

Ulysses S. Grant, 19, 30
Unity, 18
US20, 19, 29, 31, 33
US 24, 23

Wisconsin, 29–32

INDIANA
Battle Ground, 62–63
Bedford, 58

Cannelton, 61, 65
Clifty Falls State Park, 66
Columbus, 58
Cox Ford, 58
Crawfordsville, 58

Delphi, 62–63

Freetown, 58
French Lick, 60–61
French Lick Scenic Railway, 60

Hindostan Falls, 59
Hoosier National Forest, 58, 61, 65
Huntington, 61

Indiana Railway Museum, 60
International Circus Hall of Fame, 62

Jug Rock Nature Preserve, 59
Lafayette, 63
Logansport, 62

Madison, 66
Merom, 61, 63–64

Ohio River, 61–62, 64–6
Old Route 24, 56

Parke County, 58
Patoka Lake, 60–61
Peru, 62, 64
Prophetstown State Park, 63

Route 1, 45
Route 24, 56
Route 32, 47
Route 58, 58
Route 62, 45, 62–64
Route 63, 59
Route 66, 61–62
Route 135, 40
Route 145, 60
Route 234, 47
Route 252, 40
Route 263, 63
Route 662, 61

Shades State Park, 58
Sheets Wildlife Museum, 62
Shoals, 58–59

Terre Haute, 61, 63–64
Towpath Trail, 62
Turkey Run State Park, 58

US41, 48
US52, 44

Wabash-Erie Canal, 61
Wabash Park, 62
Wabash River, 61, 63–64
West Baden Springs, 60
Wilkins Mill, 58
Williams Covered Bridge, 58
Williamsport, 63

MICHIGAN
Adventure Copper Mine, 102
Alberta, 108
Alpena, 80, 91–92
Au Sable River, 91

Baraga County, 108–9
Bay Port, 88–89
Bergland, 109
Big Bay De Noc, 112, 118
Big Bay Road, 114–15
Blaney Park, 118
Blue Water Bridge, 84
Brockway Mountain Drive, 104
Bruce Crossing, 109
Bunker Hill Road, 100

Calumet, 105
Cheboygan, 82, 92–93
Copper Country, 103, 105, 107
Copper Harbor, 103–5
Crystal Falls, 106–7, 110–11

Dansville, 100
Delaware Copper Mine, 103
Delton, 96
Dexter Trail, 98–100
Dogpatch Restaurant, 116

Eagle Harbor, 104–5
Empire Mine, 113
Escanaba, 110, 112–13, 119

Fayette State Park, 118
Firefighters Memorial Museum, 105
Fort Gratiot, 65, 85
Fort Gratiot Lighthouse, 85
Fort Mackinac, 93
Fort Michilimackinac, 77–78, 93

Fort Wilkins State Park, 103
Forty Mile Point Lighthouse, 92

Garden Peninsula, 118
Garfield Inn Bed & Breakfast, 88
Gay, 103
Gilmore Car Museum, 96
Grand Island, 116
Grand Ledge, 94, 97
Grand River, 94–95, 97
Grand Sable Sand Dunes, 117
Gregory, 99
Grindstone City, 87–88
Gulliver, 118
Gwinn, 113

Hancock, 102, 105
Harbor Beach, 86
Hastings, 96
Hell, 98–100
Hell Creek, 99
Hickory Corners, 96
Hoeft State Park, 92
Houghton, 90, 102–3

Ingham County, 98
Ionia County, 94
Ionia State Recreation Area, 95
Iron River, 106, 110–11

Keweenaw National Historic Park, 105
Keweenaw Peninsula, 65, 101–4, 109

Lac La Belle Road, 103
Lake Gogebic, 109
Lake Independence, 114
Lake Michigan, 68–72, 75–79, 82, 86, 93–95, 110, 112
Lake Odessa, 96
Lake Superior, 101–5, 108, 110, 112, 114–17
L'Anse, 108, 114
Lansing, 94, 98
Lexington, 86
Little Bay De Noc, 112
Lumberman's Monument, 91
Lyons, 95

M13, 89
M25, 84–89
M26, 102–5, 109
M32, 80
M36, 99–100
M43, 96
M50, 96
M52, 99–100
M64, 102, 109
M66, 95–96
M100, 94, 97
M106, 100
M107, 101–2
M179, 96
Mackinac Island, 65, 77, 93
Mackinaw City, 65, 76–77, 82, 84, 89, 93
Manistique, 118
Mansfield Mine, 107
Marquette, 65, 74, 77, 106–7, 112–13, 115
Marquette County, 106–7, 115
Mason, 98–100
McClain State Park, 105
Michigan Iron Industry Museum, 113
Miners Castle, 116–17
Miners Falls, 116
Munising, 115–16

Nahma, 118
Nashville, 96
Negaunee, 113

Oscoda, 90–91
Ossineke, 91
Ottawa National Forest, 109

Palmer, 113
Pictured Rocks National Lakeshore, 66, 116
Pinckney, 99
Pinconning, 89
Porcupine Mountains Wilderness State Park, 101
Port Austin, 88
Port Crescent State Park, 88
Port Hope, 86–87
Port Huron, 84–85

Port Sanilac, 86
Potterville, 97

Rogers City, 80–82, 92
Route 25, 85

Saginaw River, 89
Saginaw Valley Naval Ship Museum, 89
Sand Point Lighthouse, 109, 112
Saranac, 95
Sebewaing, 88
Seney, 112, 117–18
Seney National Wildlife Refuge, 118
Silver City, 101–2
Sleeper State Park, 88
Standish, 89
St. Clair River, 84
Stonington Lighthouse, 119
Stonington Peninsula, 112, 119
Sugarloaf Mountain, 114

Tawas City, 90
Tawas Point State Park, 90
The Thumb, 85

Unadilla Road, 99
Upper Peninsula, 82, 85, 101, 105–8, 110, 113
US2, 107, 109–11, 113, 118
US23, 80–82, 84, 89–92
US41, 103, 105, 113, 115
US45, 109

Vermontville, 97

Watersmeet, 109–10
White Rock, 86

MINNESOTA
Arrowhead Country, 131

Big Falls, 127, 134
Big Ford River, 134
Bronko Nagurski Museum, 135

Caledonia, 129

Detroit Lakes, 126
Duluth, 124, 130–32
Duluth Skyline Drive, 130–31

Eagles Bluff Park, 136
Ely, 124–25

Fergus Falls, 126–27
Finland State Forest, 124
Forest Service Highway 15, 125
Forestville, 128
Forestville Mystery Cave State Park, 128

Gooseberry Falls, 124, 132
Grand Falls, 134
Grand Marais, 132
Grand Portage State Park, 132
Grand Rapids, 134–35
Great Falls, 127
Great River Road National Scenic Byway, 136

Harmony, 128
High Falls of the Pigeon River, 132
Hokah, 128

International Falls, 126–27, 134–35
Itasca County, 134

Koochiching Museum, 135

La Crescent, 128, 136
Lake Superior, 121–22, 124, 130–31, 135
Lake Superior Scenic Railroad, 130
Littlefork, 135
Lutsen, 132

Minnesota, 121–31, 133–37

Niagara Cave, 128

Otter Tail County, 126

Park Rapids, 126

Red Wing, 136–37

Route 16, 136
Route 26, 136
Route 44, 128
Route 61, 131

Sawtooth Mountains, 132
Silver Bay, 124
Silver Creek Tunnel, 124, 131
Smokey Bear Park, 135
Split Rock Lighthouse, 124, 132

Tettegouche State Park, 124
Two Harbors, 124–25, 130–31

US52, 128
US71, 126–27, 134–35

Wabasha, 137
Winona, 136–37

OHIO
Adena Mansion Historic Site, 148

Bainbridge, 148–49
Beach City, 158, 161
Bellaire, 163
Black Hand Gorge, 144
Bolivar, 158
Bottle Kiln, 162
Buckeye Furnace, 142

Campus Martius, 156, 164
Chillicothe, 148
Chilo, 168
Clear Fork Reservoir, 145
CR424, 152

Defiance, 152–53

Erie Canal, 152–53

Flint Ridge, 144
Fort Ancient, 147, 150
Fort Hill State Memorial, 149
Fort Lauren, 158
Fort Wayne, 152–53
Freeport, 160

Gallipolis, 166–67

Hammondsville, 159
Hannibal, 163
Hills Covered Bridge, 156
Hocking Hills State Park, 143
Hockingport, 165
Hopewell Culture National Historical
    Park, 148

Irondale, 159

Kiedaish Point Park, 163
Kingston, 148

Lake Tappan, 160
Lancaster, 147
Lewisville, 157
Lexington, 145
Little Miami River, 150
Little Muskingum River, 156
Logan, 143, 148
Logan Elm, 148

Marietta, 154, 156–57, 163–64
Massillon, 158
Maumee River, 152
Maumee Valley Scenic Byway, 152
Middleport, 142, 166
Mid-Ohio Sports Car Course, 145
Monroeville, 159
Mound City Group National Monument,
    148
Muskingum River, 154, 156, 164

Nashville, 145
National Road / Zane Grey Museum, 154
Nellie, 144
New Richmond, 162, 169
New Rumley, 159
Northwest Territory Museum, 164

Ohio River, 140, 142, 154, 156, 158,
    162–69
Ohio River Museum, 156, 164
Old 24, 152

Point Pleasant, 169
Pomeroy, 166
Portsmouth, 167–68

Rankin House, 168
Ripley, 168
Route 7, 142, 162–64, 166
Route 52, 167
Route 93, 161
Route 123, 150
Route 212, 158
Route 213, 159
Route 327, 143
Route 350, 150
Route 555, 154
Route 646, 160
Route 668, 143

Seip Mound, 148
Serpent Mound, 149
Somerset, 143–44
South Bloomingville, 143
SR124, 165–66
Steubenville, 163
Sugarcreek, 161

Tarlton, 147–48
Tarlton Cross, 147
Toledo, 152
Triple Nickel, 154–55

US50, 143, 164–65

Walhonding, 145
Wayne National Forest, 156, 163, 167
Waynesburg, 159
Wellston, 142–43
Wellsville, 162
Western Scenic Railroad, 154
West Lafayette, 161
Woodsfield, 156–57

Zoar, 159

WISCONSIN
Antigo, 193

Apostle Islands National Lakeshore, 172, 181
Ashland, 180–82

Bagley, 197
Baileys Harbor, 186
Baraboo River, 176–77
Bayfield, 180–81
Bayfield Peninsula, 180
Black Earth, 178
Black Hawk Park, 198
Blue Mounds, 176–79
Boscobel, 175
Brisbois Store and Fur Museum, 198
Brownstone Falls, 182

Cassville, 195–97
Cave Point County Park, 185
Chequamegon Bay, 181
Chequamegon Nicolet National Forest, 182
Cherney Maribel Caves County Park, 188
Copper Falls State Park, 182
County road B, 187
County Road-GG, 182
County road T, 185
Crandon, 192

Dodge State Park, 176
Dodgeville, 176, 179
Door Peninsula, 183, 185–87
Dyckesville, 187

Eagle River, 191
Egg Harbor, 187

Fort Crawford, 198
Fountain City, 199

Great River Road, 172, 195, 199, 201
Great River Road Interpretive Center, 199
Green Bay, 187, 192–93

Harrison Hills, 189–90
Hayward, 180, 182
Hodag, 190–91, 193

House on the Rock, 176

Jacksonport, 186

Keshena, 191–93
Kewaunee, 183–84
Kickapoo River, 174

LaCrosse, 198–99
La Farge, 174
Lake Superior, 172, 180–81
Lake Superior Scenic Byway, 180
Lancaster, 175
Langlade, 192–93

Mellen, 182
Menominee Indian Reservation, 193
Merrick State Park, 200
Merrill, 189, 193
Mid-Continent Railway Museum, 177
Mississippi River, 172, 195–99, 201
Mt. Horeb, 178

National Fresh Water Fishing Hall of Fame, 180
Natural Bridge State Park, 177
Nelson Dewey State Park, 196–97
Nicolet National Forest, 182, 191
Northern Great Lakes Visitor Center, 181
Northport, 186

Old Stage Road, 187
Ontario, 174

Pepin, 200
Point Beach State Forest, 183
Potosi, 195–96
Prairie du Chien, 197–99

Rawley Point Lighthouse, 183
Readstown, 174–75
Reedsburg, 176–77
Rhinelander, 190–91
Rock Mill, 188
Rock Springs, 177
Route 13, 180

Route 17, 189
Route 23, 176
Route 27, 180
Route 35, 195
Route 42, 183
Route 55, 191
Route 60, 178
Route 70, 191
Route 77, 182
Route 78, 178
Route 131, 175
Route 133, 195

Sauk City, 178
Sister Bay, 186
Soldiers Grove, 175
Spring Green, 176
Stonefield, 196–97
Sturgeon Bay, 185, 187
Sturgeon Bay Ship Canal, 185

Taliesin Museum, 176
Tennyson, 195
Tomah, 174
Two Rivers, 183, 188

US2, 181

Villa Louis, 198
Wildcat Mountain State Park, 174
Wisconsin River, 175–76, 178, 189, 197
Woodman, 175
Wyalusing State Park, 197

GREAT LAKES CIRCLE TOUR
40 Mile Point Lighthouse, 225

Adventure Mine, 260
Aguasabon Falls and Gorge, 257
Alberta, 264
Algoma, 244
Alpena, 225
Ambassador Bridge, 207–8
Amherstburg, 209
Apostle Islands National Lakeshore, 259
Ashtabula, 211

Barrie, 227
Battle of Fallen Timbers, 205
Bay City, 226
Bayfield, 259
Bay Mills Indian Reservation, 267
Black River Drive, 259–60
Blind River, 220
Blue Star Highway, 249–50
Blue Water Bridge, 215–16
Brimley, 267
Brockway Mountain Drive, 261–62
Bruce Caves, 217
Bruce Peninsula, 214, 216–19, 227, 266
Bruce Peninsula National Park, 218
Buffalo, 210, 248–49

Calumet, 263
Caseville, 226
Cedarville, 223–24
Charlevoix, 236
Chicago, 229, 233, 242, 246–48, 253
Cleveland, 211–12
Conneaut, 211
Copper Harbor, 260–63
CR519, 260
Cross Village, 237
Curley Lewis Highway, 267

Da Yoopers Tourist Trap, 265
DeTour Village, 223
Detroit, 206–10, 230, 247–48
Detroit River, 207–8, 247
Devil's Kettle Waterfalls, 258
Dixie Highway, 206–7
Door Peninsula, 241, 243–44
Drummond Island, 223
Duluth, 258–59
Dunham Tavern Museum, 211
Dunville, 210

Eagle Harbor, 262–63
Eagle Harbor Lighthouse, 262
Eagle River, 262–63
Elk Rapids, 236
Elliot Lake, 220
Empire, 234
Erie, 203, 205, 207–13, 248

Escanaba, 239, 241–42
Espanola, 220

Fairport Harbor Marine Museum, 211
Fayette State Park, 241
Fort Erie, 208, 210
Fort Malden National Historic Site, 209
Fort Meigs, 205
Fort Michilimackinac, 237
Fort Wilkins State Park, 262
Fox Point, 246
Frankfort, 234

Garden Peninsula, 241
Gay, 261
Georgian Bay, 214, 217–19, 221, 227–28
Gillette Sand Dunes Visitor Center, 252
Gooseberry Falls, 258
Grand Haven, 251–52
Grand Haven State Park, 251–52
Grand Marais, 258, 266
Grand Mere State Park, 249
Grand Portage National Monument, 258
Grand Traverse Bay, 235
Great Lakes Commission, 203
Great Lakes Naval Memorial & Museum, 231
Great Northern Highway, 255
Green Bay, 241–44
Greenland, 260
Grindstone City, 226

Hancock, 260–61, 263–64
Harbor Springs, 236
Harley-Davidson Museum, 246
Harrisville, 225
High Falls of the Pigeon River, 258
Holland, 250–51
Holland State Park, 251
Huron City Museum, 227

Indiana Dunes National Park, 247
Inland Seas Maritime Museum, 212
International Bridge, 208, 221, 255
Interstate Falls, 259
Ironwood, 259

Iroquois Point, 267
Ishpeming, 265

Kenosha, 247
Keweenaw Mountain Lodge, 261
Keweenaw National Historic Park, 263
Keweenaw Peninsula, 260, 262–63
Kincardine, 216

Lac La Belle, 261
Lake Erie, 205, 207–13
Lake Express, 230, 246, 253
Lake Huron, 203, 214–17, 219–21, 223–27, 229
Lake Huron Circle Tour, 214–15, 217, 219, 221, 223, 225, 227
Lake Michigan, 214, 216, 224, 229–37, 239–53
Lake Michigan Circle Tour, 229, 231, 233, 235, 237, 239, 241, 243, 245, 247, 249, 251, 253
Lake of the Clouds, 260
Lake Superior Byway, 259
Lake Superior Circle Tour, 254–55, 257, 259, 261, 263, 265, 267
Lake Superior Provincial Park, 256
Lambeau Field, 243
L'Anse, 264
Leamington, 208–9
Leelanau Peninsula, 234–35
Leland, 235
Les Cheneaux Islands, 223
Lion's Head, 218
Little Sable Point Lighthouse, 232
Lorain, 212
Ludington, 230, 233, 241–42, 244
Ludington State Park, 233
Lutsen, 258

M-13, 226
M22, 234–35
M25, 203, 226
M28, 260, 266–67
M35, 242
M107, 260
M-109, 234–35
M119, 236–37

Mackinac Bridge, 224, 237–38
Mackinaw City, 225, 237–38
Magney State Park, 258
Manistee, 233–34
Manistique, 240–41
Manitoulin Island, 214, 219, 227
Manitowoc, 230, 244–46
Marblehead Lighthouse, 212
Marblehead Peninsula, 212
Marquette, 221, 231, 233, 239, 252, 265
Marquette Maritime Museum and Light-
    house, 265
McClain State Park, 263
Menominee, 242
Michigan City, 248
Michigan Maritime Museum, 250
Milwaukee, 229–31, 234, 245–46
Miners Castle, 265–66
Miners Falls, 265
Monroe, 206
Montague, 232
Montreal River, 259
Munising, 265
Munuscong, 223
Muskegon, 229–32, 246, 252–53
Muskegon Lake, 230–32, 252–53

Naubinway, 239–40
Neebish, 223
Newberry, 266
New Buffalo, 248–49
New Buffalo Railroad Museum, 248
Niagara Escarpment, 217, 266
Niagara River, 210
Nipigon, 257
Northport, 235

Oconto, 242–43
Old Fort Erie, 210
Old Michigan City Lighthouse and
    Museum, 248
Ontario, 203–5, 207–10, 215–16, 219–21,
    227, 239, 254–58, 266
Ontario Route 69, 227
Ontonagon, 260
Oscoda, 225
Ouimet Canyon Provincial Park, 257

Owen Sound, 217, 221, 227

Palms Book State Park, 241
Paradise, 266–67
Pennsylvania, 205, 211
Pere Marquette Park, 231, 252
Peshtigo, 242–43
Peshtigo Fire Museum, 242
Petoskey, 236
Pictured Rocks National Lakeshore, 265
Pierce Stocking Drive, 234
Pinery Provincial Park, 216
P.J. Hoffmaster State Park, 251
Point Betsie Lighthouse, 234
Point Clark Lighthouse, 216
Point Pelee Provincial Park, 209
Porcupine Mountains Wilderness State
    Park, 260
Portage Canal Bridge, 260
Port Austin, 226–27
Port aux Barques Lighthouse, 227
Port Huron, 214–15, 226–27
Port of Milwaukee, 230, 246
Port Rowan, 209–10
Port Washington, 245
Port Washington Lighthouse and
    Museum, 245
Presque Isle Park, 265

Quincy Mine, 263

Red Arrow Highway, 249
Red Jacket Fire Station, 263
Ridgeway Battlefield Museum, 210
River Raisin Battlefield Museum, 207
Rock & Roll Museum, 211
Rogers City, 225
Route 2, 211–12
Route 3, 208–10
Route 5, 210–11
Route 7, 211
Route 13, 259
Route 17, 220–21, 255–57
Route 21, 216, 227
Route 26, 227
Route 32, 246
Route 42, 209, 244–45

Route 61, 257–59
Route 134, 223
Route H-58, 266

Saginaw Bay, 225–26
Saginaw Valley Naval Ship Museum, 226
Sand Point Lighthouse, 241
Sarnia, 215–16
Saugatuck, 250
Sault Ste. Marie, 220–23, 228, 254–55, 267
　　Michigan, 222, 254
　　Ontario, 255
Sault Ste. Marie Michigan, 221–22
Scenic Route CR-1, 217
Seul Choix Point Lighthouse, 240
Sheboygan, 245
Sibley Peninsula, 257
Silver City, 260
Silver Creek Tunnel, 258
Silver Lake State Park, 232
Sleeping Bear Dunes National
　　Lakeshore, 234
Sleeping Giant Provincial Park, 257
South Baymouth, 219
South Haven, 250
Splitrock Lighthouse, 258
SS Badger, 229–30, 245
Standish, 225–26
St. Clair River, 214–15
St. Ignace, 224, 238–39, 241
St. Joseph, 221, 249
St. Louis County Heritage and Arts
　　Center Historic Union Depot, 258
St. Mary River, 221, 223, 255
Stonington Peninsula, 241
Sturgeon Bay, 243–44
Sturgeon Point Lighthouse, 225
Sudbury, 227–28
Sugarloaf Mountain, 265

Tahquamenon Falls, 266
Talbot Trail, 205, 208
Tawas City, 225–26
Tawas State Park, 225
Thunder Bay, 255, 257–58
Tobermory, 218–19

Toledo, 205–6, 212
Trans-Canada Highway, 220, 228, 255
Traverse City, 234–35
Tunnel of Trees, 236–37
Turnip Rock, 227
Two Rivers, 244

US2, 211, 238–42, 259–60
US12, 247–49
U.S.-23, 225
US41, 242–43, 247, 260–61, 263–65
U.S. Coast Guard Museum, 211

Vermillion, 212

Wallacetown, 209
Warren Dunes State Park, 249
Waukegan, 247
Wawa, 256
Welland Canal, 210
Whitefish Bay, 246, 267
Whitefish Bay Scenic Byway, 267
Whitefish Point, 266–67
White River, 232, 256–57
White River Lighthouse and Museum, 232
Wiarton, 217–18
Wiarton Willie, 218
Windmill Island Gardens, 251
Wind Point Lighthouse, 247
Windsor, 207–8

Made in the USA
Monee, IL
10 June 2023

35555443R00164